This is a remarkable modern quest romance with the Divine, embodying one of the most important strands of contemporary non-establishment spirituality and linking together cultures in two different hemispheres. It shows how, with an unrestrained eclecticism, traditions from and different peoples can be brought together in a seamless whole. It also provides one of the best illustrations that I have ever read of the personal process of encountering spirit worlds, and the constructive uses to which those encounters can be put in order to advance human evolution.

Professor Ronald Hutton, Head of History at the University of Bristol, Fellow of the Royal Society and of the Society of Antiquaries, Commissioner of English Heritage.

Once I began reading this book I couldn't put it down. Barbara has delivered a powerful and timely message. Through accounts of her own experiences and the timeless wisdom passed onto her by many wise teachers, we are taken on a journey of discovery of ourselves, leading us to a deeper and more profound awareness of all that we are.

Dr David Hamilton, scientist, speaker and Hay House best-selling author of *How Your Mind Can Heal Your Body*, and *Is Your life Mapped Out?*

Barbara's book is alive, a sparkling journey that enchants whilst reminding us of the magic that both surrounds and lives inside us. By accessing our soul's knowing; the living past, via the once treasured, but now little remembered, 'rites of passage,' we have the ability to make of this life something truly wonderful, co-creating it with the Source of all life. This book really does teach us how to learn from our experiences, from any lifetime, and move toward being the authentic manifestation of our soul.

David Wells, astrologer and author of *Past, Present and Future* (Hay House)

A beautiful recognition and celebration of the ancient rites of passage, so needed in our modern-day lifestyles. We know there is something profound missing in our everyday experiences, my feeling is that 'The Shaman Within' holds a most important key to unite and bring deeper meaning to the purpose and wonderment of our lives. This book is the accessible bridge between the devic and human kingdoms, the mystical gateway that opens to the timeless wisdom within our souls and the Great Mother. Such magic in these pages.

Anaiya Sophia, author of *Womb Wisdom* and *Sacred Sexual Union*

Discover a shamanic understanding of the universal web of life and the fundamental inter-connectivity of the whole-world. Barbara re-envisions ancient and re-emerging wisdom in a wonderfully relevant and timely way. By describing her own profound and revelatory experiences, she demonstrates their universal insights, truths and awareness for all of us – if we are willing to let go of our limited perceptions. Thank you for such a heart-felt guide that empowers everyone to discover their Shaman Within.

Dr Jude Currivan, cosmologist, healer and author of *The 8th Chakra and HOPE – Healing Our People & Earth* (Hay House)

A beautifully detailed personal odyssey full of challenges, changes, insights and revelations. I felt myself taken on Barbara's journey, experiencing her travels, seeing the sights, feeling the land, hearing the spirits and enjoying the wonderful characters who pass on their ancient wisdom. A magical book with much ceremonies to put into practice to help you on your way.

Leo Rutherford, MA, founder of Eagle's Wing College of Contemporary Shamanism

Stories are so central to our human experience of being and becoming, allowing us to explore, reflect and learn; stories are at the heart of all Pagan spiritual traditions, guiding us forward. 'The Shaman Within' is a very personal story, glinting with wonder, enthu-siasm and gratitude, balanced by self-reflection, and growing understanding.

Emma Restall Orr, Druid expert and author of *The Wakeful World: Animism, Mind and the Self in Nature* (Moon Books)

At the centre of 'The Shaman Within' is a pool of ancestral knowledge into which we can dive once again to heal whatever ails us, both as a race of beings and as individuals we can find true peace, health and wealth, through the authenticity of our soul's purpose. As a healing practitioner myself I highly recommend what this book has to offer. It explains clearly how you can bring about change in your life today by healing the past, shoring up the present and helping you to co-create a better future.

Wayne Kealohi Powell D.D. Holistic Health Educator and founder of Shamanic Bodywork

English surname - medieval
origins meaning christmastide
but ultimately from the pre 7th
century "goel" - Norse - viking "Jol"

william yoel in the court Rolls of the
manor of Wakefield, Yorkshire 1297
Many different spellings
charles
CARLO, CARLOS, CARL - USAGE italian,
portuguese spanish

The Shaman
Within

Before the
conquest in 1066
my name has
a coat of
Reclaiming our Rites of Passage arms.

It means a man

Sexy classy
Masculine.

TO CARLA,

Little and womanly
Strong one
woman of strength. WITH LOVE

BLESSINGS

BARBARA

The Shaman Within

Reclaiming our Rites of Passage

Barbara Meiklejohn-Free

The Highland Seer

MOON
BOOKS

Winchester, UK
Washington, USA

First published by Moon Books, 2013
Moon Books is an imprint of John Hunt Publishing Ltd., Laurel House, Station Approach,
Alresford, Hants, SO24 9JH, UK
office1@jhpbooks.net
www.johnhuntpublishing.com
www.moon-books.net

For distributor details and how to order please visit the 'Ordering' section on our website.

Text copyright: Barbara Meiklejohn-Free 2013

ISBN: 978 1 78279 305 2

A CIP catalogue record for this book is available from the British Library.

Design: Stuart Davies

Printed and bound by CPI Group (UK) Ltd, Croydon, CR0 4YY

We operate a distinctive and ethical publishing philosophy in all
areas of our business, from our global network of authors to
production and worldwide distribution.

CONTENTS

Dedications

This book is dedicated to Swein McDonald, the Highland Seer. Without his visions and help this book would not have seen the light of day.

To Ed 'Eagle Man' McGaa, my first Native American teacher. He taught me of the ways of the Lakota and the connection of 'One Tribe, One People'; red, yellow, black, white all nations as one vision.

To Naha the Hawaiian Kahuna who touched my life with aloha, sharing her ceremonies and songs with me.

To Two Eagles, wherever he may be, whose visions inspired and guided me.

To Wallace Howard, Leonard Crow Dog, Mary Summer Rain, Dave Swallow, Gerald Ice, Jim Beard, for their teachings and leadership of the Sun Dance.

To Cherokee Elder, Grandmother Jean C, for your wisdom, teachings and friendship; a blessing indeed.

To my spiritual brothers, Shaun, Alan, Rondie, Steve, Mark, Tim, Simon, George, Olaf, Kam, Nick, Sherif, Wayne and Yuri. And my spiritual sisters, Pat, Annie, Claire, Diana, Elaine, Linda, and Linda Lou, Lynn Taos, Janet, Jenny, Jo, Gail, Julie, Karen, Marjory, Ocean, Teri, Tree, Juliette, and Olivia.

To all the teachers in school who said I was not good enough, and to all the people who put me down, rejected me, abandoned me, misled me in this lifetime, for without your help I would not be who I am today. I have experienced what I don't want in my life through these great teachers.

Foreword

My friend, the author, states that this book walks with you to reclaim your natural rites of passage, and create your own path to enlightenment. By tapping into the teachings our ancestors have accumulated since we first walked on Earth, Barbara holds – we access – the 'Shaman Within' which lies within each one of us. The key is to find it. Rites of passage, for we Sioux, our ceremonies are a key source from which we may discover this enhancing mystery.

I was blessed to experience two powerful Sioux Holy Men (Shamans) that affected and changed my life. The first Spirit Calling ceremony prepared me for deadly combat. I flew an F-4 Phantom Marine fighter, 110 Vietnam missions and then later, after my predicted (by the entering spirit to Chief Fools Crow's Spirit Calling ceremony) safe return, I attended another ceremony conducted by Chief Eagle Feather wherein six bodies buried under snow and ice were found. All the entering Spirit's predictions came vividly true in that Spirit Calling too. Spirits are real! Organized religion cannot connect or communicate with them because their leaders lack sincere focus and fruitlessly detour themselves to and through materialistic gain, accentuated fear, superstition, false ego and control. Not only Native Americans have cultured and kept alive this gift but the British Isles Celts also administered such spiritual communication is my strong belief. Some adherents believe that there existed a co-sharing of Nature-based beliefs long ago.

Dominant society-organized religion has ruthlessly destroyed all influential vestiges of the old, practiced Celtic Way. It is quite foolish, my opinion; to go to organized religion to seek practical, applicable knowledge regarding genuine input into one's Spiritual beliefs and advancement. The Natural Way, the Celt Way, (the Shaman Within) has been rekindled by my tribe, the

Lakota, after it (our spiritual beliefs and practices) were unconstitutionally (unlawfully) banned by lobbying Christian missionaries to our legislative Congress.

We Sioux were great fighters and initially defeated the American Army, namely their mounted cavalry which were ordered West to defeat us. We were mounted as well and like Genghis Khan, whom we are descended from; we had better horses, expert riders and easily captured their guns and horses for close to two decades. What we thought was an end to the fighting was the treaty of 1868 which we would not sign until the Army burned all their forts down in our territory. Their losses were so evident that they signed but in less than a decade the White Man's greed for discovered gold made them break the Treaty.

We were confined to Reservations eventually and the destruction of our 'Shamanic Way' began. During this sad, hungry time of despair, our Medicine men and women (Holy Persons/Shamans) stubbornly clung to their beliefs and ceremonies. Our reservations were so vast that the missionaries and their lackey Sioux-converted spies could never entirely penetrate our secret. The Olde Nature's Way was the 'Right Way' for us, especially after we viewed the many atrocities displayed by the Christian missionaries, namely Paedophilia, Greed, Superstition, Cruelty and Un-truth perpetuated against us.

But fortunately we suffered less than a century of the U. S. Government occupation complete with their bullying, disrespectful missionaries before the advent of Martin Luther King's Civil Rights Movement which freed our return to the Olde Natural Way, which the majority of my tribe prefers to go back to. Our ceremonies have returned, our Shamans have emerged from the Underground where the old full blood families kept the smouldering embers of Spirituality glowing during our Reservation confinement. A century was not enough to destroy us and now our annual Sun Dances of Thanksgiving flourish upon our reservations and the lesser ceremonies as well – Sweat Lodge, Vision Quest, Pipe Ceremony... and yes – the powerful Spirit Calling is also among us.

We have succeeded to re-birth the Natural Way, the Celtic Way, the Shaman Within. Over 60 annual Sun Dances of Thanksgiving now flourish upon our Dakota/Lakota reservations. Back in my time, as a young child there were no Sun Dances allowed. Finally, as a young adolescent sitting beside my Grandmother, I watched Chief Eagle Feather boldly defy the missionaries and bring back the Sun Dance on a hot August day. Chief Fools Crow, whom I would later dance six times in six years under, pierced Eagle Feather before a pitiful small crowd. In my final years of Sun Dancing this crowd would grow into thousands. Now you are ready. The Shaman Within will guide you. Read on!

Ed McGaa, Eagle Man, Oglala Sioux- OST 15287, best-selling author of *Mother Earth Spirituality, Rainbow Tribe, Nature's Way, Creator's Code* and many others published by Harper Collins.

Introduction

Behind all material things and all the change in the world rests one fundamental, universal principle – the way things are. The ultimate reality which is unfathomable and unknowable yet manifests itself in laws of unfailing regularity. The purpose of human life, then, is to live life according to the way things are – or the unfailing cycles of Nature. When we achieve an understanding, acceptance and appreciation of these cycles and our part in them, then we will be free to choose to continue within, or to move beyond them...
Taoist teachings

Shamanism is simply the way of being in harmony with all living things; it transcends all conventional divisions and is the oldest belief system known to humanity. Our *Rites of Passage* come from this knowledge and instil in our emotional and physical bodies clear guidance and direction, preparing us for the next stage of our human evolution... Atlantis is not a myth, Atlantis is 'now'. Plato wrote that during the final 'Golden Age' the people could access the fifth dimension and live in harmony with one another and all that was around them. It was Heaven on Earth.

We have walked full circle and the test of time will emerge from the question, *'Will we actually get it this time around?'* Our alarm clock is set and time is ticking. We are the ones we have been waiting for. We are those strands of life intricately woven in time and space to connect back with the past to intertwine it with the future possibilities of a chosen destiny.

It is our personal responsibility to gain a deeper understanding of the way in which our beautiful Earth works. She reflects back to us a mirror of our emotions that have been bubbling beneath the surface, like a volcano waiting to erupt. If we wish to flourish, the acceleration of dis-ease and illness within us has to stop. We are the cause of this 'plague of illusions' distorting and depressing our greatest possibilities. It is *the* wake-up call. So how do we answer it? By tapping into the teachings our ancestors have accumulated since we first walked on Earth – by accessing the 'Shaman Within' who holds the key, and the key is our rites of passage. This book walks with you to reclaim your natural rites of passage, and create your own path to enlightenment.

We yearn to be whole and sacred once again, to fill the great void that lies within the very centre of our hearts. We seek outside ourselves in order to try to rediscover, joy and desire. We hope to be truly free of the suffering that we find in and around us and follow the cycle of life, whether we are aware of it or not. Our ancestors walked the great Wheel of Life, from the Celtic wheel of the year in the North to the Medicine Wheels of the West, and had an intimate connection with Source. They knew it worked because they lived by it, through the ebb and flow of life. It was the golden age, an epoch, embracing the oral traditions of rites of passage.

Mother Earth has always maintained a very sacred connection with Wisdom Keepers, known universally as Shamans or Medicine Keepers, but the 'Shaman Within' exists in us all, waiting to be re-awakened. Our personal 'vision quest' (discovering our purpose in life) has been lost since our spirit was crushed and suppressed by systems of control and manipulation, and our individual souls expelled from existence. How can we regain our souls – our true, authentic selves, our very meaning? By reintegrating our rites of passage into our core foundations, the industrialisation that has traumatised our instinctive feelings will be removed. Then we will once again experience a sense of purpose in our everyday lives and satiate our need for the search of profound belonging.

For the last forty years I have listened and learnt from Mother Nature, the Grandmothers and Grandfathers, Elders and Teachers of our Earth-centred traditions from around the world.

What I embarked upon in the process was the greatest treasure hunt of my life. This has brought more meaning and momentum to my life's work to help others. I was led into the world of oral traditions and connecting with the native peoples of North, Central and South America and into the mysteries of Upper and Lower Egypt, all of which strengthened my connections to the Gods and Goddesses that have informed and inspired millions for millennia. I left my Celtic lands in search of completion, a fitting together of the missing pieces of the jigsaw puzzle and I have now come full circle back to my ancient soul rites. What I needed to do was 'die' to my old story so that a new story could emerge and be created – rebirth and renewal.

I will share with you my journey of following the voice of Spirit to find the Shaman Within. It is a journey you may sometimes find strange, funny, painful but often magical, as we explore the ancient rites of passage: vision quest, soul naming, inner child, sacred marriage, the four losses, the give-away, elder-hood, and death and rebirth. Once reinstated they will help you to evolve through life with greater ease, joy and appreciation of the beauty in being H-U-M-A-N (History Uniting Mankind And Nature). This visionary approach transcends all languages, cultures, beliefs and indoctrinations. The dream weaver sees the world as it truly is, one and whole.

Ed McGaa Eagle Man, of the Oglala Sioux, my first Native American teacher, said to me, 'Barb, you've learnt enough now, go out and teach.' Likewise my first earthly guide and mentor, Swein McDonald, one day said to me, 'After you have reached fifty years of age you will have gained enough wisdom to share with others having learned and studied with the indigenous people, walking the fourfold path of seven years each. You live your life guided by Spirit so go and share the wisdom, when the time is right, with people of like mind, who live from their heart wisdom. Heaven is on Earth, the centre of the Universe is the centre of our hearts, the core of our awakening.'

I was shown a vision so powerful that it changed my entire life, and is waiting to be shared with others who are being called. This incredibly deep and profound heart-wisdom is accessible to each and every one of us. Through our personal life experiences and individual rites of passage, Spirit is waiting to help and assist us through the transitional journey to awaken and sing our souls back home. And now it is your time...

Chapter I

The Calling
Yule & Vision Quest

Our world is incomplete until each one of us discovers what moves us – our passion. No other person can hear our calling. We must listen and act on it for ourselves.
Richard J. Leider

'I've got to go, they are calling me!' I said aloud without thinking. Shaun looked at me and smiled, 'Who's calling you? Where do you have to go?' I explained about the visions I was having, that I was being shown to go to Albuquerque in the USA.

'What will you do when you get there?' he asked.

'I will follow my heart and trust what I am being shown.' I was so excited; Spirit had gifted me yet another revelation. Nothing was going to stop me from following my calling. I needed to know more about *Rites of Passage*. I had gone through many different rituals and ceremonies in my life but when I had asked questions I was always told 'all in good time, be patient.'

My mentor, Swein McDonald, explained once, 'There will come a time when you will be able to share your stories, but until then act as if you know nothing. Go to the rituals and ceremonies as if for the first time. Learn, even though you may already know, and then watch and observe others whilst keeping humility in your focus.'

I knew that rites of passage marked a person's progress, a journey from one stage of life to another. By working through and integrating our initiation ceremonies (our rites of passage), we become whole and complete. In traditional cultures, rites of passage were there to serve and support individuals in recognising their unique gifts and potential for the benefit of not only themselves but also for the whole community. Today we have become disjointed and fragmented, separated from our tribe, our people, not knowing how to facilitate our transition from self to soul, girl to womanhood, boy to manhood.

I was ready, booked my ticket, my calling had begun. I landed at Albuquerque airport, New Mexico, in America and the Sun was shining. I felt good and, as arranged, Mary was waiting for me. I had told her about my vision in the dreamtime over the phone a few days before I arrived and she offered to drive me around the area. I checked into a local motel and as soon as I lay down on the bed I fell fast asleep and drifted into another time and place. I found myself standing on a mountain top facing east, watching the sunrise. A new chapter in my life was beginning heralding endless possibilities. From the very depths of my being my spirit connected once again to the ancestors of the ancient land of 'Turtle Island'. I felt Creator, Great Spirit, surround and embrace me – like a long lost child returning home. I was on the land of my ancestors once again. This was the heartlands, the land was alive and the birds were singing in the dawn of a new day.

I started to cry with joy. As my tears fell to the earth they created a river that flowed into the oceans of immortality. It was then that I saw him for the very first time. He was sitting on the mountain top in front of me watching the same sunrise. I felt the presence of a very old and wise medicine man. He turned around and looked at me and said, 'Look to the gatekeeper.'

I asked, 'Where will I find this gatekeeper?'

'Look to the gatekeeper,' he repeated and with that the medicine man disappeared and I woke up. I lay in my motel bed seeking answers from Spirit about my dream. I did not get a reply. It was now four o'clock in the morning and my body was still on UK time. I switched on the television. The local news was highlighting the 'Annual Native American Powwow' taking place in Albuquerque that weekend. That's it! I thought, that is where I have to go. I believed my answers were there, but little did I know what was to come…

The next morning, I sensed that something wonderful was going to happen. I was ready for Mary when she picked me up at ten o'clock and as we set off in her car, I asked her if she knew where the powwow was being held. She didn't, but suggested we drive around until we find it. After half an hour's fruitless scouting, we began to head back towards the motel when we noticed several marquees near a very large sports arena called 'The Pit'. Many Native Americans were heading through a gated area, so we drove right up. Sitting there, guarding the gate, was a man. I opened the car window and asked if he knew where the powwow was taking place. As he stood up I felt a cold shiver run down my back. This Native American's presence was all-encompassing He was very tall, had long plaited hair and wore dungarees. He bent down and as our eyes locked he said, 'I knew you were coming. I have travelled a long way to meet you.'

I was overwhelmed and began to cry. Mary asked him about the powwow and he told her that the arena was the very place, although the event was to start the next day for the public, which was Friday, and today was for vendor set-up and pre-selective dance competitions. When I finally composed myself long enough to speak, I asked him why he was at the gate.

He said, 'I am a police officer for the native people. I am guarding this gate today to ensure that only authorised people are able to get in.'

I burst into tears again for here was the 'gatekeeper' foretold to me by Spirit in the dreamtime. Once I calmed down I started to explain why I was crying.

'No need to explain,' he said, 'I already know. My name is Two Eagles and I am from Hickman, near Memphis. Come back tomorrow, we will spend some time together.' He wished us a good day and went back to guarding the gate.

Mary and I were ecstatic as we drove away. 'Amazing!' I

exclaimed. For the rest of the day we explored the local area and at the end I returned to my third-floor motel room where, I discovered when I looked out the window, the powwow arena was in clear view. It was only a ten-minute walk away! What I came to find was right on my doorstep! That night I slept well, dreaming of my power animals coming to me who sang sacred songs of their ancient ways. It was an incredible experience, which continued on from my dreamtime into my waking consciousness, singing the songs alive which echoed in my heart.

Early morning I was up, dancing and singing. I could not wait to go to the powwow, so I phoned Mary to tell her I was walking over to it myself. As she had to drive from Santa Fe we agreed to meet up on Sunday, rather than her meeting me that day. I was first in the queue to buy my ticket and once inside I looked for the gated area where I had seen Two Eagles the day before. He was there again! I felt like an excited child who just discovered that fairies do exist. This was all my dreams coming true. Two Eagles got up and greeted me like a long lost friend. I had the most wonderful feeling about him, as if I had known him all my life.

He told me that he knew he was going to meet and teach me the sacred ways in order to help me remember who I was. I started to tell him about my dreams and visions and he just smiled knowingly, as he listened to me joyfully rambling on. The next three days spent with Two Eagles, at the 'Gathering of Nations', were among the most inspiring times I experienced. Two Eagles explained many things that I had been questioning. On the third day, both Mary and I walked around the powwow with Two Eagles. We caught up with people we had met through other trade shows; like reuniting with members of an extended family.

Two Eagles told me it was time for him to give me my Spirit name. I knew that to receive one's Spirit name you offered a gift as a sign of deep respect for what was about to take place. I went off and bought Two Eagles a beautiful eagle bone necklace and returned to him with the gift.

After Two Eagles accepted my gift, he looked at me and said, 'Your name is Hawk Woman. This is a sacred name and is part of your medicine way.'

I thanked him as I remembered the presence of hawks surrounding me since I was a little girl, walking in the wilds, talking to the animals, the ravens would chase the hawks away. My pagan name of Raven, gifted to me so many years beforehand by Swein McDonald, the Highland Seer, now sat side-by-side with my Native American name of 'Hawk Woman', gifted to me by Two Eagles.

As Two Eagles and I walked back to meet with Mary, he turned around and said, 'I am leaving now.'

I looked up at him, 'But the powwow is not over yet.'

He smiled. 'My work here is done. Time for me to go.' He handed me a powwow programme with his address and phone number written on it and told me that I was welcome to contact him whenever I needed him, adding that I should go to Santa Fe where more would be revealed.

As we reached the main arena, where the grand entry of the dancers was about to take place, Two Eagles turned around and said, 'When you turn around next time I will be gone.' Sure enough, one minute he was right behind me and the next minute there was no sign of him. I found Mary and told her that Two Eagles had gone. She did not seem bothered by this news because she was focussed on getting a seat in the arena for the grand entrance. So I decided to look for him myself.

Despite all the people making their way into the arena, I knew it would be easy to spot Two Eagles because he stood well above nearly everyone there. After searching inside, I went out to the parking lot where I knew he kept his camper van. I could not find it either. I went to the gate where I had originally met him and asked the guards if they knew where Two Eagles might be. They looked at me and asked, 'Who?'

'The native man, he was six foot four inches tall. He's been at the gate for the last three days.' I attempted to jog their memories. They looked confused and said they had no idea who I was talking about. This was weird.

I looked at them and said, 'You know me, right?'

They all agreed.

'Well, how can you not know Two Eagles? He's been the gatekeeper here for the last four days,' I insisted.

They just shook their heads. 'Sorry, we still have no idea who you mean.' I made my way back into the main arena stunned and perplexed, questioning everything that had just happened.

Confused I went to the trade stand of my friends Tom and Mary. They smiled and said, 'Angels come in many disguises. Don't worry. All will be revealed in due course.'

I walked around in a dream state, going over all the events that had unfolded over the past four days. What next? The only clue I had was Two Eagles' message to go to Santa Fe and so I left Albuquerque with Mary on Sunday night to go there. Once in Santa Fe I hired a car and drove to a local motel. After a rather restless night's sleep, I went across the street to a diner for breakfast. Whilst eating, I nearly jumped out of my seat when I glimpsed a man entering the diner who looked just like Two Eagles. He was the same height and had the same braided hair, yet he was a white man!

He sat down at a nearby booth and struck up a conversation with me. He told me his name was Joseph and after a few minutes of telling him of my recent days at the powwow, he invited me to join his drumming circle on Thursday night.

'But I don't have a drum,' I sheepishly replied.

'Go to Red Bird at the Cochiti Pueblo and I'll see you on Thursday,' was all he said before paying his bill and casually heading out the door to begin his working day. I checked out of the motel and drove half an hour or so to the reservation. Once inside the reservation, Spirit led me straight to a small house. I got out of the car and walked round to the back yard. A native man had his back to me as he sat carving a two-headed skinned drum. I walked over and said 'Excuse me. Are you Red Bird?' Without turning around or looking up, he said, 'The Elders told me you were coming. I must teach you the native drum because you will be sharing this wisdom with many.'

We talked for a while about why I was here in New Mexico, both the vision that led me to the powwow as well as the practical side of my trip. Because the business Shaun and I ran involved me sourcing original merchandise from around the world, I had promised Shaun that I would take the opportunity, while in New Mexico, to go to Gallup, the central trading town of Native American jewellery and crafts. Red Bird suggested that he accompany me on the four-hour trip to Gallup because he could then use the opportunity for some drum business there. Surprisingly, without hesitating, I agreed. While Red Bird went inside his house to pack, it dawned on me exactly what my family and friends would say if they knew I, a 30-something lone woman, was driving off with a man I had only just met!

On our way I told Red Bird about the drumming circle I was invited to. Red Bird knew the two-headed drums he made were not yet right for me, so he suggested we stop along the way at his friend's shop in Albuquerque to look for my first drum. We walked in to a shop where many All-One-Tribe shamanic hand drums were on display. One immediately called to me. Pictured on the hexagonal drum was a hawk in the centre surrounded by ravens in each of the four directions. I placed it against my heart and cried as I felt the joy of coming home to my long lost friend. I knew this drum could express the feelings that, until then, I was unable to voice from my head. The voice that needed to speak was from my heart and not my head. In a few seconds I could feel the difference between head talk and heart-talk. My first drum had found me!

We resumed our drive to Gallup and Red Bird continued his storytelling all about his family's tradition of making Native American drums handed down from generation to generation. This was his life's work and passion, and through his deep understanding of how the spirit of the drum works. The spirit of the drum shows us how to change our ways of both thinking and living in a natural environment. For the next three days we did our separate business during the day and then met at the motel during the evenings in order to continue with his storytelling and teachings. His wisdom and knowledge of the drum helped me to form a deep relationship with my own drum so that I could listen to what it was teaching me.

The first words the drum spoke to me were, '*Get out of your head and into your heart, then you will know where to start. It's not the thinking, it's the feeling, it's the knowing and believing...*' There, my first song was gifted from the spirit of the drum. Little was I to know at that time, that it would lead me to the awakening of my heart-voice and that I would go on to record many CDs of songs and chants.

Very early the next morning, we checked out of our rooms and drove from Gallup to a sacred mountaintop for my Sunrise Naming Ceremony, which Red Bird had informed me about the night before. I did not want to offend Red Bird by telling him I had already been gifted a name by Two Eagles, just four days ago, so I chose to say nothing about it. During this ceremony on the mountain, amidst burning sage and prayers, he lifted up his arms just as the Sun broke the horizon and spoke loudly in his native tongue. Then in the middle of the words which I did not understand, I clearly heard 'Morning Star'. He continued to pray, whilst I was asking Spirit what I would do with both native names of Hawk Woman and now Morning Star. At that very moment I heard a piercing cry. I looked up to see a beautiful red-tailed hawk circling above us, and knew my name to be Morning Star Hawk Woman. Both Two Eagles and Red Bird had gifted me with my Spirit name. When Red Bird had completed the naming ceremony, I told him Two Eagles had given me the name of Hawk Woman and that when the hawk had flown above us, I had seen the vision of the two names coming together as one.

Red Bird said, 'Time to become your medicine name, to gain a deeper understanding of its meaning. Only when you are ready, and not before, will you use your sacred name as you call to the Spirit of your ancestors. You have been on a journey, gifting you many visions, and will now lead you on to discover the rites of passage that will heal your life.'

Red Bird gifted me with a deeper insight – it was the understanding that there is no separation, that we are all connected to the One. I had spent four days with each of the medicine men, walking the sacred wheel and honouring the four directions. It was time to head back to Santa Fe for the evening's drumming circle with Joseph. As we started back down the mountain I thanked Red Bird for all his teachings, I felt sorry to leave this sacred place, but knew one day I would return.

I phoned Joseph that night when I reached Santa Fe. I had a quick shower and met him in the motel lobby. We set off with my new drum firmly clutched in my arms. We arrived at the meeting house and I was introduced to the other drummers in the group. I was so excited to play my drum for the first time with other people. Joseph explained that the intention of this evening's circle was a group journey into the lower worlds to meet our power animals. As I sat on the floor I could feel the vibration of my drum coursing through me. I could hear voices talking in very soft whispers but as I looked around the room I noticed that nobody was talking. That's strange, I wondered, who's speaking? Joseph picked up his drum and commenced drumming with a very fast beat. I was aware of all the drums coming together as one voice. It was like a high pitched drone. I tried to recall where I had heard this sound before, it was so familiar.

The next thing I remembered was spiralling down a tunnel

into the Earth while observing my drum and hands having a life of their own. I asked, 'Who is drumming?'

Spirit replied, 'Let go of control and just trust.'

I saw a fire in a forest clearing. Trees, wolves, eagles, bears, snakes and many other animals were being pulled into the flames and then transformed before my eyes into drums. Once again I started to question what I was being given from Spirit. They answered with, 'Find the drum-maker of your drum. Then bring back the drums to your land and share the spirit of the drum with others.'

I found myself being called back from my vision by Joseph's drum who was drumming the call-back beat. After a while I realised I was back in the room with the other drummers.

We took turns sharing our experiences of what happened when journeying in the lower worlds whilst passing around Joseph's 'talking stick'. When it came to my turn to express my experiences and adventures, I found it very emotional and started to stammer my words.

Joseph said, 'Barbara slow down, let your heart do the talking, not your head.'

I looked at him with tears streaming down my face and said, 'Thank you.' After that I was able to share my experiences with everybody. When the drum circle had finished one of the drummers came over to me and shared with me that All-One-Tribe were the makers of my drum and they were to be found in Taos, just a short distance from Santa Fe.

By opening hours next day, I was parked in front of the show-room of All-One-Tribe Drums. I met Feeny, the owner and founder and Lynn, the current holder of the original designs. Throughout the day I was shown the processes the native people from the nearby Taos Pueblo used to make their drums and beaters. I met many different native medicine men and women who would become powerful influences in awakening my inner shaman. At that time they were working with the company to promote mainstream awareness of the transformational powers of the drum. I met Standing Deer from the Taos Pueblo, a well-respected elder who teaches singing and drumming in ceremony. He had travelled extensively, with his 'Mother Drum', sharing his songs, knowledge and native teachings to all who would listen. Standing Deer has to use oxygen for his breathing and finds it difficult to talk. As soon as he picks up the beater and sings his songs, his voice is amazing transcending the physical body into pure Spirit.

After a magical day in Taos, it was time to leave and return to Santa Fe. In the boot of my rental car were twelve, wonderful, new drums from All-One-Tribe and as many more from a neighbouring drum maker called Taos Drums; all destined to leave with me a few days later for the United Kingdom. As I stood looking down on my drum mentors, I took the opportunity to reflect on my very first calling which I would like to share with you.

Many of us have heard the saying, 'When the student is ready the teacher will appear.' For me, the experience of this wisdom began when I was twelve years old and met Swein McDonald. I had been crying out to Spirit for help. Spirit listened to me and upon hearing my heart, responded. Swein's eternal wisdom teachings awakened my soul's 'knowing'. My mind expanded to embrace an incredible journey that would take me to the heavenly heights of the soul and the hellish depths of the self. I discovered, in both the Inner and Outer Worlds of our creation, Wisdom Keepers are waiting to appear to us. It is our choice whether we follow our calling – to awaken from the deep sleep that we have been subjected to and make the journey. Teachers come in all forms, and are not always who or what we are expecting them to be. My experiences are summarised by the first thing I always say when running courses and workshops, 'Have no expectations.'

Understanding Your Calling

Storytelling is the oldest form of sharing and teaching traditions, which have deteriorated with the disbandment of tribes, clans and cultures. I have experienced sacred storytelling around campfires and hearths, when the nights are long and dark and the stars are bright. So what is the 'Calling' and how does it happen? It can come in many ways. Most of us are gifted with our calling in the dreamtime and through visions. It is a profound inner knowing. Everyone has a calling, be it to climb mountains, travel the lands, sail the oceans, become a nurse or doctor, nun or priest. Many saints and seers have referred to the beginning of their true life's purpose as a 'Calling to serve God'.

Your calling is the 'highest purpose' for your life. Great prophets and oracles of the past like Muhammad, Buddha, Jesus, Gandhi, Alexander the Great and Joan of Arc, to name a few, had to fulfil their calling, even if it meant death. These people did not fear death; they knew it only as a transition from one form to another. They had reached for the impossible dream, to go and do what no one has done before. Captain Kirk's quest to 'go where no man has gone before' is the calling that lives within every one of us today. The greatest Universe of all is the one within you that still needs to be explored and traversed without damaging or spoiling the integral landscape.

We came to Earth from the Spirit World to follow our calling. This desire has propelled us through time and space to be in the here and now. If anyone should ask you to explain what drives you forward, your honest response will come from an unquestioning faith, for when you have no more questions you will not be asked to explain yourself any longer. I discovered how much easier my life became when I eventually surrendered to the Great Mystery and put away for good my 'girlish ways' of anxiously wondering what's next. The calling to awaken your life purpose arouses your soul. Following your calling is your proclamation to willingly become the best, the most content, you can be.

So what happens to keep us from following our calling, awakening our soul, knowing and walking on Earth on our own, unique journey? Look at your life now. Are you awake? Are you following your calling? Do you know the history of your soul path? If not, why not? What has stopped you? Perhaps it's because of your fears, doubts and worries or maybe you are reacting to other people's fears, doubts and worries. Many times I have witnessed people not following their calling because they were worried about what other people would think, do or say about their most heartfelt decisions. Expressions like, 'Anything for a quiet life' become common excuses. Despite the fact that we have bills to pay, to live in the materialistic world of today, we can all still be 'walkers' between the middle world of self and the upper and lower worlds of spirits and souls.

Our unloved and unloving selves are almost always birthed from our own emotional and psychological wounds experienced during childhood. I was in a local supermarket and overheard a conversation between a mother and her young daughter. The little girl asked, 'Why do we have to buy our food in the shop? Why can't we grow it ourselves and have lots of animals around us?' The mother's response to this wise little one was, 'Shut up. You come out with such stupid ideas. Don't question me. You are only a child. You know nothing.'

Many of us are told that our visions of what we will be when we grow up are silly fantasies. When I was in primary school, singing and dancing in the school play, I told my mum that when I grew up I was going to be on stage. I also told her that I would help lots of people get well by giving them lots of love because they were walking around with holes in their hearts. The response was, 'Don't be so stupid, how could you possibly know that? You're only a child?'

Before I became a teenager, I again shared with my parents my dreams and visions, telling them that I knew what I was going to do and I would do it. I was belted and told, 'Don't go telling

I remember to be treated to be a nun –

– people do think im crazy and weird

anyone what you have just said. They will all think you are crazy and we don't want anyone thinking that about our family. We have morals and standards to keep up.'

I believe that as children our souls communicate very clearly to us about what it is that we want to do, but we become conditioned to be afraid of being hurt or hurting others when we act upon our inner knowing. We are confused about what is truly selfish and we really struggle with why it seems we must abandon everything and everyone we've valued to follow our dreams and goals. I was further humiliated by my dyslexia, so I buried my visions deep within my soul and waited until I grew up. I knew I had a calling and when the time was right nobody or nothing was going to tell me otherwise.

I will share with you a story of my dear friend Nicolas Standing Bear. As a child he was ridiculed for his poor health and every time he would rise up, something always knocked him down. Over the past couple of years he has travelled all over the world searching for answers. His calling was to find out who he is and why he is here. His Journey led him to many sacred places including Egypt. Here Nicolas' goal was to climb Mount Sinai. On his first attempt he got three-quarters of the way up the mountain before the climb became too much. When he returned with my group in January 2009 he was determined to make it to the top. I decided to remain at base camp that morning. When Nicolas returned to our base, he was very disappointed.

With tears flowing he confided, 'I nearly made it. I am such a failure. I was so close to the top but could not quite do it. I could even see the top. I'm so upset with myself.'

I sat him down and said to him, 'Nicolas, stop looking at what you have not achieved but rather look at what you have achieved. You have climbed the mountain twice now and both times you have seen the top of the mountain within arms' reach. Remember as you look down the mountain see how far you have come on this journey.'

Our calling can feel like the proverbial 'voice in the wilderness' and in a way it is when we don't remember how to find our way back to our soul. It would be very helpful if we had signposts that showed us the way of our calling or a satnav directing us to our souls! When we realise we are at a crossroads in our lives we are in a place of power because we have a choice to make. Many times the directional signs we are seeking are literally right in front of our faces. How many times have you looked for something you have lost and you go back to where you started and find it is right in front of you. If I had looked out of my motel window in Albuquerque I would have seen the powwow site that I had spent time searching for.

When we start to ask questions such as, 'Who am I?' and 'Why am I here?' we open our hearts to receive the answer to our very own life purpose. When we hear our soul's response, our calling, we begin our 'awakening' by trusting our deepest sense of knowing. Upon making the commitment to journey, we cease questioning. You become one with all of life, filled with a deep joy and sense of wholeness. Those who truly love you will support you every step of the way with words and actions of encouragement. Supporters want you to be happy and to share with them the joy and rapture you are feeling in your success. Look at how happy some parents are for their children when they do well. I wish it was applied to everything we do.

Living the Dream

My first vision quest was to come to this Earth plain to learn and grow with the many different cultures and traditions from around this world. I have met and worked with many elders and Wisdom Keepers, the shamans who have helped many people to connect to their first rite of passage, their vision quest healing. I have come to realise that while others can help us discover ourselves, the one thing that does not change, no matter how far away from home we venture, is Spirit.

The shaman within is a self-realised 'IN-DIVI-DUAL'. Shamans go with-IN, see the DIVI-sion of the self and the soul and recognise the DUAL-ity of the Creator and Creation as one. My greatest teachings and learnings have come from the self-realised shaman within awakening me to my calling and my journey throughout this life. How can we come to this moment of self-realisation, self-mastery?

One of the surest ways of knowing our life purpose is to go on a vision quest. Since the beginning of time people have gone 'walkabout'. We've climbed the highest mountains, gone deep down within the womb of our Mother Earth by entering her sacred caves, ventured into dense jungles, journeyed across deserts and sailed on uncharted seas, all for one purpose. We were crying out for a vision, seeking our life's purpose and answering our calling. Today with modern technology we can see into the deepest oceans, yet the depths of our souls remain the last bastion to be navigated due to lack of support by the system, that will cover up, at any costs, the real meaning of your life's purpose.

A look through history reveals stories of just such personal journeys. Greek mythology is clearly about vision questing; heroes and heroines would journey for months, if not years, to find the 'Golden Fleece'; their pot of gold at the end of the rainbow. They encountered and overcame monsters and demons for the single purpose of awakening within life's greatest gift of self-realisation.

Where are the heroes and heroines of these ancient tales in today's world? Are they lost and forgotten? Today they are replaced by celebrities. Are they to be our roles models? Have they replaced the myths and deities of a golden age that forged the foundations of great wisdom through storytelling? Have television and gaming replaced our sacred storytellers?

In the deepest recesses of our soul awaits the 'quester' of our vision; the one who knows. There have been many films which inspire us to use our imagination to remember what it was once like. From Harry Potter, to the Sorcerer's Apprentice, Pirates of the Caribbean, The Golden Compass and many more, we get lost in the excitement wishing we were a part of the film. One of the greatest epilogues we have at hand is our own life story and by travelling our timelines back into our soul's history, we can discover riches beyond our wildest desires. From my experiences of vision questing, I have found that when I journey to a sacred place and whole-heartedly rest my intention on what it is I am searching for, I always receive the answers. It's about knowing how to press the on switch to activate the archives, to show you the moving pictures of your time lines which so many see fleetingly flash across their vision in an instance. By slowing down time, which we all have the ability to do, we can access what has been lost and forgotten.

My first initiation into the art of the vision questing ceremony was in my homelands of Scotland. One day when I went to visit Swein, he decided that we would go for a walk. He picked up a blanket and said, 'We will be out for a while, so we'll make sure you are warm.'

We climbed the hill behind his croft where there was a forest of Scots pines. We found a secluded area.

'This is a sacred grove, a special place where our ancestors have gathered for thousands of years,' Swein explained to me. 'Here you will be safe. The Spirits will take you on a journey to help you find the visions you are seeking.' He stood at what seemed to be an entrance into the grove and started talking to the Spirits, asking permission to enter into the other worlds. I stood behind him holding my breath, and felt as if everything in the forest was doing the same.

Time stood still, the land surrounding us changed and came to life. Everything was connected. Nature looked like a giant spider's web as luminous threads floated through the air from tree to tree and from bird to bird. Then I heard the buzzing sound for the very first time. I thought it was from bees. When I could not locate any sign of a hive or nest, I shook my head to clear out my ears.

Swein laughed and asked, 'Are you okay, lass?'

'What's that noise?' I asked.

He smiled as he replied, 'Oh, you mean the fairy folk. It's them talking. It sounds like the humming of bees, the droning you hear are spirits talking to one another.'

I imagined recording my voice on tape and then speeding it up one hundred times to make a sound like that.

I asked Swein if he meant the spirits of people were talking to each other. 'Much more than people, lass. You are hearing the Creator and creation as one voice,' he replied and then he took his staff in his left hand and held it out in front of him as he walked around me in a clockwise direction. He moved into the circle and struck the ground three times, leaving his staff in the ground in the centre of our sacred space, declaring, 'The circle is now open so we can communicate with the other worlds. You are protected and safe within this sacred place. It is time for me to leave you so that you can journey and become one with all of Nature around you. The elements are your teachers. Go into the silence and listen.'

My desperate questions tumbled out, 'How long? What will happen? Will I be ok on my own?'

Swein replied, 'You are never alone. You are very safe here. I will not be far away. I will light a fire and be your watcher. You are about to become the quester.'

'What am I seeking?' I asked.

Swein re-assured me, 'Soon enough you will find the answers to your calling.' He handed me the large tartan blanket. 'This will keep you warm. You will be staying here until the morning when the Sun comes up,' he said with a firm, but gentle voice and with a glint in his eyes.

So I sat down in the circle and pulled my jacket around me.

Thank goodness I was wearing my warm clothing and had the cosy blanket. The Sun was just disappearing on the horizon and it was quickly becoming dark. I was a little afraid. All sorts of thoughts were running through my head. I shouldn't have listened to all those ghost and witch stories which abound in the Highlands of Scotland. My friends and I had shared these tales during many long nights around log fires in their homes. Now my imagination was going wild and fear was creeping into my bones as if it were dampness. Through the trees I noticed Swein in the distance silhouetted by the fire. He looked like a great magician with his beard, white hair and his staff in hand. He was staring at the fire and talking to it. I sat feeling sorry for myself in the damp and for a moment I was jealous of Swein sitting by the nice fire, keeping warm.

Suddenly, I heard a noise behind me. I thought, this is it... the bogie man is coming for me! I held my breath until I saw a deer come into the clearing. She was beautiful. She took a long look around to make sure all was well. Then I noticed the fawn, the baby deer. I found my breath taken away again, this time in wonder at the tenderness of what I saw. After the mother was content that her little one was safe, she lay down and the little one followed. I was not alone. My fear left as soon as the deer had entered the circle. I knew I had to remain still because any movement or loud noise would scare the deer away and I did not want to cause that. So I gently lay down and wrapped Swein's blanket around me. I made a pillow for my head out of one of my jumpers, and looked up at the night sky. Near the horizon was an incredible blood-red crescent moon. It was alive, like the fire Swein was communing with. As I watched the clouds passing by the moon, I beheld a magical dance of fire in the sky. Many times I had dreamt of the Earth going through transitional changes with the elements of Earth, Air, Fire and Water all playing their part in the process of renewal and rebirth. My dreams and premonitions always showed me that there was nothing to fear.

I could now begin to see the shimmering Milky Way spread across the sky above. As the Moon edged over the horizon, I was transfixed by the millions of stars coming into view. I remembered the time when I was four years old pointing up to the stars and saying I wanted to go home. I now understood that I was home. I was not separated from the stars. I was the stars. In a rush I felt the Earth. It was like a roar, I could feel the ground tremble and the trees surrounding me shook. I felt strange, as if I were caught up in a vortex of energy. I saw spirals, like the ones I had been drawing for as long as I can remember. The teachers in the schools always told me off for day-dreaming when they found me drawing these spirals over and over again, as I travelled into the other worlds, during classes. I would explain to the teachers that the symbols and signs I was drawing were singing and talking to me. Now I was actually experiencing visions of these spirals in this sacred place.

I felt as though I was travelling at 'warp speed'. It took my breath away. I had stopped breathing. I remained breathless for what seemed forever until I came to the end of the spiral and stepped out into a place of nothingness.

I heard voices say, 'We are the Gatekeepers and Guardians of the Great Mystery. You have come to the Great Void to experience who you are and where you have come from. You are a star child, as are all souls of the Earth. You have remembered who you are and that you have come to the Earth at this moment in time to help others awaken to this knowing. The spirals you have been drawing are the keys to the doorways of different worlds of your one reality. In time you will come to understand their full meaning, but for now it is enough for you to just know you are a Wisdom Keeper and Gatekeeper of the Earth.'

I was told to share the fruits of my experiences. In this way, many people would come to me. The voices continued, 'You are here in the place of creation; the Milky Way. This is where you chose to extend the very creation of your divine being. You will travel to sacred sites and connect with fellow Wisdom Keepers. You will access the portals that have been left on Earth. The signs and symbols there are keys to sound travel and in time you will understand their meanings left by your ancestors about who you originated from.'

I cried as the old ones, the wise ones, now appeared before me. I remembered being here in the Great Void since time began. 'Here in the Great Void you will recall everything. You are on a journey of more than fifty years. Until you share what you know, use your time little one, to learn, grow, travel and prepare. The golden years are upon the Earth. There are many changes coming. Now is the time of the great serpent, death and rebirth. You are a part of the needed change of consciousness on this planet. The spiral which you draw is your key, the portal to the stars. We are here always, for we are not governed by time. When you wish to connect with us, find a sacred place. We are waiting for you wherever and whenever you create a sacred space.'

As I stood up I heard sounds coming from them. They were singing me back home! My whole being was filled with vibration, the vibration of the sound of symbols being sung into me. I saw the spiral once again. This time it looked like a long snake. I slid down its back to Earth.

The next thing I remember is Swein saying, 'Come on lass. It's time to go back to the croft for breakfast.'

Breakfast? But I had only been in this sacred space for a few minutes. I looked around me and noticed that the mother deer and her baby had vanished and the Sun was streaming through the trees.

Swein said tenderly, 'You have had your quest to the stars, lass. I sent the deer to protect you so you would not feel alone. Remember many people do not know who we are and it is best to keep it this way. Let them think what they want, only speak to those who are ready to understand the true message. Take your time to prepare for what is to come. Learn and watch. Even if you already know things, do not say so to others until the time is right. Our ancient traditions tell us we must learn for thirty-two years before we share.

I told Swein the ancient ones told me I would be in my fifties before I was ready to share my knowledge.

Swein responded, 'The timing is perfect. Be patient, for you are a quester and this is your calling.'

Rite of Passage: The Vision Quest

How will you become the quester of your vision? My journey has included vision quests on my native lands of Scotland in the spring, a 'walkabout' in Australia during winter, an empowering ceremony in the rain forests of South America in the autumn and visions of a Sun Dancer on Turtle Island in the summer.

Before Sun Dance, the dancers climb to the top of the hill to experience what the Lakota tribes call 'hanbleceya' translated as 'crying for a vision'. Many different peoples and cultures practice some form of vision questing. Whether we spend just a day in Nature or devote four days and nights of fasting we gain an insight into our calling. So how can you take time out from your 'linear', busy work schedule and make sacred time to connect with Spirit out in Nature? Make the time to be with your soul to go within and find something far greater than you have ever known before. You will be questing for your own personal power – the true vocation of your calling.

Today, one of our greatest fears is spending time alone in Nature. Media hype, exaggerating the dangers of lone travel, has caused many people to develop a deep fear about going walkabout alone. Yet vision quests often require us to travel to the remote destinations to find a quiet, sacred space without the usual distractions that keep us from connecting with Spirit. When I did my first quest with Swein, my head was full of ghost stories and my imagination created all sorts of fears that would not normally have been there.

As we walk the wheel of the year through the Gates – North, East, South then West – working with our rites of passage, it will attune us to the seasons, bringing a rhythm of balance back into our lives once again. What is important is that you do what feels best for you in your own time and in your own way. The healing rites of passage in this book serve as a guideline only; they are not set in stone. They have shaped and changed my way of living and being, something I now wish to share. So I invite you to take what you need and shape your wheel of life your way.

I was given a vision to write this book by Spirit showing me eight rites of passage and the Celtic festivals. I was guided to start with 'Yule' – the new birth from the universal womb of life. This is the time of the year known as the Winter Solstice (Alban Arthuan, Saturnalia or Christmas).

Winter Solstice marks the shortest day, Nature's least productive time in the Cycle of the Wheel. The time of endings and beginnings, the re-emergence of light out of the darkness of winter, bringing renewal of life as the Sun is reborn and starts to burn brightly once again. Our Celtic ancestors celebrated the birth of the Sun as did the ancient Persians, and later Romans, who celebrated the rebirth of Mithras, a Sun god, born on 25th December. We are invited to emerge from a period of deep personal reflection during the dark winter slumber, now stepping into new life, and a new year – from death to rebirth.

It is now time for you to prepare for your vision quest by calling on your spirit guides and power animals, to help you discover the answers to the questions you seek. Firstly, it is important to find a sacred space, a safe place to hold your rite of passage ceremony. This may be a place that you already go to out somewhere in Nature. Walk around the area, making sure of your personal safety in case of extreme weather conditions. Make sure you are not sitting too near trees, just in case of a lightning strike. Yes, it is a sign of a shaman if you are struck by lightning; however, speaking from personal experience it is not advisable as anything electrical goes haywire when you touch it. I have gone through too many cars, phones, and computers, so save yourself some money and be safe.

Also make sure you are not near a cliff edge, as I don't want you going into a trance and falling off. Some people prefer to be hermits and go into the womb of Mother Earth. A cave is a wonderful place to do a vision quest. However, please make sure it does not have any unwanted guests in it or you could end up meeting a new-found undiscovered power animal in the flesh, which might not be of your choosing.

It is very important to ask permission of the ancestors before walking onto and working upon the land. Place seeds and food for the animals and tobacco for prayers as a giveaway and thanks. Once we have prayed to the ancestors and received their blessings, we then create a safe and sacred circle in which to hold our vision quest. If your vision for the quest includes building a purification lodge I would suggest finding a Wisdom Keeper who is experienced and knowledgeable in preparing a lodge for you to sweat before and after your vision quest.

The most important thing you need to do is set your intentions before going out onto the land. Many of us will start preparations for a vision quest at least a year in advance. We will be shown in vision how long we will be on our quest. This can range from one day to four days in ceremony. When I assist people as a watcher, I build a fire nearby and sit like Swein did all those years ago for me, offering protection for those in my care. If you have medical problems let the watchers know before embarking on your vision quest.

If your calling is to journey alone into Nature, make sure that someone knows where you are going and for how long. This is your responsibility, not only to yourself but also to others. The whole time you are vision questing it is not just solely about you. Your supporters are praying with you, eating and drinking for you, tending the sacred fire for your strength and protection until your safe return. What greater gift can come from a friend than their support as your watcher? When you return, your watcher or vision quest leader will be there to assist you in interpreting your signs and encounters, both with the land and nature spirits. This will be done during the concluding ceremony of the purification lodge.

It is important to have warm clothing as you will most likely be out all night. I find this is the best time to be out, and have had amazing experiences and visions watching the shooting stars. A warm blanket is very important, as at night the temperature drops. Spirit food is also of great significance, to feed the spirits who will be watching over you. Please bring water, medicines and also food for yourself for after the vision quest. Remember though, the purpose of fasting is to assist you with your visions; you also need to be sensible about your health and well-being. Carry with you your own personal medicine tools. Bring a drum or a flute. Pack a note book and pen for writing down your experiences.

Once you have gathered everything together, go to your sacred place, beseech the ancestors, get permission, create your sacred space, cast your circle before you sit down and listen. All will be revealed. It will often take a while for your mind to stop interfering, so slow down by dropping into your heart space. Listen for your heart-talk; the still, small voice that you will need to hear above all other voices. Then once you have connected with your heart-voice you can communicate with the wonderful spirit of Nature and of all creation. Your vision quest will awaken your soul's knowing. Enjoy your journey for it will be an astounding experience that you will never forget. Welcome home!

(If it is not possible to go outside to do your vision quest, then you can create a sacred space indoors for this rite of passage. Again trust your intuition; there is no wrong or right way. Follow your heart.)

If it is your calling to vision quest with a watcher or gatekeeper then find someone who has worked in the shamanic field and has run vision quests before. Approach them by either writing to them with your request or by meeting them personally. A true medicine man or woman will listen and honour your request. It is important to find out from them what they have done with regard to leading sacred ceremonies and what their qualifications are that cover taking responsibility for you whilst on the vision quest. It is always befitting to bring with you a gift, whether tobacco, chocolate, or something that you know the medicine person likes. The Vision Keeper will arrange a sacred place for you and perhaps others at the same time but with a distance between you. They will ensure there is a purification lodge for you for before the vision quest and for when you have finished your questing. They will light a sacred fire and tend that fire the entire time you are on your vision quest. They will pray for you, watch over you, protect you, and make sure you are safe. Their intention is to ensure your well-being throughout your journey.

When your vision quest is finished the keeper will interpret your visions and answer any questions you may have about your experience. A true shaman will have your best interests at heart for they will have experienced many vision quests and will have the wisdom, knowledge, integrity and clarity to help you on yours. Remember to gift a donation for all the work they have done. This is the 21st century and our valued Wisdom Keepers need money to pay the bills for firewood, preparation, etc. After all this is completed, and you have decided how, where and when to do your personal vision quest, take the time to focus on what it is that you are asking Spirit for. This is a great undertaking, not to be taken lightly. This is your commitment between you and Spirit, only you will know what to say when the time comes. All I can say is simply surrender and just 'be'. Keep your thoughts and feelings pure of mind and heart; this sacred time is between you and Source. Have no expectations and miracles will happen.

I leave you with some questions to ask of yourself, if you do not have an understanding of your life purpose or how to access your soul's history. Please don't beat yourself up with frustration. Working with the eight sacred rites of passage will unfold and reveal to you in time what you have always wished to know. 'All good things come to those who wait' and 'patience is a virtue' are sayings which apply to your personal vision quest...

- Who am I? *CARIA Morgen 33 mother of two - good person*
- Why am I here at this moment in time? *- To be a spiritual teacher*
- What have I forgotten? *How to love myself*
- Do I have a life purpose? *yes*
- Who do I trust? *not many - spirit*
- Where am I going? *on many journeys*
- Where do I belong? *in nature*
- Where do my fears originate from? *- Bad family*
- What is spirit? *reincarnation*
- What am I looking for?

Chapter 2

The Awakening
Imbolc & Naming

Those who see through the illusions of the self and strive to discover their true nature will reach their ultimate truth, the light of their soul and their inner knowing.

Barbara Meiklejohn-Free

People are often afraid of what they don't understand or cannot comprehend. It takes great faith to transform consciousness, to let go of this lifetime's erroneous conditioning and programming and to surrender to happiness greater than all the riches in the world. Happiness is the life force energy that empowers us in everything we do. Without awakening to this happiness we are empty and alone, void of Spirit's love of all life. Neither will we find happiness by going to the Spirit world before our time. Asleep, we remain unaware of our personal power. This power is our ability to know, feel and understand all that we have carried with us since our first thought. All our actions and thoughts create the world we live in today. It would be wonderful if there was a Wisdom Keeper waiting to gift each of us with the understanding of our life purpose.

The moment we were able to understand and communicate, as little children, is when we were at our most open and intuitive. To have someone there who would understand everything we see and sensed would have helped us greatly in the enhancement of walking between the worlds. The tribal community ensured that each child had an Elder/Wisdom Keeper to guide, teach and nurture them and imbue them with spiritual awareness and strengthen the connection to Nature. Long ago in India, for example, the children lived in the forest and sought guidance from sages. Appointed keepers of ancient wisdoms who guide, love and understand a child's spiritual development are missing in today's societies.

Introducing You

Most of us born into this contemporary world have no choice in our name. My birth name of Morag Jamieson was given to me by my blood mother before I was put up for adoption. My mum called me Barbara Margaret when she adopted me nine months later. By the age of nine months I had been given two different names, which would change the course of my destiny. The nine months from my birth to adoption was another womb time for me while the course of my history was being changed. When I met my blood mother I thanked her for putting me up for adoption because it changed my life. I truly believe I would not be who I am today had it not be for the intervening hand of Spirit. I am now walking my shamanic path. It gifts you with the courage to teach others through your own life's experiences.

Had I listened to my adopted mum's wise words when I was young, I would have forgone lots of heartache, but that strengthens you and enriches your life to a deeper level of understanding of what not to do! You only burn your fingers once. The second time you have a much deeper skill of communication. I was always one who if my mum said not to walk on the grass, I would straight away go and walk on the grass. I always did and always will question everything, I will never conform to restrictions or conditions placed upon me. We are free to be who we wish to be. Let no one or nothing ever stand in your way of being who you wish to be.

Our Birth Day is a celebration of our birth onto Earth after about nine months of being in our mother's womb. Our primal scream resounds throughout the Universe as we announce our arrival into the world of sound. Our birth is our first rite of passage in human form. With us we bring all the memories of our previous lifetimes. Our soul lines are intact, for this day is our reincarnation day. We have come to Earth to experience and fulfil that which we chose to undertake before coming to this world once again. This is why our names are very important to us when they reflect who we are and why we are here. My first Spirit name of Raven was given to me by Swein when I sat in Nature and the ravens surrounded me. My second set of Spirit names, Morning Star and Hawk Woman, were given to me by Two Eagles and Red Bird in a period of less than a week. It would take me a couple of years to integrate my Spirit names into my being. It is a responsibility that I could not take lightly. A Spirit name signifies a sacred undertaking or a personal attainment, a bringing into form of who we truly are.

Riting Wrongs

The chapters of this book focus on various rites of passage for our Soul. We combine these rites with insights into the eight Celtic festivals of the year to gain a new and deeper understanding of how these events affect us in our everyday living. In the first chapter we focused on our Soul's Vision Quest, our Journey in response to our Calling, the reason why we are in the here and now. The very core and foundation of your cosmic make-up is known by accessing and acknowledging who you have been before. Once this wisdom has been activated you are prepared to celebrate your awakening with a Naming Ceremony honouring your Birth Day. This ceremony will help you to reclaim your birth right as Children of Earth, extending from infancy through our teenage years to our coming of age and into our old age as well.

During my early years there was a lack of Earth-centred rites of passage. No wise man or woman was there to help me through the difficult times I experienced as I was growing up. Until I met Swein at 12 years old, I did not have a choice. I was baptised at the age of five in the Catholic Church, which took the place of the naming ceremony I would have received had I been brought up in my natural shamanic ways. I recall being dragged to the church kicking and screaming. Much to my parents' annoyance, I was never the perfect child in their eyes. I did not like what I was forced to do and let them know it. I was reluctantly confirmed when I was 12, which again took the place of my rites of passage into womanhood. Like many children, I was not asked if I wanted to undergo these church ceremonies but felt forced into them.

I was not impressed wearing a white veil on my head and a white dress. In my early years I was the tomboy, climbing trees and playing Cowboys and Indians. After the confirmation ritual, I ran outside, climbed the old Yew tree which was in the church grounds and would not come down until I was ready to. I recall asking the spirit of the tree why I had to endure this, it was not my way. They explained to me that to understand other people's traditions I needed to walk in their footsteps.

I cried out, 'I'm in the only church I wish to be in, here in your arms. You are the tree of knowledge; you are the only teacher I wish for.'

The tree spirits were great. They never said I was wrong. I always felt comforted in the many different trees I grew up with. Each one had a different voice, a different wisdom to impart to me. I experienced how the trees protected and cared for those in need, just like in *The Lord of the Rings*.

The next thing I remember was my mother's voice, 'What are you doing up there? You are in a lot of trouble. Look at your dress. It's filthy.' I was taken home, beaten with my father's belt and sent to bed without any tea. My mother did not know at the time that I had a stash hidden under my bed of biscuits, chocolate, cola and other goodies that I bought with the pocket money I was given when I was good! I was always happy when I was sent to bed since it meant I could have a feast all to myself eating what I wanted, not what my parents forced me to.

It was not until my early thirties that I experienced a rite of passage that honoured my Awakening. This was my first Native American Naming Ceremony with Red Bird, which was very different to the one I had with Swein much earlier in this lifetime. Whenever I had visited Swein I would go outside to Nature and sit in the Scots pine trees behind his croft while my friends' mothers would have readings with Swein. The ravens and the crows would always visit me. I sat for hours on end watching them as they watched me, becoming the watcher and the seeker. Swein shared with me that to know the raven I had to become the raven. So every time I was at Swein's or out in Nature I became the raven. I started to experience shape shifting after many hours of watching them. I could not separate them from me. We were one. At night when I fell asleep I became the raven and flew in the dreamtime. This I loved. I was free. I had wings and could see everything. I was always disappointed when I had to wake up because I loved to fly so much.

'Why can't we be like the birds and fly free?' I asked Swein one day.

'We can,' he replied. 'It is only ourselves and other people that stop us from being free to soar on high, to reach the endless possibilities of who we truly are and can be if only we are given the deep understanding that all of us have wings. We are all angels come to Earth, to learn, grow and share with everything around us. What has the raven taught you?'

I declared, 'Freedom, strength and the courage to be who I wish to be and not what other people expect of me. Not to have my wings clipped by other people.'

Oddly enough ravens at the Tower of London have their wings clipped to stop them flying off. We are told the reason for this is it will bring bad luck if the ravens leave the tower.

I am reminded of a true story. An eagle was captured and tethered to a stake. It walked round and round the stake, for this is all it knew. It soon forgot how to fly and stopped flapping its wings. After many months of capture, one day a wise man saw the eagle and knew he is meant to fly free and not be tied to a stake. He unbounded the eagle and said, 'Go! You are free again to fly.'

The eagle continued to walk round and round the stake because this was all he could remember. He had forgotten he was an eagle and could fly. This story applies to each and every one of us in today's world. (We must remember that we have the abilities to soar like eagles)

'How many times has Raven visited you in the dreamtime?' asked Swein.

I told him I was with Raven nearly every night.

'Good. You have become one with Raven. Raven has gifted you with looking within the body to see what the outer eye cannot see. In the future you will work with the Raven in different forms of healing. The Raven will assist you.'

I am smiling as I reflect back today on Swein's words of how Raven would help me. I pick up the raven wings I was gifted many years ago by Spirit to use in shamanic healing as I call on Raven to help me in the healing of others. Understanding the medicine of Raven is a lifetime's commitment. Calling myself 'Raven' is an acknowledgement of the forces of Nature at work within me. This is what is known as *becoming your name.*

What's in a Name?

Do you know what your first name means? This is the name you were given at birth. If you can, ask your parents what names they were trying to decide between for you. Ask them why they chose the name you have today. Have you spent the time to trace back to find out about your family tree, and where your first name and your surname come from? This is an important way for each of us to discover our roots and foundation.

Our names influence the course of our life purpose and our destiny. Our name also affects the family members around us. I have looked deeply into the histories of both my adopted family and my blood family. My Scottish blood connects me to the clans of Gunn, St Clair, Jamieson, and McGilvery, back to the times of the battle of Culloden and before.

I played as a child on the battlefield of Culloden near my childhood home in Inverness. It was then covered with Scots pine trees. I would always play near the well where the last McGilvery was killed. Without knowing why at the time, this was the one place I was always drawn to. I was only later to find out that I was from this clan. I was playing and connecting with my ancestors at the same time without even realising what was happening on a much deeper level. The people of the land took the clan leader's surname, and here I was connecting to my bloodline, my people. This deep understanding of how, as a child, I could intuitively connect to my blood ancestors who once walked upon the land is easily explained. My ancestors took me to their graves and bones and the land to connect with their spirit. There are no mistakes. Spirit will take us if we're willing and have an open heart connected first and foremost to who we are. I was being taught by the Spirit as my forefathers and foremothers had been taught for thousands of years before me.

When we look at all the different cultures from around the world and how they name their children, a lot of things come into play. Some elements are the time of birth, the place of birth, who attended the birth, who the parents are and the grandparents. My Egyptian brother Fergany was born in a pyramid of Giza and continues to be honoured as the 'Man of the Pyramids'. As I am writing this chapter, I can look out of the top floor flat of Fergany's home to a magnificent view of the Great Pyramid with the Sphinx in front. It's not by chance that Fergany, Man of the Pyramids, has a house directly in front of the Sphinx and leads groups from all over the world into every sacred site in this amazing land called Egypt. When my husband David and I walk around the Giza plateau and Egyptians come up to sell us something, all we need to say is we are staying with Fergany. We are respectfully left alone. Fergany's surname holds great respect here in Giza because of his father and his father before him. Not only is Fergany known because he walks his talk. He walks his name into his personal power.

Many children of different cultures are named after gods and goddesses. In the Hindu tradition the naming ceremony is very important and involves looking at the child's horoscopes to determine the date and time of birth, the birth star, the forefather's name, the deity's name, and the name the child will be called by in everyday life. Here in Egypt the tradition is to give the child a name that has an honourable meaning and will benefit and bring blessings to the child throughout his or her life. In other African villages children are first given a name which is later changed when they reach their rite of passage called puberty or coming of age. Some tribal customs for naming children include calling upon the local medicine man or woman to cast the bones to see the destiny of the child about to be born. They prepare a great feast for the Birth Day of an old soul into a human life form once again.

For most of us living in the UK, our bloodline comes from many different cultures. Our native roots go back to the Gaelic, Norse, Pictish, Welsh, Gaulish, Germanic, Latin, Greek, Hebrew and other ancient cultures. With all the people who now live in the UK, it is truly a marvellous melting pot of many different cultures. This is the true meaning of this land, a United Kingdom, uniting the people as one.

My Highland ancestors valued clan names not surnames, so it would be Barbara of the clan Jamieson, Gunn, St Clair, and McGilvery. The name I use today is Barbara Meiklejohn-Free for the following reasons. Barbara means mysterious one, hidden depths, limitless and unending. Meiklejohn means 'truth conquers', and Free came from my former marriage with Shaun. I wanted to keep my name of Meiklejohn as well as his surname of Free, which means a free man or woman of the land. So I combined them all to form an individual name that describes who and what I am: the mysterious one who comes from the stars, sharing the truth of ancient wisdom with one and all to set the people free. I was gifted this expanded information twenty years ago in a reading by Marcia Day, an astrologist at the Arthur Findley collage. At that time I had not added Free to my name, yet the name I had chosen before I came into my earth walk was already written in the stars. My destiny was changed at nine months old to become who I am today.

Until the Domesday Book of 1086 was compiled by William the Conqueror a surname wasn't important. The Native Americans did not use surnames until the whites colonised them. We all remember the names of Red Cloud, Black Elk, Geronimo, Sitting Bull, Chief Seattle and many more. Would we have remembered if they were called John Smith?

As you probably know, John Smith came from the very common name of John who was the blacksmith of the village, hence the full name of John Smith. We started using surnames to separate ourselves from one another when we had too many Marys and Johns in the same village. There are still places in the world today where people do not use surnames. It's only in this legal world that we are required to state our given names.

Intrinsic Power

Take your time and find out more about what your name means in today's world, and look at how you can become a free man or woman of the land you live upon, in more ways than one. You are not a 'legality', you are 'egality'. It is time to emerge from the seas of unconsciousness onto the shores of awareness and reclaim your ancestral birthright. Let us first look at our names and how we can go about starting the foundation of a new you.

- Who are you and where do your ancestors come from?
- What day does your Birth Day fall on?

- Do you know the time of your birth, and where you were born?
- Do you understand the meaning of both your first name and surname?
- Have you traced the history, traditions, culture and the geography of your first name and surname?
- Do your names come from your father's bloodline or your mother's?
- Have you had your astrology chart done to discover your path of Destiny?
- Have you looked into researching your family tree? This is your axis mundi, the world tree with the very core and roots for understanding the complexity of your ancestral lineage line.
- Do you know your soul's lineage, tracking your soul lines?
- Have you walked on the lands of your forefathers and mothers to connect with who you are?
- Did your ancestors change their name due to relocation, not wishing to be known, or due to records that have been lost or destroyed?
- Has your family kept secrets from you about your birth line? Maybe you were adopted.

Our names hold great meaning, but this understanding has been almost lost. By tracing your ancestors through your name you can discover a lot about yourself. When I visit the USA, many Americans I talk with are happy to know I am Scottish. They tell me that their grandmother was Scottish or English or Irish. They are so proud of their heritage and where they have come from. They love my accent, would love to visit the UK and walk the land of their ancestors because it means so much to them. They feel a part of them is missing because they don't fully know their roots. I explain that this yearning for a pilgrimage is a calling for their souls to go home.

Let's look now to the naming ceremony and how we can apply it to our lives today. This ceremony is for those seeking a spirit name and for those wanting to gift their newborn children with a deeper understanding of the power of their given names. I speak to many people in workshops and talks and ask them if they are happy with their names. The response I usually have is about half the people in the group wish for a new or soul name. The Naming Ceremony, or gifting of a soul name, is based on Earth-centred traditions found in many different cultures from around the world. This beautiful ceremony is a welcoming of the child's soul to the Earth plane from the Spirit world.

Tribal cultures from around the world have many different ways of welcoming their children onto the Earth. They honour that their newborns come with great wisdom and understanding, for these souls have come directly from Spirit. Newly born souls still have an unbroken link with the Great Spirit and can remember who they are and where they have come from. You can see this by the memories they carry with them from previous life times. Unfortunately they soon fail to remember as they get lost in the seas of forgetfulness and are carried not by the tides and Nature's flow of the Earth's movement, but by an unnatural and controlled way of living. They are integrated into a strange world, devoid of feelings, totally different from the spirit world which they have just come from; in Heaven only love and truth exit.

The Naming Ceremony is our first rite of passage on our Earth walk. In certain traditions before children are gifted with their name, the child is observed over a period of time to see what the child is drawn to for an understanding of what they will grow up to become. For example, the elders would have watched to see if early on you were a great hunter, or were drawn to working with herbs and tinctures, or demonstrated a gift for writing, singing or dancing. If my adopted parents had taken the time to watch me, they would have seen that I lived in Nature and did not enjoy living in their house, that I slept on the floor and not in my bed, that I sat for hours on end gazing into the fire in the living room hearth until I fell asleep in front of it, that I built a tree house in an old oak tree at the bottom of the garden, that I was always wearing feathers in my hair and bringing home all the stray cats and dogs I could find. Swein watched me and saw straight away my true nature.

In many cultures the baby's name represents many aspects of Nature, mystical entities, saints or other names from holy books. Sometimes the name given by the parents to the child has such a deep meaning that only they know its truth. This name will protect the child from unwanted energies. The naming ceremony gives the child a sense of safety and belonging, honour and respect. Also important is to observe children as they grow up to see how they are living the true meaning of their soul name. Many children inherit the name of a passed loved one. This is a great honouring of the ancestors to remember them. The child who has just come into the world as a newborn is honoured as well, for they are completely unique and different from the ancestor who has gone before them.

Often when doing readings with people who wish to connect to their dead loved ones, I find that the loved one chose to come back again to Earth as their child or grandchild. I was doing a reading for a lady called Susan who had just lost her father William. He came through and said he had promised that he would never leave Susan. He said he would be back as her son, much to Susan's surprise. She told me she had no plans for another child. She already had two children, and she and her husband had tried for the past five years for another but were not able to. She put this down to nursing her father in his ill health for the last five years of his life. William continued to tell her when he would be born and that it would be the same time as he died. A few months ago Susan visited my shop in Buxton with her new born son William, who was born on the same day that his grandfather had died. Her father kept his promise and returned.

What do we gift to our future generation who are being born into this world today? They are the pioneers in the next step of our human evolution. They are highly evolved spiritual souls, who need our guidance and wisdom now. These ceremonies help us to be grounded in this physical world. We need to feel safe, protected, honoured and respected by our family, friends, loved ones and our community around us. Gone from modern life is the kinship of the tribes. Most of us live in little boxes devoid of contact with our true soul family. Elders and children are left in nursing and foster homes because nobody has the time to look after them. This would not have happened in a tribal family, because all were taken care of. Old people were not cast out as witches but were honoured as wise men and women.

Cosmically Sacred

The naming ceremony is a welcoming of your soul into the physical world. This is why it is so important to integrate this Earth wisdom now. You are all Wisdom Keepers who deserve to honour your soul, I spend a lot of time doing soul retrieval, helping people remember their soul which has not been honoured and awakened into its true life purpose. So whether you are two or 72 it is time to call your soul into being. Your soul will know your real name and who you truly are. It takes great courage to be on the Earth in the physical body.

To live in human form on the Earth is the greatest adventure of all. The trick is to live with yourself forever, and that is an art in itself. This is what we are here to experience and learn. It is important to integrate your mind, or the conditioned self, with your body which is a great teacher and your soul who has been a part of you since the beginning of time. Then your spirit comes into true form. Your soul knows when the time is right to prepare for your first rite of passage. The naming ceremony celebrates your Birth Day. Your name is sacred.

Many years ago I was invited to my first gathering of elders and Wisdom Keepers in the USA. When the elders entered the room, they announced to the assembled people who they were, their tribal ancestry, and the names of their grandfathers. Since then, I have witnessed this proud introduction of lineage in other native gatherings all over the world. One of the most amazing and colourful events I continue to attend is the annual Native American Gathering of Nations Powwow in Albuquerque. During the Grand Entry, each tribe and every elder is announced as they enter into the sacred space of the arena. Here is where representatives meet as one people from nearly every tribe in the North and South Americas, from Alaska and Canada to the southern tip of Argentina. How I wish we of the modern world would put our differences aside and look to their example of coming together as one people. Here in the West, the only time our name is called out in ceremony is when we are at a wedding or a function. We have lost an important part of our heritage.

So how can you find out more about your bloodline? From the moment I knew I was adopted, I wanted to find out who I was and where I had come from. The first thing I did when meeting up with my blood family about ten years ago was to ask about my lineage. Since then I have been on a mission to find out more about the blood that flows through my veins. This is our connection to the pulse of life, to knowing our ancestors. I could not find the truth about my birth when I was younger. My adopted parents told me a lie, saying my birth parents were killed in a car accident. You can imagine my surprise when I got a phone call from my brother thirty years on saying I had an entire family. I have six blood brothers and I am the only girl.

Not coincidently, I was living outside London when I was reunited with my blood family. The entire family lived within fifty miles of me. They had also all moved from Scotland to England as I had done. Technology can now help us trace our bloodlines back to where we have all come from on our evolving planet. DNA studies show us that people living on the Earth today have one thing in common. All our ancestors living before recorded history came from Africa approximately one hundred and fifty thousand years ago. I have travelled all over the world and I keep coming back to the Egyptian part of Africa every year to write and rest. It feels like home because it is home.

As a nation we can truly find ourselves once again by going to the roots of our tree of life, our family tree. It's called a family tree because your tree of life is your soul family, the connection to all the worlds both seen and unseen. Our personal story connects us to our common history. When people come to me for readings to trace their family history, I help them by speaking with their loved ones in the spirit world to connect with grandparents they never knew. People gain some answers to the questions they have about who is in their bloodline and where they come from. I then combine a deeper understanding of who they have been since the beginning of this world time by tracing their soul lineage. I weave this wisdom together with the knowledge of their ancestral bloodline for a powerful understanding of who they are.

Also when connecting with loved ones from the spirit world during readings, I am asked to describe who I am talking with and to ask the spirit for their name. As soon as I give them the loved one's name as a confirmation, they are happy. It is evidence of survival beyond death, and we all need to know in one way or another that we continue to live on. Our soul name is the key to unlocking our innermost potential. Our soul name resounds throughout space and time, singing our souls back home.

Rite of Passage: Naming Ceremony

Now it is time to prepare for your naming ceremony. This ceremony is a heartfelt 'soul awakening' experience. You undertake to connect to all life. You belong, feeling the bond deep within the innermost sanctuary of your knowing. You are birthed as your soul awakens once again and soars to its highest potential. Your heart sings and your soul rejoices for you have found the one you have been looking for. It is a sacred ceremony and therefore whatever aspects or meanings that are brought into this ceremony are held in the greatest respect.

You can choose to do this at whichever part of the year feels right for you. However, 'Imbolc', halfway through winter in early February in the Northern Hemisphere, or early August in the Southern Hemisphere, is a most auspicious time. This is the time when the days lengthen, when the land is preparing to birth again in the spring; a time of emergence as new shoots appear from the ground, early flowers begin to blossom and we witness the start of the renewal of life. This was an important time for our ancestors, as fresh milk and dairy products once again became available, meaning the difference between life and death after the cold, harsh scarcity of winter. At Imbolc today it is still a Pagan tradition to pour fresh milk on the ground to honour the Earth Mother and to ensure fertility for the coming season in the agricultural communities. It is a time of purification in preparation for the coming year portrayed as the young virgin Maiden aspect of the Celtic Triple Goddess. She is the young girl awakening to womanhood just as nature begins its fertility cycle.

And so it makes for a wonderful time to birth your soul name. There are many ways of undertaking this ceremony. Your local spiritual church can perform naming ceremonies, or you can seek out those who work within the traditions of your birthland. Every culture has a wise man or woman who can perform this ceremony for you. Remember, your name is the foundation for the other rites of passage that follow, so choose wisely. I have both a Shamanic name and a Native American name. I also have a hidden name known only to the gods and goddesses which I use in high ceremonies when invoking the ancestors of the lands I walk upon.

You may want to go on a vision quest first to seek your name, or you can go to a wise person of your traditions and beseech them for a name. Always bring a gift to them and remain aware of which land you are on and the traditions of the gift, be it tobacco or chocolate. Ask someone who knows the elder you are approaching which gift is appropriate to bring with you. At a chosen time you will approach the elder and ask for a soul name. If you already have your name gifted to you by spirit in your vision quest, you can let them know you had a vision of your name and would like a naming ceremony. The elder will go away and sit with spirit to pray for a name for you.

They will call on your ancestors, the appropriate gods and goddesses of your traditions, and the ancestors of the land you are upon. These prayers give the elder deep insight into the name that will be given to you. When the elder is ready for your naming ceremony, you may be on your own or with others. There is no right or wrong way of working with ceremony. Your honest intentions are the most important aspect of the ceremony.

Naming ceremonies normally take place at sites sacred to both you and the elder. The elder and his or her helpers will have prepared the site. Please remember when you are gifted your name do not be upset if it is not at first to your liking, it may be because the name gifted to us is what we most need. Later we will see the true meaning of the name given. Your soul name is Creator's way of reconnecting you to your true form of Spirit. You are Nature, not a part of or separate from, but complete and whole as one living life form called Creation. Once you and your elder have chosen the place for your naming ceremony, first ask the ancestors of the land for permission to hold the ceremony within the chosen sacred space. When you walk upon the land you will feel the boundaries of sacred space. This is the space between the mundane world of the head and the sacred space of the heart. You will go from the thinking to the feeling. Your soul's knowing will guide you to the right place where the veil is thinnest to the world of spirit. You might be drawn to a tree, a well, or a stone circle. This pull is the transition from the secular to the sacred. Rites of passage help you to reclaim your true birthright. You may have waited a long time for your naming ceremony to announce the name you are called by from within.

What if your Calling is to host your own Naming Ceremony? You might like to spend the night before your Birth Day at your chosen site, and wake up with the Sun rising in the east to start your ceremony. Imagine yourself as an acorn that has been planted in the Earth for a long time. The Sun's light and warmth are the rays of your soul, now shining onto the acorn as the acorn sprouts through the Earth for the first time. With the index finger of your left or right hand, whichever feels comfortable, draw in the sky the circle that follows the Sun's heavenly journey from east to west each day. As you do so, see and feel the brilliance of the Sun's rays fill your sacred space.

Stand facing the East, open your arms to the Sun and hold them up high. Proudly declare to the direction of the East, *'My name is ...* (say your name)...' three times. Then listen to the calling of the spirits around you. Take your time, there is no rush. Let the elementals guide you.

Once you have done this, cross your hands over your heart centre and say, *'I integrate my soul name into the embodiment of my knowing. May I walk in the beauty of becoming my soul name.'*

When you are ready, turn next to the South with opened arms and declare again three times, *'My name is ...'*

Once you feel that your connection with your name is complete, place your hands across your heart and say, *'I integrate my soul name into the embodiment of my knowing. May I walk in the beauty of becoming my soul name.'*

Turn now to the West and open your arms to declare, *'My name is ...'* three times.

Notice the difference in each direction as you call to the guardians and gatekeepers. When it feels that your connection is complete, place your hands over your heart and speak your heart words to your soul, '*I integrate my soul name into the embodiment of my knowing. May I walk in the beauty of becoming my soul name.*'

In your own time, turn and face the North. Open out your arms and embrace the direction. Let the ancestors of the North welcome you home. Declare your soul name three times, then listen for your name being called back to you from the silence of your knowing. Yes, this is your soul name, the name you have been waiting to hear for a very long time. Own it, claim it as yours. Awaken its memory and become one with your name. Place your hands over your heart and speak your name to your soul.

Now sit on the Earth and feel your connection once more. Place your hands on the Earth and speak from your heart to our Earth Mother, '*I have come here today to honour who I am and where I have come from. My heart is open, and my heartbeat joins with you my Earth Mother to once again evoke my inner knowing.*'

Let the words and tears flow from you onto the Earth, '*Blood of my blood, tears of my heart, I welcome you back into my life. Lost and forgotten I have been, now no more forever unseen. My name is my Calling back to my soul. Awaken now and forever unfold. My destiny, my birthright it's all very clear. My name is my key to the Great Mystery.*'

Take the time to integrate what has just happened. When you are ready, stand and lift up your arms to the sky. Speak your heart words to Father Sky, '*Great mystery of life, you have opened my eyes. Let me reach to the stars and dream in your skies. The Milky Way is my place of birth, from whence I came onto the Earth to live out my destiny and seek the Source of love's true gift for one and all.*'

Once you feel yourself becoming one with all that is, place your hands over your heart and journey into your centre, '*Into my heart this journey will take me, discovering new depths from within. The answers I seek are really quite simple; it's not all that difficult to see. From my head to my heart I take my passage, surrendering to all in my wake, from thinking, to feeling, to knowing, to trust. That's it. I'm we.'*

Take your time coming back into the middle world. You may want to spend the rest of the day in your sacred space. This is your Birth Day. You have just gifted yourself with your soul's name. This is a great time for inner reflection and meditation. Enjoy the day whatever it may bring, for it is the first day of the rest of your life on beautiful Earth.

Chapter 3

The Transition
Spring Equinox & Inner Child

The spiritual path assists mortal man in gaining and under-standing of his or her place within the Divine Order and allows mankind to experience the greater purpose of evolution from a more universal perspective.

Akhenaton

I knew my transition from childhood to adulthood was not going to be easy. I did not like what I saw when I observed my parents in their day-to-day life. My father was always at work and when he did come home, he drank and fought with my mother. If this is what I had to look forward to, then I did not want to be a part of it. I became more disillusioned with life. I did not want to grow up and become an adult. My childhood was filling up with unhappy experiences of family life, when this should have been my happiest time. I would rather be surrounded by Nature; the trees, the elementals, the animals and birds. I was safe in the arms of Mother Nature. I hated going home when mum blew the whistle to inform me it was time to leave. That shrill sound would always cut across the silence to find me wherever I was playing locally. I knew if I did not go back, when she called, I would be in trouble. But I had been belted so many times, from both the headmaster at school and my mum, that I was becoming immune to it. It was worth the pain just to get an extra few minutes of freedom each day. I loved watching the Sun going down on the horizon, and I would not come in until it got dark.

I did not have many friends at primary school because I was considered strange and outspoken. I was constantly getting into trouble with the teachers, spending far more time outside the classroom than in it – I was the outcast. The few friends that I did have were boys. I was a tomboy and could climb any tree and fight just as well as they could, and I excelled at sport. Mum said once, 'If you were as good with your homework as you are with your sports you would be top of your class.' But I was top of my class; I won every sports trophy going and yet that was not enough. No matter what I achieved I was always a grave disappointment to my parents.

In those days there was no understanding of learning difficulties. I hated reading and writing because the written word made no sense. My parents and the teachers knew nothing about dyslexia. Had they known, maybe I would not have gone through all the harsh treatments at the hands of adults trying to enforce things I did not comprehend. I was constantly told that I was stupid, worthless, and a troublemaker. I was not loved. What was the point of sticking around? So I decided to run away.

Not This Life

The thought of running off to London with my friend Lynn, who was also a tomboy, did not bother me in the slightness. It would be an adventure. We got our inspiration from the hippies who were into free love, freedom, travel and fun. It was the end of the 'Swinging Sixties' and the start of the Seventies and we wanted to be a part of it. It's amazing how naive we were. We did not think about all the dangers to ones so young. We thought we were invincible and nothing or nobody was going to hurt us in London. I did not for one moment consider where we were going to get the money to survive. Running away just seemed a great idea.

I smile now as I look back on what I put mum through. 'I didn't bring you up to behave like this,' she said too often. Of course, the wildness and freedom was in my blood, the bloodline of my ancestors. I understand now why I did what I did as a child. I was following both the calling of my ancestors and my soul's lineage line. Nothing and no one could stop me. My soul was on fire. It did not matter how many times they beat me at home, school or church. I remembered suffering much more in previous lifetimes when I endured burnings, beatings, hangings, and drowning.

In this lifetime I was on a mission not to be imprisoned like everybody else around me through fear and conditioning. I packed my school backpack carefully with the sweets, biscuits and other things I would need for my journey and left it ready underneath my bed, which was the one place my mum left well alone. Lynn and I had planned our escape to the last detail, or so we thought. I said an early goodnight to my mum, adding that I was tired. After about an hour in bed, I climbed silently out of my bedroom window with my backpack and cycled to Lynn's house. When I arrived I went straight upstairs to her bedroom.

I did not pay attention to her mother, who picked up the phone as soon as I arrived as I was so caught up in the excitement of the adventure about to unfold. We were going to catch the night train to London by sneaking on board and hiding in one of the compartments of the train under the seats. Lynn had also gathered food, and we were ready. But the next thing we heard was my mum's voice downstairs, asking, 'Where is she?'

I soon learned that in her excitement, Lynn had told her brother, who told his mum, who had called my mum, who quickly came to take me home. I did not go home without a fight. I sat on Lynn's bedroom floor crying my eyes out, I was so unhappy. My cries went unheeded, as I was unceremoniously dragged down the stairs and into the car where my father was waiting. Once home I was severely beaten and locked in my room. Mum said this was the last straw, and that in the morning she was calling the authorities to put me in a foster home. This was all too much for me. I was merely following the true nature that flowed within me. I lay in bed sobbing my heart out after being told by my mum yet again that I was wicked, an embarrassment to them; all I did was cause problems. As I write this the emotions come flooding back; desolation, rejection, loneliness and the total lack of love. It makes me wonder how many others have gone through this and been left to feel a lack of support, care and attention throughout their lives.

The next morning I woke up in a bed full of blood. I screamed. When my mum asked what's wrong, I said, 'I'm bleeding. I'm dying.'

'No,' she replied, 'it's your curse. You are now a woman, and this is your punishment. You need to grow up and stop this childish behaviour of trying to run away.' With that she walked away to return with a large piece of padding.

She tossed it to me saying, 'Here, make do with this. You are not leaving the house until I say so. Now get out of bed and wash your sheets.' I spent the day crying in my room. If this is my life, I didn't want to go on living.

I was not allowed to be who I wished to be, and was forced to do things I did not want to do. I was not allowed free choice of food, clothing, school, or church, which went totally against the grain of my entire being. That night I decided I would run away and not come back. I was happiest when I was asleep in the dreamtime or in nature when under the trees or looking up at the stars. That's where I wanted to be, not in this place of pain. Once the house was quiet and my parents had gone to bed, I got up, dressed warmly, and climbed out of the bedroom window. I went to my willow tree, picked up my favourite blanket, and without turning around started running down the street as fast as I could. I was not able to use my bike, as they had locked it up as part of my punishment for running away.

In the sky above the full moon was showering me with moonbeams. It was a beautiful night, warmer than usual. The silence echoed as I slowed my running to a walk. I was far enough away from home by now, so I could take my time. I drew my breath and looked in front of me. The steep hill path, called the Godsmans Bray, would take me down to the Islands. As soon as I started to walk down the steep embankment I knew I was changing my destiny. It felt so exhilarating that I ran down the bray. Nobody can catch me now, I thought.

At the bottom of the hill is the park. As I passed it I could hear the laughter of spirit children echoing around the swings and roundabouts I used to play on. It was as though they were calling to me to come and play. 'I must go on,' I said, 'I cannot stop and play.' My destination was the Islands, a place that I had been coming to since I was a little girl. It was my playground ever since I can remember. The river Ness runs from Loch Ness right through Inverness, and here was the place where the waters divide into two before joining again further down the river.

Upon the Islands was nearly every tree I could imagine, and lots of nooks and crannies for places to hide where nobody would be able to find me. One of the entrances to the Islands on the east side was a suspension bridge. I stopped when I arrived at this first bridge, for what I saw in front of me took my breath away. The moon had a full rainbow of colours encircling it, and the mist swirled along the river's edge creating the effect of a doorway into unseen worlds. As I looked at the bridge, I felt I was crossing over the thresholds of the seen and unseen to a mystical place. I had come here for a purpose. The passion of my spirit, coupled with the strength of the primal drive within me, was so great that I knew something within must be done.

I heard a voice saying, 'There is no going back. Your passageway to womanhood awaits you.'

The wind came out of nowhere and pushed me onto the bridge. Okay, I thought, if this is what you want so be it. I walked head held high, crossing the bridge of time into the world of spirits. I stopped half-way across the bridge and looked down at the water surging underneath. Maybe I should jump over and be done with it.

I felt a deep peace surround me, as if loving arms enfolded

me. I heard an owl calling hauntingly, 'twit to-woo-ooo-oooo.' It sounded like, 'Not now, not you.'

With that I looked at the moon, tears running down my face, and said aloud to the elementals, 'What's the point of all of this? I'm so unhappy. I want to come home. You listen to me, talk with me, and understand me.'

Again the wind picked up. 'Little one, trust us. We are watching over you. Come with us now to where the rivers divide; this is your place of transition.'

I wiped the tears from my face and slowly walked over the remaining half of the bridge. On the other side of the bridge stood the great guardian, an old redwood tree. I walked up to this amazing tree and asked the spirit of the old redwood to grant me protection as I walked to my destination. As I stood in front of the grandfather tree, it brought back happy memories of the old oak tree in my garden at home. In the centre of that oak tree is my very special place, my tree house, where I go to rest and hide away from everyday life. Often I fell asleep in my tree house, journeying in the dreamtime through the doorway of the great oak to the other worlds. I could hear the spirit of the Island's grandfather redwood calling me back to the present moment. 'Come rest with me and we shall journey to wonderful lands.'

'Thank you but I must go on to the reunion point of the river. It is calling me.'

I continued on and passed by the ash tree. I remembered long afternoons in the summer, lying under its canopy of leaves whilst watching the squirrels dart from tree to tree in search of food. Whenever I bonded with the ash I could feel my spiritual heritage. Now I felt the ash helping me reclaim my true rite of passage. I hugged the tree and said a thank you. The wind responded once again, blowing me gently onwards to my chosen destiny.

I passed by the lofty pines that reached into the sky to almost touch the moon, and felt purified as I walked between them. I stopped and smelt the resin in the air coming from the trees and my spirit felt lighter. I thanked the pine trees for their gift of purity. I was carried away by the familiar smell, and got so lost in the moment that I walked straight into a holly tree. I had nearly forgotten that it was straight across the path, and that everyone had to walk round it. No one trimmed this tree, so it grew as big as it wanted to.

This holly tree always reminded me to honour my courage and inner strength. I said thank you to the holly tree and its prickly leaves for giving me a renewed awareness of my inner sense to see in the dark. I so wanted to stop at every tree that I knew so well, but I knew it was time to move on. My heart beat faster as I approached the clearing towards the fork in the river. In front of me the elder and alder trees seemed to merge together. I didn't remember seeing them bonded like this before, but then again I had not come down to this sacred palace at night before. It amazed me how everything seemed so different in the moonlight. After a few more steps I entered a place of regeneration and rebirth; I could feel all the worries lift away from me as the healing influences of these trees enveloped me. As I passed between the elder and the alder I thanked them for being guardians of this ancient land that I walked upon and was so dear to me.

I was alone with the Gatekeepers of the land, as if for the first time. In front of me was the old yew tree that guarded an unmarked grave. Nobody knew whose grave this was. It had been left alone out of respect. Ivy covered the broken stone that was entwined within the yew and I had always felt that the yew had been planted over the grave in honour of whoever lay below. The old Highlands hold many secrets beneath the ancient trees.

The wind picked up gently to urge me onwards. Only a few more steps and I reached the point of the river where two trees hang into the water's edge. On my left was the weeping willow tree, and on the right was a silver birch. I walked to the stone that divided the great river, 'Which path must I walk?' I asked to the moon as she shone brilliantly above me. I stretched out my arms to the moon and held her in my embrace and cried out, 'Please help me Great Spirit! What must I do? I don't want to be in this world any longer. I have only ever experienced pain and sorrow. I don't have any happy memories of my last twelve years. The only time I have been happy is when I am with You.'

As I looked to the moon, I heard a soft feminine voice ask, 'Are you happy now?'

'Yes. I am with my family,' I replied.

'Look to the river,' said the voice. 'Here a great river divides in two. Whichever side of the river you choose to follow, you will find that after it has completed its separate journeys it joins together, once again, having learnt new ways of understanding. It is still the same river. Nothing can change that. But in the course of the river flowing in two directions, it experiences different views and perspectives. This is how you will live your life, seeing it from the two different viewpoints of yourself and of others. Include other people's points of view and you will have a deeper knowledge that all things come from the same source.

'The source of the river comes from the well of creativity that lies deep within the Earth, so its connection to all the waters of the Earth is one and the same. So, too, are people's thoughts and beliefs connected. They all spring from the same source, it's just that over time, each individual will claim the one source as their own. You were born of Spirit and came to this beautiful Earth to experience the human form. You chose the experience you are now living. Yes, little one, I know it seems hard to believe, however, from this lifetime you will learn the transition from fear, pain and doubt into something stronger than you can ever imagine. '

'I am so afraid. I feel so alone, with nobody to talk to, no one listening. Why should I stay here, what's the point? I talk to dead people. I talk to the trees and to the elementals. Nobody believes me.'

'Do you believe in what you are experiencing right now?' came the Voice.

'Yes, with my whole heart and soul. I would give up everything for You. You are the only Ones who have ever listened. All I have ever done is love people, and I have been rejected.'

'This is the path you have chosen little one. To love, to give love freely, unconditionally, no matter what others say or do to you. For thousands of years you have walked this path, helping people to understand that love is the only choice.'

I asked, 'Where do I go, what do I do now?'

'You have still many hardships to go through on your Earth walk. One day you will look back and understand.'

The river flowed towards me with great force, hitting the stone I was sitting upon. I became mesmerised as I watched with great intent, the twisting and spiralling of water. I felt as if I was falling into the water.

'Look to the left,' I heard the Voice say. The reflection of the moonlight was shining down on the water flowing past me on my left. I could see pictures of all my previous lifetimes. 'This is your past. This is who you have been. You sit now at the great divide of death. Now is the time to make a choice, for this will change the course of your destiny. You are at a turning point of your life, and there is no going back,' the Voice said.

'I would rather die than lose my spirituality,' I replied. 'I talk to dead people who are more alive and caring than those who live around me. My friends are the trees and the elementals who watch over me.'

'This is the world of spirit manifesting on the Earth. You are here to help others touch what seems to be the unseen, the world of Spirit. Your words and gifts will help many who will listen and understand the choice for happiness that all can make. That is why you are at the great divide in the river. Now look to your right,' I heard her say.

As I turned to face the other side, I saw who I would become in the future.

'The choice is yours. You can let fate take control of your life and allow others to tell you what to do. You can be controlled, bullied, and have your spirit broken to please others. Or you can use your free will to create your own destiny. Follow your heart's calling. Let no one tell you how you should live your life.'

After what seemed an eternity, I was brought back into my body by the call of the owl once again. I caught my breath as I looked up to see the owl's silhouette glide across the moon. Suddenly I had this immense urge to get into the water. This is crazy, I thought. Just when I am feeling better and no longer want to throw myself into the water to drown, I was now feeling compelled to go in. Okay, but I'm not getting my jeans wet. I took off my jeans, knowing the water would be cold. I sat on the stone with my legs dangling over the side until I felt ready to slip into the water. Beneath the stone was another stone covered by the water. The cold hit me with great intensity.

'What am I doing?'

Spirit replied, 'You are washing away the sins placed upon you by others. You are cleansing and clearing all that has gone before you. The blood is pure, not tainted and defiled by the words and actions of others. What you are now experiencing is natural. This is the blood of your birth and of your ancestors. It is time to honour who you are.'

I now felt an energy flowing up from my feet, into my legs and warming my whole body.

'You are now at a point in your life when you are no longer a girl, but a woman. You are stepping into the great power of womanhood. Be proud to be a woman, from whence all new human life comes. Let nothing or no one take this away from you.'

I could feel the blood surge from my body into the water, where it was carried away by the river in both directions.

The voice of Spirit continued, 'This is the path you have chosen, to be the walker between the worlds.'

I looked up and could see the man in the moon smiling down on me. I felt well, safe and whole. Here in Nature I received all the answers I was searching for. Here was my comfort and hope for my future. I lifted myself out of the water, dried off with my woollen poncho, and slipped back into my jeans. I heard a rustling of the trees, and looked behind me. The weeping willow was calling to me. I walked over to the willow tree, found a soft spot between its roots, and sat with my back against its trunk. I felt at home. I could feel its branches and roots wrap themselves around me. I was safe. The wind caressed the leaves of the willow, creating the sound of music. For a moment I could not tell the difference between the sounds of the rustling leaves, the wind and the water. I closed my eyes and drifted off to the sound of voices in the winds.

In my dream state I heard singing from within the woods. I followed the sound along the path that wound deeper into the forest. Then I came to a clearing in which stood a beautiful thatched cottage with smoke coming out of the chimney. Farm animals surrounded the cottage. The singing was coming from within. I opened the door. In front of me was a woman standing over a fire, stirring a hanging pot. This felt so familiar. I sat down on the bed that was covered with sheepskins, and watched her going about her work. The joy she exuded was astounding. When she turned round I knew her face. She was totally unaware of me. Her sole intent was preparing the potion in the pot on the hearth. There was a knock on the door.

'Come in,' she called out. A man entered sheepishly.

'I cannot be long,' he said, 'otherwise I will be missed in the village.'

'That's okay,' she replied, 'it's ready.'

She handed him a potion and said, 'Take three drops a day for a week, and you will feel much better.'

'Thank you. Outside is the goat you asked for. You will get fine milk from her. I must go now, it's late and I don't want people to find out that I am here.'

The woman looked at him and laughed. 'Dear John, you have nothing to fear.'

'It's what they will do to you that I am afraid of. They are spreading rumours of you being a witch.'

She walked up to John, looked lovingly into his eyes and said, 'All will be well.'

He held her close, saying, 'I will find a way for us to be together. It does not matter what other people say.' With that he left the cottage and walked back down the path he had come on.

Suddenly, from outside the cottage came a harsh chant, 'Burn the witch! Burn the witch!' I followed the woman as she went out to face an angry mob in front of her cottage. They were holding John by his arms.

'Is this the woman who has bewitched you?' they asked as she stood framed in the doorway. 'Speak, or we shall burn you as well.'

John looked up at her and said, 'Yes, this is the woman who has bewitched me.'

The woman let out a gasp. 'How could you do this to me? I love you.'

He looked down at the ground and would not raise his eyes to meet hers.

'Burn the place to the ground, with the witch inside!' they shouted, as they grabbed her. They then threw her back into her home and blocked the door from the outside. Their torches soon set upon the cottage. 'This is what we do to witches, we burn them alive!'

They then rounded up all the animals and walked away jeering and laughing. John walked silently with them, afraid of what they might say or do to him. As I watched the cottage burn down, I asked why I was witnessing this.

The reply shocked me. 'This was you in a previous lifetime. You have just witnessed your own death and saw the work that you did. You were betrayed by your own people, and by the one who loved you and then who rejected you. From lifetime to lifetime you carry this pain with you, and this is reflected in your life now. You have come back to work out and release all the pain and suffering you have endured from these previous lifetimes.'

With that I was back under the willow tree, a little dazed by all that I had just seen. So this is why I was being persecuted in this lifetime. I won't let it happen again, I can't! Deep within, I felt as if something had snapped, as if I was released from my chains. I had a burning desire to right the wrong that had been done.

'How can I change all this? Please help me.' I looked up to see the silver birch glowing in the light of the moon, which by now was on the horizon. I walked over to the shining tree and was compelled to put my arms around her. 'Please help me release the pain from within. Help me to understand why people are condemning me once again.'

The birch leaves shook with great intensity as I heard the voice of the Earth Mother call to me, 'Daughter, little one, you are here now to complete your destiny as foretold by the ancients. Look to the shining light in the sky of the morning star. This star will guide you and help you in all you do. This is a time of new beginnings, a time to change what has happened in the past. You will help and heal others to understand who they are and why they are also here at this moment in time. You will awaken and reconnect people to who they truly are by helping them overcome their fear.'

'How am I going to do that?'

'You will see. In time all will be revealed. Have patience, young goddess, you have much to learn. Keep this night to yourself. Let no one know of what you have experienced until the time is right for you to share it with the world. Then they will understand what you will talk about. Even those who fear, have pain, and who live in their minds will be able to comprehend what you say. For the words you will speak are the words of the heart, not of the mind.'

For how long I stood hugging the tree I do not know, but I felt a deep peace within me that soothed my soul. When the Sun started to appear on the horizon, I turned and thanked the ancestors of the land. I knew it was time to make my way back to the house. I tied my hair ribbons first on the silver birch, then on the weeping willow. I will always remember this night, the night of my passage from a girl to a woman. I walked back through the Islands, thanking each tree as I passed by for all the gifts they had given me. I felt one with all. This time I smiled to myself when I reached the bridge to cross over once again.

The birds were waking up as I walked back up the bray. Rabbits and squirrels darted about in the first light whilst I was surrounded by the most beautiful sounds of the dawn chorus.

I got back to the house, unlatched the window and climbed back into the bedroom. All was silent in the house. I sank into bed and promptly fell into a deep sleep. The next thing I remember was my mum waking me up, saying, 'Come on sleepy head, time for breakfast.'

I went through to the kitchen and ate a good breakfast. I was hungry. Mum talked to me as if nothing had happened over the last couple of days, and the next week's events took a drastic turn.

My father had a heart attack and so Mum spent a lot more time looking after him and I was pretty much left to my own devices. With Mum's once harsh focus no longer on me, things got much better at school, and it was finally time for me to meet Swein MacDonald, the Highland Seer. This meeting would change my life forever.

Owning the Experience

The foundations of your life are built on your own personal

experiences. Accept nothing less than what you yourself have experienced and lived. I wonder who reading this book will resonate with the stories that I write. Many people, who read my first book, *The Heart of All Knowing*, say to me it was as if they were reading their own life story. Of course, everything we do in our everyday life is a reflection of what we feel, think, say and do. As I write this book I am hearing the deeper messages that are being gifted to all of us, if we choose to listen. That is the hardest part of all, listening to what is being said, and then discerning the voices within – the external advice from others – and the voices of Spirit.

For me, there is my head talking and my heart speaking. Over the years the voice of my heart is becoming much stronger, as I nurture and listen to the inner child. By listening to and observing her, I have gained a much deeper dialogue between what is real and what is not. I look at my childhood issues in a loving, caring way and instead of acting out of my wounds am able to solve my life's problems in a more mature way. It takes time. It's our lifetime's work to heal and nurture all the pains and fears, but I have found the rewards far outweigh the disappointments! It's about taking responsibility for our current behaviour.

We can bury our heads in the sand and choose to ignore what is going around us, or we can look with new eyes, the eyes of the heart, upon the distortions of the past to walk again in authenticity and truth. We can be in denial and fool those around us, but we cannot fool our soul. Being in the 'knowing' is our true life's purpose. Our soul wants the best for us. We can learn to say no to the chatter in our mind and instead live in wholeness. We recognise ourselves as divine children. We love, help and heal our inner children by kissing their wounds. We often teach others what we ourselves need to learn the most. When I am working at the Mind Body and Spirit shows in the UK, I have noticed that what fellow presenters are teaching also applies to their own everyday lives. Are we paying attention to what we are teaching? For example, if I am teaching psychic protection, somewhere in my life I need to psychically protect myself. By listening to what I am saying, I also get little gems of inspiration.

It's not by chance that we are gifted with lessons. As I look back on my life, I am so grateful for all the lessons that life has gifted me. Two sayings which I use a lot in my readings are, 'You know you are your own worst enemy and also your own greatest teacher', as well as, 'It's not the enemy without that poses the greatest threat, but the enemy within'. Who are these enemies within, and how can we make them our allies? We can begin by recognising the child within who wants to be the grown-up, and the grown-up who wants to be the child. We take time out for ourselves, to experience our feelings, with no attachments whatsoever.

One way of validating our true emotions and experiences is by telling our stories. We recognise the wounded child within crying out for help by expanding our inner senses to listen with our inner ears. Our wounded child's injuries stem from childhood traumas that are never our fault. With greater awareness we can even accept that our parents are not at fault either, since they were not taught how to love themselves either. It is the inhuman conditioning from generation to generation. Only a hundred years ago the grandmothers chained themselves to the railings demanding independence as women. Much existing history portrays children and woman as chattel who did not have a say. The key to lasting liberation is releasing our wounded children. By doing so, we free our ancestors of their wrong or misdoings.

I meet people from all walks of life who blame their parents without comprehending the bigger picture. 'It's my parents' fault for what happened to me. They made me like this.'

When we do not take personal responsibility, we project onto those who have hurt us the most, who are often the ones in which we have the greatest emotional investment. This is the same in all relationships of the heart. At the College of Psychic Studies in

London I was giving a reading for a woman who wanted to know what was going to happen in her future. I explained to her that I do not tell the future, that we create it and have free will to choose. In the reading her deceased mother came through apologising for all the pain she had caused her daughter by ignoring her when she most needed her. The mother went on to explain in great detail what had happened in her own life and asked for forgiveness. I encouraged the woman to release the grief and to forgive her mother. This would help her create her true destiny, without doubts and fears. Once she faced her past and honoured her inner child, she would be free and a new life would ensue. At the end of the reading, I asked her if she had any questions.

'No thank you. I am fine now,' she said as she smiled, thanked me for all my help and left.

A month later, she wrote explaining she was not happy with the reading. She still had breast cancer, she did not want to speak to the spirit of her mother, her troubles were her mother's fault, her life was a disaster due to her mother and she would never forgive her. She wanted her money back. She was angry and upset that I had not given her what she wanted.

This is the wounded child refusing to take responsibility. Contributing to this woman's breast cancer are unresolved issues with her mum to do with nurturing, the feminine. The illness trapped in the body was due largely to suppressed emotions. We can only help those who wish to receive help. That day I spoke to her mum in spirit and asked for the woman's healing. I prayed that she would feel the love and compassion that her mother has for her from the spirit world. A couple of weeks later I got another call from the woman, her mother had come to her in the dreamtime seeking forgiveness.

'I am so sorry,' she said, 'I just couldn't see the truth, I was blinded by anger and bitterness; can you forgive me?'

'There is nothing to forgive,' I replied. 'A healing has taken place, all will be well and your life will take a new path of your own volition.'

At the beginning of a reading, I explain to my clients how I work. I set my boundaries and emphasise that to create our destiny we must first look at past wounds and heal them. We forgive those who have hurt us and move into the present moment by taking responsibility for our existing behaviours and patterns of the self. With understanding, we free ourselves from the untruth of the past. This is our gift of the present. By being present and observing the self, that wishes to control and manipulate us and others, we gain a deeper understanding of what happened in our childhood, and how it has affected our day-to-day living as adults. We see in a blameless way how we interact with ourselves and our loved ones.

Mythology abounds with deep-rooted belief systems and stories of heroes and heroines. Ancient tales tell of a quest to find lost treasure, hidden, yet in plain view for those with eyes to see. When we delve into what appears to be out of reach from us mere mortals, we see a story starting to emerge. The story is of how we came from the lands of heavenly bliss, born into this world pure, innocent, and untouched. Then our journey begins through the labyrinth of earthly life, on our personal vision quest to discover why we are here in this lifetime and in this form. Immortality is gained by releasing all pain and fear, surrendering to a greater power within – the divine child.

Over and over again in world culture and mythology we read stories of the wounded and abandoned child, Isis and her son Horus or Mother Mary and Jesus. So, do we get our belief system from our own inner knowing which we brought with us from previous past lifetimes, or from those who have influenced us in our early childhood such as our parents, teachers, siblings, and religious authorities?

Most of us accept what we are taught without question. I would not accept what I was being told because it did not feel right. The first seven years of our lives is when we are influenced the most by others. This is when we form our first impressions of life. As children we are very observant, watching those around us for guidance and clarity. We build the foundation of our life from other people's words and stories. Our kith and kin learnt from the great teachers of yesterday, just as we formed our options based on what we have learnt from others. But what have we learnt from ourselves, our soul's knowing? Until we personally experience what we are taught, read and hear from others, we need to keep an open mind.

Living the Moment

Everything that I write about in this book is my personal experience. I have seen it, felt it, lived it, become it, believed in it and integrated them all as one. The very core of my being is the Shaman Within. My personal experiences with my first drum during those early weeks back in the UK from my amazing Albuquerque trip were enthusiastic and childlike. I wanted to see it, feel it, and play with it through the eyes of a child, with no expectations. This got me thinking what it would be like to share my childlike wonder with children. Sandra, my neighbour and long-time friend was a school teacher. I visited her and shared my vision of bringing my collection of drums into the classroom for children to interact with. Sandra loved the idea and promised to discuss it with her head teacher. The next afternoon she was very excited when she visited me. Lillian, the head teacher proposed that I give a talk about the Native Americans as part of a history lesson, and at the end of the lesson I could let the children play with the drums.

It was an extraordinary day. The children loved everything I had to share with them about the native people of 'Turtle Island', an ancient tribal name for the Americas. I showed them pictures of my adventures with Native Americans and passed around postcards with hundred-year-old photos of chiefs, tepees and buffalo herds that I had collected from various trading posts around the reservations. I wore my leather native dress that I'd made by hand with Tom and Mary Grey Elk's help in 1989. I brought in a bow and quiver, shields, staffs, dream catchers, flutes and feathers and set up my big powwow drum for the children to sit around as they eagerly listened. I invited each child to choose a drum to play. Not one of them questioned me about what to do with the drum or how to play it, they all just knew. I sat there with tears flowing down my face as I watched and listened to tomorrow's ancestors.

Amidst all this enthusiasm I experienced a profound vision. I was standing in front of a mother drum and as I was drumming it was giving birth to baby drums. Then red, yellow, black and white children from all the nations of the world came and picked up the baby drums. As they drummed together there emerged one beat that started to vibrate the Earth. The animals, people, trees, and stones that surrounded the mother drum all started to sing with one voice. I became aware that the singing was in fact coming from the room I was sitting in. Back in the classroom, the children were all playing their drums and chanting together. Some of them got up and started dancing around the room, still singing. They were totally uninhibited – completely in the moment.

'Let the children be your teachers,' I heard from the spirit world. 'They are here to remind you to see the world through the eyes of a child, to sing, dance, play and laugh.'

At that point Lillian walked into the room, clearly overwhelmed by what she saw. Immediately the children stopped and sat down. Not one of them spoke until Lillian asked them if they had enjoyed themselves. Their poor response indicated that they did not want to share their stories with her. Why were they suddenly so shy, I wondered? Lillian thanked me and as soon as she left, the room exploded with the children's pent-up excitement.

They turned to Sandra and said, 'Please Miss, can we do this again? It was fantastic. Can we have the drums to take home with us? Please, please, please!'

I asked why had they not wanted to tell the head teacher how much they enjoyed themselves?

The responses I got astounded me. 'We didn't want to tell her because she would not have believed us. We get told off for having vivid imaginations, for telling stories and for lying about the ghost people we see.'

They looked at me hopefully and continued, 'You believe us Miss. You saw all the spirits in the room when we were drumming. You heard all the sounds. You saw all the animals in the room with us. Didn't you?'

Of course I did. What I had assumed to be my vision alone, was part of a group vision. I had been honoured to see what they saw for the future as a vision of what had been in the past.

After this amazing experience with the children I spent more time in my spirit room at home. I used this room in my house only for connecting with Spirit. It had an altar, a healing bed and all my spiritual tools, statues and pictures that I had collected from around the world. It was my sacred space in which I would light my sage and candles and sit holding my drum to my heart. Spirit told me that if I wanted to communicate with the drum, it would be through heart talk and not through the mind. The drum did not understand the language of the forked tongue. As I sat holding my drum tightly, I could see my heart opening up and expanding to the drum. At the same time I could feel the skin and wood of my drum expanding, surrounding and protecting me. I felt the safety of being wrapped in the arms of Mother Nature.

I started praying with my drum, asking the spirit of the drum to teach and show me how to be in a right relationship with my drum. The deeper I went in prayer the more the visions came to me. Spirit told me drumming is about being in 'right relationship' both with self and others. They taught me to become aware of the drum by treating it with respect and honour. To know the drum, I must love the drum as I would myself and my beloved. It is a sacred marriage. I could think of the drum as my lover, as an interaction between two spirits of the heart. The more love I give to my drum, the more fulfilment I receive from drumming. The sacred union of two spirits is the connection and awakening of the sacred fires of knowledge. We free the mind and body by letting go of earthly burdens. We become Source, the One, as an embodiment of light in divine bliss and ecstasy.

I had not borne a child in this lifetime, yet as I sat holding my drum in my arms I felt a bonding as if I had just given birth to a baby. I looked down at my drum with great respect and awe. I felt the responsibility of being the drum's life-long caretaker. Birthing my drum meant nurturing and playing it as my drum's spirit wished to be heard in the world. I took my drum with me every-where, even sleeping with it in bed, much to Shaun's surprise. The more I drummed the more I noticed that my entrance to the spirit world of visions was through my heart. I could feel and know and see so much clearer. This brings me to an experience in Dublin…

Stand on Solid Ground

I finished a talk on Power Animals at a Mind Body Spirit show in Dublin, and invited people to discuss it at my stand. Many came and finally I took a break when I heard, 'Excuse me, I want to know about Bear.'

I explained I would be available in less than five minutes.

The response was, 'I have already hung around here waiting for you to finish. I haven't got all day.'

With that I got up, smiled and said, 'Bear has come to help you understand the real you. It is a time for introspection and resolution. The impatience and forcefulness you feel comes from a lack of love as a child – not being heard. You studied and showed to the world your knowledge. From this place of pain, you are emerging into a new and deeper place of healing and supporting yourself. Now come out of your cave and share, listen and experience love. Share your strength and wisdom with others. You are compassionate and caring. Listen to your inner knowing; hear the heart for it speaks the truth.'

She asked, 'What is your birth sign?'

I smiled and told her Capricorn.

'What's your tree?' she asked. 'I have many trees that I connect with for many different reasons. It depends on what is happening in my life, and the medicines that are called for at that moment in time.'

'Well,' she replied, 'your tree is the Silver Birch. The Native Americans say the silver birch is for your star sign.'

'Which tribe do you speak of who shares this wisdom?' I asked.

Her curt response was, 'It says in my book that you are the silver birch.'

Again I asked her which tribe this came from.

She looked at me angrily, 'You know nothing.'

I wished her well as she walked off muttering to herself. I put my thoughts up to Spirit for a healing to take place. I asked Bear to visit her again, to help in her transition from the wounded child to an enlightened adult. The message was already given to her, but not listened to. She did not hear the voice of the heart words, but only her internal wounded child's words.

But whilst in this place of abandonment and neglect we can change. We can remove the self's pain by going back to our roots; the very foundation of who we are. I have lived with tribal cultures to gain first-hand knowledge of their ways and rites of passage. This for me is a natural way of living. That is why so many of us today are seeking other tribal traditions for the missing pieces that we feel we have lost. We find our essence and become the 'knower' by journeying to other lands. We discover parts of our spiritual ancestry that have been buried deep in the recesses of our inner knowing, which we thought had been lost and forgotten.

If we want to save the world, then we need to heal ourselves first. Instead of seeking substitutes, such as working too hard and eating too much, we need to observe why we do these things. I know that when I am feeling sad I eat lots of chocolate. It's about all things in moderation. It's about having a balance of work, rest and play. If you like to smoke tobacco, drink alcohol or work with sacred plant medicines then that's your free choice. I honour each individual's free will and choice. It's when it is to excess that it's a cry for help. A great saying is, 'I'm drowning my sorrows.' And that's what happens. We drown, submerse our feelings. 'Please love me!' This is what our inner child is saying to us. The voice of the inner child is calling for help and it's time to listen.

The child within is not one to be suppressed, but respected. For healing to take place within me, I listened to my inner child and took the time to heal the wounds. I remember my parents saying to me, 'Children should be seen and not heard'. The idea was to crush my spirit so they could control me. This is similar to society's way of making us co-dependent on other people, systems and the government. We can all survive in today's world physically, but on a mental, emotional and spiritual level we feel empty. Our inspired childhood is lost and forgotten and we grow up feeling dead inside.

Often the people who come to me for a reading don't know why they need help, they just expect me to tell them. This is a story of one lost soul who came to me for a reading in Scotland last year. When Amanda walked into the room, she burst out crying, I held her in my arms until she had stopped. I could see that she was in terrible emotion pain. In the last few years she had lost both parents who she had taken care of, her marriage had broken up when her husband went off with another woman, and she had lost her job. To her, it was the fault of everybody else. Amanda's belief system controlled her mind, and memories of her painful experiences dictated how she felt in the present.

We looked at how and why her inner child was screaming for love. Once we had worked through this, I moved forward into her destiny. I could see boxes in her house. She was going to an ashram in India for six months to study yoga and meditation. She would go on to teach, meet her partner and together they would work for change. The reading showed it was new beginnings for her and time for healing to take place. She confirmed that all her personal possessions were in boxes, she was in a rented house, and her dream was to go to India. She had always wanted to teach yoga.

We talked for over an hour and I discussed how she could heal her past and walk into her destiny. Suddenly she said, 'Well, that's all very well and good, but you have only talked about the next six months. I want to know my future. I went to another psychic, who told me my future and told me that I was going to meet a man, get a new job, and I was going to be taken care of.'

She admitted the psychic did not explain how it would happen, or when and where it would take place. 'I told the psychic what I wanted and she confirmed that it would happen.'

I smiled at her and said, 'Amanda the choice is yours. To follow your destiny, step out the door and take the first steps of your journey.' I gave her a hug and wished her well.

The journey from the head to the heart is the hardest path of all, for it takes great courage to find the equilibrium, the middle ground where harmonious voices can be heard and understood. That's when the transformation can take place. 'Be gentle with yourself. Love yourself.' I gave her a leaflet on 'how to heal your inner child' and invited her to read *The Heart of All Knowing*. Three months down the line and Amanda still sat at home waiting for the perfect job and the man of her dreams to come to her front door. If you don't play the lottery how can you expect to win?

To create your destiny you must stop living in the past. Your destiny awaits you if you have the courage and support. I continue to talk to Amanda over the phone, and she is taking the first steps to loving herself, talking to her inner child, and focussing on creating her perfect life by following her true destiny. Changing our way of thinking changes the way we respond to our ever fluctuating emotions. We can say 'No!' to the inner voice that is judgemental. We can all walk out of our pasts and live in the awesome power of *now* on solid 'wholly' ground.

So let's have a look at how we can heal our inner child and transition through one of the most important rites of passage in our lives. Have a diary or journal to write down all your feelings as you experience them. This is this lifetime's work. There are no quick fixes. It takes a lot of audacity, time, and persistence, but it does work. What we are going to do is focus on the positive aspects of inner child work. It is always better to light a candle than complain about the darkness. When there is darkness within, the only thing you can do is light up your world.

- Make time to love, nurture, protect and trust the inner child.
- Don't be so serious in life; take time out from work for you.
- Take days off for loved ones. Leave your mobile phones switched off and unplug the TV and computer. Go to a theme park. It's not just for children. It's for grown-ups to unleash our inner children.
- Get out the old photos of your family and make a collage that brings back happy memories. Put it where you can see it.
- It's time to do the things you want to do, not what other people want you to do. Stop feeling guilty because you don't live up to other people's expectations and demands. Receive graciously instead of being the one who provides all the time.
- Be honest with others about your feelings. Share your

thoughts with loved ones who will listen. Don't bottle them up inside.

- Do you feel joy, pleasure, excitement, about life? If not, why not? What stops you from feeling this delight?
- What in your life would you change, and what is stopping you? Make the decision and change it. You will be glad you did.
- Wake up each morning look forward to the day ahead. Don't wish your life away. Live for the moment. Remember to tell yourself that you are a child of creation, perfect in every way. You are the beloved of the Beloveds, created in love, whole and holy.

We learn something new every day, and I find my inner child most of the time teaching me compassion for myself. I am the navigator of my own destiny. What I have discovered is that the closer I get to knowing myself, the more I realise that I have much to learn. This takes me to the lesson I have just learnt by writing this book. For the past year my book of learning has been the dictionary, and thank goodness for spell check on the computer. For me speaking is easy. To take words of the heart, and transpose them into head words was a totally different way of working.

Until fifteen years ago I would not go near a computer, until my dear friend Dr Gerald Sinclair said, 'Barbara, we need to keep in touch by e-mail.' This was how I started writing, and thanks to Gerald I am now writing my second book. I had completed a chapter and was so pleased with myself for having achieved so much that I sent my manager and friend, Kate, an e-mail, 'I am so proud of myself. I have overcome dyslexia and taught myself spelling, and grammar.'

Kate wrote back, 'And so you should be.'

I promised her that I would send the next draft of the book the following day, once I had gone over it with David so that it not only made sense to me, but also to another.

I got up in the morning with a great sense of wellbeing. When I later opened my computer and looked for the draft file, it was not there. I had been saving the file throughout the day, and the computer automatically saves it, so where was it? I was in tears, it had simply vanished. 'That was the best day yet,' I said to David through my grief, 'My spelling, my grammar, it flowed through me. I was so inspired. Now it's gone.'

He hugged me for a long moment until I followed his gaze through the balcony doors onto the lush green fields. 'What do you see?' he asked.

'I see beauty,' I replied.

David looked at me, 'Then write from your beauty, not from your grief. The words will come when you listen again to your heart.'

Although I smiled and thanked him for the wise words, the wounded little girl inside me was also chattering. I went out for the day to Luxor as a break. I dismissed what had happened, stuffed the emotions within and convinced myself it was just one of those things. I will start again tomorrow were my thoughts as I went to bed that night crying and feeling sorry for myself.

Suddenly, I was back in the classroom as a seven-year-old. I had drawn a beautiful picture of an angel and I was eager to show the teacher. But right now it was English lessons. I could not understand the words on the paper.

'Okay,' said the teacher, 'we are going to make the sound of a car, vrrooom, vrrooom.' I opened my mouth and nothing came out. She came over to me and demanded to hear me make the sound of a car. I looked at her and said I can't. With that she grabbed my hand and made me stand on my desk. 'Now do it!'

'Please miss I can't.' By this time my whole throat had closed up.

She took her belt and starting hitting me across the back of the legs, 'Barbara's stupid. She's a dunce. She cannot spell. What do we do with dunces? We put them outside the classroom.' As she started to pull me outside I grabbed the picture of the angel I had drawn. She took it and said, 'You won't be needing that,' and tore it into pieces in front of me without even looking at it once.

I woke up sobbing. I thought I had forgotten this painful memory, but it was locked away in my heart. I went through all sorts of sensations that morning. I curled up in bed in a foetal position and journeyed into the depths of my emotions. I found my inner child curled up in a corner in the dark.

'How can I help you?' I asked.

'By listening to me. You need to take time out, stop working so hard, and play with me. You help so many other people; it's time to help yourself. You have been working all year and now it's time for us to play. I am here to remind you to enjoy the moment.'

I held her close and said, 'You are so wise. Thank you.'

I was brought back into the room by the laughter of the little girl, Haba who lived next door. She was singing and dancing in the street. When I walked downstairs and opened the door, she came running into my arms. Tears flowed down my face. Here was this beautiful four-year-old, in total trust, radiating love. It shone in her eyes, no need for words. Here was a great mirror for me. We walked down the road hand-in-hand. It was time to play, and what better way than to go and get some chocolate at the corner shop?

By the time we arrived at the shop, there were seven children playing with me. I bought them all chocolate, and sat down with them on the shop steps. Together they all hugged me at once. It was the most amazing feeling, I was little once again, but this time I was happy laughing. I had found my playmates, and I was healed.

Honouring Your Inner Child

It's time now to look at how you can honour your inner child and gift them with a rite of passage befitting one of the most important times in your life. This book is about how we can repair the wounding done to us through no fault of our own. There is a deep lack of understanding about initiation rites of passage for the 21st century. Many of us have gone through our lives without help or the understanding of the process of awakening our soul to its life purpose. At each stage of our life's passages, we forgo the experiences that could ease us into the next stage of our lives. Instead, we are often traumatised, deeply suppressed and missing out on what should be a truly magnificent celebration of our lives. It seems we go from drama to crisis, without understanding why. We feel incomplete, sensing that we are missing something, but not knowing what it is.

The most significant times of our lives are our transitional rites of passage. They help us build a firm, lasting foundation for a healthier relationship with ourselves. And our teenage years are important times of our lives. Some of us experienced the separation of going from primary school to secondary school. It was a very scary rite of passage. We were suddenly separated from the friends we had grown up and played with, and moved to the betwixt and between. We had to start all over again to establish new boundaries which we could trust.

I stood petrified at the school gate, not wanting to go. When I asked my mum to accompany me to the new school, I was told I was too old to be escorted to school, so grow up. So there we were between worlds, wondering what to do next. We reintegrated by learning new ways of surviving. It was an assault course over which we had to scale many walls and fences to survive our test of endurance. This is what happens throughout our lives, whether we are aware of it or not…

- The separation; spirit to form, mother at birth, parents to school, school to work, home to another home, parents to partner, partner to work, work to children, children to grown-ups, work to retirement, retirement to death, death to spirit.

- Being between the worlds of spirit and here on Earth, as we struggle to establish new directions and boundaries.
- Re-adapting to new situations, settling in once again.

A lot of us have problems with abandonment in relationships, saying, 'It's too good to be true, it cannot last forever.' In today's western society we do not have clearly defined thresholds in which to lead lives of totality. There are different cultures today which still acknowledge puberty as the age of conscientiousness, fruitfulness and accountability. By working with our tomorrow's ancestors – our children – we form a bond to help them transition through a difficult time in their young lives.

The stages of the transformation of the butterfly are from crawling to flying. Puberty is the most critical time in our young lives. The evolution of our inner butterfly depends on it. For thousands of years our children have suffered at the hands of the adults. In many cultures around the world female children especially have suffered in silence because they were told too little about this transition from childhood to adulthood. They suffered pain, trauma, stigma, mutilations and fear for the sake of others' beliefs.

Rites of passage today are created with love, and only love. Pain does not increase the transition from childhood to adulthood, as once believed by many ancient cultures. It creates a fear-based society, and that is not what we want for our future generations. Every man, woman and child has free will and choice. It is our birthright to seek an alternative path if we so choose. We are created by the love and in the image of our Creator. We can re-educate our ways of dealing with life, welcome our youth with compassion and redefine our rites of passage so that they are done in a loving and supportive way.

There is no need to cut bits off our body. Spirit does not ask this of us, only the self asks for sacrifice. Spirit loves us, and never judges. They would never ask us to live in anything other than divine bliss. We don't need to suffer for our sins any longer. Enough is enough. The original sin story has run its course; it is time for a new story, time to create a new harmonious, loving and peaceful world. Aloha, salaam, and shalom all start with you, light a candle within and let it shine for all to see.

One of the most beautiful and moving rites of passage for a girl is the 'Apache Sunrise Ceremony'. I was honoured to witness this fantastic ceremony in Ruidoso, New Mexico, with Dr Sinclair. The Mescalero Apache Reservation surrounds the area where he lives and once a year, in July, they hold this ceremony which marks the important transition from childhood to adulthood. The four-day event takes place during the summer after the girl's first menstrual period. All the woman of the family come together to nurture and support her. The women then choose a spiritual mother to teach the girl about sexuality, growing up as a woman and to also support her during the four days of the Sunrise Ceremony. They also instruct her in important life issues regarding work and home. It is important that the young woman is physically fit for all the singing, dancing and praying that invokes the qualities and attributes of White Painted Woman. The young women re-enact the story of the first woman of the Apache.

The young woman is covered with a mixture of pollen and clay, which is left on for the entire ceremony. When the dawn comes the young girls first face the east, then the other three directions to welcome the new day. This honours the four stages of life, from infancy, to childhood, to adulthood, then wisdomhood. White Painted Woman gifted the Apache nation with the Sunrise Ceremony. White Painted Woman's beloved is the Sun, with whom she birthed her first son. Her second son was birthed from the rain. After a passing of many years she became old, and one day she walked towards the Sun. As she came near the horizon she met her younger self. They merged together and became one. She became young once more, and continues to be reborn with every new generation to help, guide and show the young girls the path of White Painted Woman. She is one and part of all of creation.

So what can be done now to retrieve your inner child and make the transition from wounding to healing in order that your inner child can continue to be part of your creativity, rather than dragging you back into emotional poverty? Everything you say, think and do in a negative action affects both yourself and others on an emotional level that ripples out into the stream of consciousness that pollutes our emotional waters of life. Only you can make the difference between healthy water and muddy water. Remember the first waters from the oceans of creation, billions of years ago, are still being filtered and drunk today with the added pollution of hundreds of years of insanity. It's now time to write down in your journal your feelings about the following questions...

- Describe your inner child. What does s/he look like?
- At what age did they retreat within? What trauma triggered off the introspection?
- When are you aware of your inner child? Can you hear her/him trying to communicate with your adult self?
- Do you listen to or suppress the cries from inside your heart?
- What do you need to say to the inner child awaiting reassurance?
- Has your inner child come to you in the dreamtime? Have you dreamt you have given birth, and from what part of the body?
- How willing are you to comfort and nurture your inner child? If you have a fear of them, what is it and how does it affect you?

- Do you practice life affirmations to nurture your inner child?
- Do negative thoughts cause problems on a day to day basis? Where do they originate from?
- Do you feel you suppress your inner child? If so, why? Are these suppressed feelings having a negative effect on your life?

Rite of Passage: Healing the Inner Child

For this meditation find safe surroundings; somewhere private where you will not be disturbed. Check that all the phones are switched off. Then create your sacred space with candles, incense, and flowers. Think about what your inner little girl or boy would like. Make sure you have your blanket and a pillow with you to be as comfortable as possible. As a child where did you go, where did you feel safe? Create that place for yourself. How about creating a little den or a hideaway so nobody can find you? Use your imagination and be creative, for your inner child likes to play.

You might decide you want to go outdoors around the time of Easter, during the Spring Equinox is good. It is the first time of the year when day and night are of equal length. Signs of new life blooms. This is a period of fertility, the birthing of Nature which our Celtic ancestors celebrated, as the harshness of winter subsided and the growth of new crops meant food for the people and animals and the difference between life and death for communities. Easter traditions originate from this time celebrating the Celtic Goddess Ostara, relating to her association with new beginnings and fertility, as does the Easter Egg.

In Pagan tradition, the shell of the egg represents the cosmic egg of creation and rebirth, the yolk symbolises the Sun and the white, the Goddess in her Maiden form. All of this makes for a most auspicious time for you and your inner child to create a new relationship. If you do go outdoors, make sure nobody is about, or better still have one of your friends facilitate being the Gatekeeper, watching over you from a distance to protect you and keep you safe. It is always a nice feeling to know someone is there for you as well. In nature there are lots of hidey holes in the forests, in the hills, or down by a waterfall. You might be able to find a cave. Just check it out first before you settle in, you might find one of your power animals in there waiting for you who are great friends to have along for the journey. Remember this is an act of love, done with gentleness compassion, and trust. It is important to bear in mind that your inner child might be a little hesitant at first, as this may be the first contact. So go slowly, and with patience.

I would suggest you lie down for this, if possible curling up in a blanket. You want to create that feeling of being a little girl or boy again, underneath the blankets safe and sound. It is important to trust what you see, what you feel, don't rush, take your time. Now close your eyes, and breathe. Follow your breath, watching where it flows. Allow all the worries of the day to gently drift away. As you become more relaxed, keep focused on the breath, following the breath to your heart centre. As you drop down into a deeper sense of wellbeing you start to feel lighter and lighter, until you feel relaxed and at peace and close your eyes.

You now notice that your pulse has slowed right down. Now become the pulse, connecting to your heartbeat of life. As you merge with your heart centre you start to feel an expansion from inside your heart. It feels like a warm glow, the flowing rivers of eternal life and the elixir of bliss. Now expand this feeling throughout your whole body and as you do so, you drop down into this wonderful feeling of lucidness. Your inner eyes now open to see in front of you a sail boat, with its sails billowing gently in the breeze, as it floats towards you on the mists of time. You step into the boat and sink down into the luxurious materials of silks, wools and finery draped in the bottom of the boat. As you begin to relax you hear the lapping of the water gently rocking you to sleep. You drift along on the seas of tranquillity, taking you back in time to when you were a child.

The next thing you become aware of is the sound of laughter and play. You are lying looking up at a clear blue sky, the Sun is shining, and you feel a deep sense of peacefulness. The laughter is calling to you to follow it, so you get up and climb out of the boat onto a beautiful sandy beach. The Sun's rays permeate into the very core of your essence, filling you with a radiant feeling of euphoria. You feel as if your whole life is about to change forever. You hear the laughter again and turn around to see a group of children playing in the distance near the cliff face. They are running and jumping over the rocks and fish pools. They are immersed in what they are doing and do not notice you at first. You feel overjoyed by once again being in a place of happiness and wellbeing. You also notice that all your pains and fears have left you. You cannot think, only feel, the awareness of sensitivity. What deep joy it is to feel this feeling, to be free of cluttered thoughts.

Instinctively you start walking towards the children, for you want to join in with their playful antics and become a part of what you once lived when you were a child. All of a sudden they turn around and see you.

'Quick,' they say to one another, 'there's an adult coming to take us away from our secret place. Let's hide in the caves, they will never find us in there.'

They scatter in all directions as you call out, 'Please don't go, I will not hurt you. I just want to play with you and have fun.' They do not listen to you, for they cannot hear your words, the words of an adult who has forgotten how to talk with children. You start walking after them calling out, but your words are lost on the winds. You carry on walking towards the caves for you have seen a little one who keeps stopping and looking back at you. You feel a deep connection to this little one as if you know them. This feeling drives you onwards to discover the bond between you.

You arrive at the caves where you see there are numerous passageways leading deep into the Earth. 'Which one will I take?' you ask.

'The path of the heart,' comes the response from deep within the cave, 'for here is your inner child waiting for you.'

With that you look up at the sky and say, 'Spirit, please help me in this journey I am about to undertake. Show me a sign so that I may find my inner child and bring them home to me so we can become one.'

The next thing you hear is the beautiful sound of birds singing. You look behind you. On the tree are the most brightly coloured songbirds you have ever seen. Their singing fills you with deep insight and an awareness of the language of communication between the birds and you. They are telling you which cave to go into. They are singing your soul back home. You turn around and without thinking walk straight into one of the passageways.

As you start to descend into the Earth, you become aware of a feeling of deep serenity within yourself and your surroundings. The passageway is lit by the beautiful glow of all the crystals that illuminate and radiate a sense of therapeutic wellbeing. For how long you have been walking down this crystal passageway you do not know. You have lost all perception of time. Then you enter into a magical crystal cave deep within the Earth. In the centre of the cave is a fountain with a stream of iridescent flowing water coming out of the Earth. You notice that the water flows into channels cut into the crystal bedrock, carrying the water in four different directions out of the cave. It creates a deep resonant sound of tranquillity.

You sit down on the edge of the fountain, and dip your hand in the water and take a drink. As you do so you are filled with an overwhelming sense of peace. You look into the water and see your reflection looking back at you. Something is missing, your eyes seem lifeless. You take a deep breath.

'Please Spirit, free me from this aching feeling in my heart. Let me be whole and complete again.' There is something so familiar about this place, as if you have been here before. The sound of the water coupled with the hum of the crystals, awakens feelings from within that you have not felt for a long time.

'What happened?' you ask yourself. 'How did I manage to cut myself off from my feelings?' In that instant you become aware of someone looking at you. You lift your head to see in front of you the most amazing eyes, soulfully looking up at you.

'Hello,' you say.

They reply, 'I knew you would come for me one day, I have been waiting for this moment since forever. When I saw you on the beach, I recognised you.'

'Then why did you run away?' you ask.

'To see if you would follow,' was the reply. 'I ran away years ago, but you never came looking for me. After a while I felt sad and lonely, so I decided to go where you would not find me, unless you changed your way of thinking.'

'Where are we?' you ask.

'In the world of the imagination; the place of the heart. Here we can play with the other children, until the adults come to take them back home to their hearts. I have been very happy here.'

With that the little one comes and sits beside you. You look deeply into their eyes and say, 'I am so sorry I abandoned you. I was so wrapped up in my own grief that I did not notice that you had left.'

'I tried to talk to you,' comes the response, 'but you were not listening. You were so caught up in your head you could not hear my cries for help.' The tears start flowing down your face and the little one reaches out a hand to wipe the tears.

'Don't worry, it's okay,' they say to you. You start sobbing from the depths of your soul.

'Here in this place is where we come for healing, don't be sad.'

By this time you are both holding each other, crying together with joy and laughter.

'I so missed you,' both of you say at the same time. You look into each other's eyes and see happiness.

'Can we go home now?' the little one asks of you.

'Of course we can,' you reply.

'Is it okay if I come back and visit this place?'

'You can visit whenever you want, as long as I am with you as well,' you answer. Holding each other closely you say, 'Let's go home.' With that you feel your heart opening, as the little one integrates into your very essence, becoming one. Once again that empty space within no longer is. You feel full up, overflowing with life. The pain has gone. You are at peace for the first time in this life, and your little one has come home to play.

When you are ready, open your eyes, place your hands over your heart and say, 'I will always love you. I will always be there for you. I will never abandon you again. I will listen to you and to what you have to say. I will make time in my life to nurture and cherish you. I will honour the inner child within me by being a very good parent. You will help me to remember what it is like to have fun, to play, to take time off for us. It's time to bring balance, enjoyment, harmony and fulfilment back into my life. Please show me how to be us.'

Chapter 4

The Knowing
Beltane & Split-Apart

*Those who understand are learned. Those who know themselves
are wise. Those who subdue themselves are strong. Those who are
content are wealthy. But those who do not lose their souls will
endure.*
Lao Tse

What legacy will we leave our children? Will they remember us
because of our pains and fears, or will they recall us through the
gift of transformation, affording them a future of love in which
to create a destiny of hope, joy and abundance? Glancing back at
my childhood and teenage years, I can see the influences on my
life today. When fears or doubts arise, I know they could stem
from a trauma that happened to me in my formative years. The
biggest part of self-healing is recognising that many problems
originate within us. I have discovered the difference between
being awake and asleep.

My friend Gwen once said, 'It's okay for you Barbara, you
know what you are doing.'

I replied, 'My work is to become conscious of what I am doing
24/7.'

Being aware of our every thought and action is a full-time job.
Whilst writing this book I am conscious of how my words might
affect others who read them. This takes discipline and it's not
easy, for the self will lead us all a merry dance given half a
chance.

In the last chapter we focussed on healing the inner child and
integrating that back into our centre. In this chapter we will be
looking at the healing of our 'split-apart'. I am really talking

from personal experience, for many of the problems I have faced since my twenties came from my childhood and teenage years. Our rites of passage through infancy and adolescence are crucial to help us to be whole and complete spiritual beings. The absence of these rites of passage creates a huge void within us which we then try to fill by being with other things, including people. From this we can learn to understand that we will not find in anyone else that which is missing within ourselves. As children we do not go around searching for another person to complete us. We are complete. It is only as we are growing up that the quest for our split-apart begins.

As a teenager it is not easy; hormones kicking in, trying to find an identity, and desperate to fit in. I was always the odd one out for I did not want to fit in. When I met Swein, he was the first person to recognise the child of nature, who I am. He saw the limitless potential of my soul and told me, 'Your life will always have the Sun shining on the horizon.' So because of Swein, and our fortuitous meeting in Inverness, I went on to meet other wise men and women who took me under their wings and guided me in the teachings of the wise ways of the ancestors and the land.

During this time my mother was focused on getting my father well after his heart attack. This gave me the opportunity to spend more time with my new friends in secondary school. I was seldom in the classroom, always preferring the sports field, swimming pool or being outside. At the pool I made a lot of friends because we all had in common a love of swimming. That is where I met Christine Macpherson. She attended a different school, but that did not stop our friendship from developing. She invited me back to her house where I met her parents and I recognised them instantly.

I had seen them at one of the evening gatherings held in Inverness for Swein. I remember them smiling at me during the meeting and nodding as Swein said, 'We need to nurture the young ones and help them to adapt to this modern way of life.

We need to keep the old ways alive, and help them boldly face their rites of passage so that they can progress to the next stage of their lives. We should help them comprehend what is before them.'

Jack and Margaret Macpherson welcomed me into their home. I asked if it was okay to visit them instead of going to church.

They said, 'Of course you can. We will see you on Sunday then.'

As I left their house I was delighted. I now had somewhere to go, and people I could talk with who understood me.

Sunday School

So each Sunday I was expected to go to church but little did my parents know that I was now going to Christine's house. I loved it there as I always felt welcomed. The home baking was delicious, and was something I did not experience much at my house. The Macpherson house overlooked the river Ness and was not far from the Islands. They had the most amazing garden with a monkey puzzle tree which I loved.

Christine's parents told us many stories about the Highlands, about the myth and magic of the lands. For hours on end I sat listening as they weaved a web of magic around us. Their stories included legends of the fairy folk, ghosts, magical stone circles, cairns, wells and hills that abound the Highlands.

'You are so lucky,' I said to Christine one day as we were walking back from her school to her house. 'I wish my parents were like yours. They support you, listen to you, and help you.'

'Yes. They take me to all the places they talk about, and we spend time together talking about the history of the land and its folklore. Would you like to come along on our next outing?' she replied.

I did not need to be asked twice. When we arrived at her house and walked in, her mother met us in the hallway. 'There you are, we were just talking about you. How would you like to come with us this weekend to the Clava Stones at Culloden Battlefield? We are having a celebration there. Friends are getting married, and it's also Beltane, so it's a double celebration.'

I had visited the Clava Stones many times, picking raspberries on the farm nearby to earn pocket money, and then continue on to explore the sacred sites around the battlefield. There are three burial cairns at Balnuaran surrounded by standing stones that are part of a line of seven extending along the south side of the valley of the river Nairn. The woodland setting is amazing, and the site of these cairns is one of the most beautiful and peaceful places I have encountered in the Highlands of Scotland. *(Once I went to the Stones with my friend David. It was dusk and just as we were about to set off home we caught site of a group of men clad in long cream robes approaching us. David was terrified and ran home. I was mesmerized and climbed a big tree nearby to get a better view of the action. It was a magical time. Though I was unaware of the meaning of the ceremony being performed it felt sacred and I felt so special for having witnessed it.)*

I was just about to ask Margaret about my mother, when she looked at me and said, 'Don't worry, I will call your mother and sort it out. Can you remember to bring with you a scarf or an old piece of material please?'

'Of course,' I answered, wondering what I would need it for. I went home that night with a big smile on my face. My mum greeted me as usual with a guilt trip about being late for tea. It was already on the table, and cold, but I was expected to eat it. I sat down and ate everything. I wanted to get to my bedroom as fast as possible. Later I heard what I was waiting for – the phone ringing, and after a moment I heard my mum say, 'Yes, not a problem.' She came to my room. 'That was your friend's mother on the phone. They are going to a wedding and would like you to go. That is fine by me as long as you do your entire household chores before you go.'

'I will make sure it's all done. Thank you,' I replied.

On Saturday I was ready long before the Macphersons arrived. I wore a dress for the celebration as Margaret had asked. I only had one dress for special occasions, and today I knew was going to be out-of-the-ordinary. I was so excited. They drove up at 12 o'clock prompt, and I ran out of the door shouting goodbye to my mum. I jumped into the car before anything or anyone could stop me. They all smiled their welcome, and I felt I was with my long lost family. We first stopped at the florist in town, and then headed over the River Ness. After about five minutes more driving, we stopped outside a church and parked up.

'This is where the wedding will be.'

I had only been to one wedding, my uncle's. As we sat down in the pews, I whispered to Christine, 'I thought we were going to the Clava Cairns.'

Margaret overheard me. 'Don't worry. We will get there. Have patience.' I was a teenager who was not very good at patience.

The music started and I looked back to see a beautiful woman wearing an exquisite white dress as she glided down the aisle. I was suddenly whisked off into a magical world of Camelot, back to Guinevere and Lancelot. I watched in awe as the couple in front of me exchanged vows, whilst I slipped in and out of this world to one of kings and knights. Before I knew it the service was over and they were walking back down the aisle. We exited the church to watch the bride and groom leave.

'Okay, let's make our way to the Drumossie Hotel for a meal.'

Meal? When are we going to the Cairns? But then the thought of food temporarily took all notions of the Clava Cairns out of my mind.

After a couple of hours of eating, followed by speeches, I had given up going anywhere. It was late afternoon and the Sun was starting to sink in the sky.

'Are you ready to go?' I was asked by Jack.

Although I answered 'yes,' I thought to myself, this is it. They are taking me home. I noticed Margaret was going around the tables speaking to people who were also getting up to leave. The bride and groom had already left, so I presumed the wedding was finished. As we walked out of the hotel and made our way to the car, people were asking us, 'We will see you there?'

I looked at Jack, who gave me a wink and smiled. 'Soon lass. Soon.'

That's strange. No one calls me 'lass' except Swein, I thought. We drove away from the hotel, but not in the direction of my house. We were heading towards Culloden. Fantastic! They have not forgotten.

We soon arrived at Smithton just below Culloden. 'We are going for a walk. Do you have your cloth, or scarf?'

'Yes, I have one. What's it for?'

'You will see soon enough.'

As we walked down the road, I noticed many other people getting out of their cars and heading in the same direction we were. I glimpsed the bride and groom in front of us. We turned off onto one of the paths, and soon Jack was walking beside me.

'I know,' he said, 'you have many questions running through your head right now. I will do my best to answer them. We are going to Clootie Well to ask a blessing for the married couple. It is a tradition of our people to go to the well on the first day of May. This is called Beltane. We will have a hand-fasting at the Clava Stones after we have been to the well.'

We passed by St Mary's Well on our way, but did not stop. 'Where we are going,' said Jack before I could ask, 'is much older in traditions than the well we have just passed. My family have been coming here for many years on this special day to tie a ribbon or piece of clothing onto the trees around the Clootie Well to ask for blessings and healing.'

Jack went on to explain the many stories that were connected to the land where we were now walking. He talked about the ghosts from the battle of Culloden and the Highlanders who had been killed there. 'It is said that many were slain at this spot.' As he pointed to a stone, I could feel a shudder going through my whole body.

I could see the entire scene as if it were yesterday. I became rooted to the spot as I watched the Highlanders being slaughtered, along with women and children. Jack reassured me, 'It's okay, lass. We know you have the gift of the second sight.'

I asked, 'How can we help them? They looked so afraid.'

'Imagine a light around them,' Jack said. 'Can you do this?'

'Yes,' I replied, but soon added, 'What is happening? They are becoming clearer and are starting to disappear.'

'Good,' said Jack, 'You have helped them go on to the Summerlands. Well done! Is this the first time you have seen ghosts?'

'Oh, no. I have seen them many times, but did not know what to do. Most of the time they just disappear. Touch the Clouds takes care of them for me.'

I went on to explain to Jack that Touch the Clouds had been with me since I was a little girl, and that he was always with me.

'Then he's your gatekeeper and protector,' Jack replied. 'We expected this. Come, let's catch up with the others.'

When we arrived at the Clootie Well, the only people there were from the wedding party. The bride and groom stood nearest the well. Jack walked over and placed his hands on the couple, then said, 'We are here to witness a blessing on this day of Beltane for our soon-to-be hand-fasted couple, Peter and Sheila.' With that he bent down and took some of the spring water in his hands and poured it over their hands.

'We ask for a blessing from the God and Goddess who walk on this sacred land. Let no harm come to them, for this water is sacred and will keep ill health away from those who leave a part of them behind. So, let us all take our ribbons and tie them on the trees that surround this sacred well. Make sure to not touch any other person's cloth tied on the tree, for if you do you will take their illness upon yourself.' With that the bride and groom tied their cloths onto a branch, followed by the rest of us.

Once we had all finished, Jack said, 'Now it is time for the hand-fasting. Let the bride and groom go on ahead to be met by those who have prepared the Cairns for this ceremony.'

It was then that I noticed Margaret was not with us, nor were about six of the other woman. I walked back to the car with Jack and we drove the mile or so to the Cairns. What greeted my eyes was a sight to behold. It was now dusk. Mist was on the ground, giving a haunted feel to the place. Hurricane lights were placed around the first cairn, and flowers were everywhere. I stood transfixed, my mouth opened in awe. I heard Jack's voice behind me. 'Many say this site is haunted, but we know it's not, don't we lass?'

I turned round and looked at Jack. He was now wearing a long cream robe. 'It's you! You were the one here that evening with everybody else.'

'Yes, and you were the one up in the tree watching us. You told Swein of your adventure, and he told us. That is why you are here now. Hail and welcome, Raven!'

'How do you know my name?' I asked.

'Swein told me,' he replied. 'Now come and join our ceremony that is about to take place. Tonight is a special night, the night when the Lord and the Lady come together as one. You will learn a lot tonight, Raven, which will change your life forever. You must not speak a word of this to anyone, for they will not understand our ways. There will come a time in your life when you can talk openly about what you have experienced, but until then say nothing of what you know. It is best.'

I took an oath. What I then witnessed was the most beautiful ceremony I had ever seen. The authenticity of the words, the sacredness of the place and the happiness of the people will forever live in my heart. That night I realised I was not alone. There were others like me. I had found my family. I was home.

Christine and I sat in the background and witnessed the whole ceremony. After the hand-fasting we made our way back in the car, smiling.

'That was beautiful. Thank you so much for inviting me.'

Christine looked at me, 'You can thank my parents. They wanted you to come as well.'

As I was climbing up the stairs to bed that night in their home, I thanked Jack and Margaret for letting me share the day with them. They were standing arm in arm looking at me smiling. 'When we heard from Swein that it was you up in the tree, and he told us all about you, we knew you had to be there with us tonight. We know there is no one in your own home to help guide you on the path you have chosen. When you are ready we will sit and talk about your future within the craft of the old ones.'

'Thank you so much. When can I start?'

'After a good night's sleep. Good night Raven, sleep well.'

It is worth noting here that as a people we tend to focus on ceremonies that bring relationships together. We bind couples in sacred marriage who love each other to come together to grow and learn. Sometimes that winding path of togetherness ends at a significant time, when energies change, and when this happens a break in a dignified way should be honoured. This can be done in a simple ceremony to unbind the souls of the said parties from any verbal vows and contracts that were made, to release them in all directions of time. It is important to do this to cut any emotional, physical and spiritual ties that bind those souls together in order for them to move on freely.

The ceremony can be done with or without the physical presence of the other person. So if they are with you take their left hand (that of the wedding ring finger) with your left hand and say, 'I thank you for accompanying me on my path thus far. I now release you from all vows made to me in all directions of time.'

The partner then repeats the phrase. If the partner is not present, make the statement and see in your mind's eye both of you being cleared of any etheric cords that have attached from said vows. Having honoured and released you both from the partnership the unbinding is complete for you to now move on, with no attachments, in all ways and levels.

The next couple of years were happy times for me. I travelled with Christine and her parents during weekends to visit the sacred sites in and around the Highlands. I learnt about herbs and their healing properties first-hand from the land. I gained a deeper understanding of the indigenous trees, shrubs, and plants. We spent many hours walking on the hills and through the glens, visiting springs, wells, and other places of the fey. We always visited ancient sites with stone circles, barrows, cairns, and spent many days working with the energy of the land and the local deities. My favourite places were Loch Ness, Glen Urquhart Castle, and the Black Isle. Haunted castles were also favourites of mine, and I began doing séances with a few of my other friends who were into contacting spirits.

I learnt very quickly that if I focused on my sports in school, I would not have to do school work. I excelled at swimming and diving. I was on nearly every women's sports team going in the athletics field, and I loved it. I was made a prefect and house captain. I was accepted at long last, no longer an outcast. I began making plans to become a sports teacher or swimming instructor. I was so passionate about sport, living and breathing it. In those few short years I won every sports trophy my school offered. I was seldom at home, spending all my time at the swimming pool, on the sports field or at Christine's house learning the ways of the Craft. Those were the happiest moments of my young life; I was on cloud nine, doing what I wanted. Then my life changed forever…

The False Prophet

I decided one morning to practise diving on the spring board at the pool. One of the dives I loved doing was an inward dive, where I stood with my back to the water, balanced on the edge of the board and flipped backwards into the water. Like hundreds of times before, I perched on the edge of the board with my toes, and bounced up. But instead of landing in the water, I crashed head first onto the spring board. I don't remember much because I passed out. Through a haze I heard my coach Donnie call to me. 'What you are doing lying on the board?' I got up slowly and staggered off the board. Donnie helped me to the shower.

'I'm not feeling well. I need to go home,' I said.

Donnie offered to drive me home but I said I would make my own way back. My next recollection is collapsing outside the doctor's surgery and waking up in a hospital bed.

I had compacted the vertebrae in my spine, causing my left leg to swing higher off the ground than my right. I had also dislocated my jaw. Any sport was impossible for at least six months whilst my battered body healed. I was lucky to be alive, they said, I could have rolled into the water and drowned. But I didn't feel lucky, my world was shattering. I was fifteen years old, ready to soar and my unbeatable body had been destroyed. It does not matter what anyone tells you, like it will be okay and you will get over it. You don't. I left school. I got a cooking job in the local hospital. A part of me had died there and then. I did not get any support from my parents. I lost all my school friends and the one family that mattered to me was moving away because of Jack's job. I felt abandoned, on a downward spiral with no way out.

However, I was once asked if I had my life over again would I choose to experience the same thing and the answer is yes. All the pain, the hurt, the fears and the doubts have made me who I am today. Because of what I have gone through, I am now able to see past traumas in others and how they are related to their present perspective. I have empathy to help them through their rites of passage into being whole and well again. This is the shamanic death and rebirth that some of us choose to experience to help ourselves and others live again with hope. After the diving board accident my adopted parents showed me little love at home. I moved in with a young man and his family who promised to take care of me. Whilst there, however, I was raped and abused so often that I lost my hair as well as my self-esteem. I became pregnant and was given tablets, by the mother of this new family, to abort the child. This caused serious damage in my womb as well as the loss of the baby.

I attempted suicide. My father died and I blamed myself for his death. My mother blamed me for his death. My second attempted suicide failed.

I then discovered that despite being told many years previously that my natural parents were killed in a car accident, they are actually alive and well. At seventeen years of age this was my experience of life. I did not want to continue. What kept me going? What is it that drives us forward to continue despite all the adversities that life presents? What I had experienced from a very early age was 'who I was not'. Today I look back on the times of pain, fear and wounding and realise that they were great lessons. It was my choice whether I would learn from them and move towards enlightenment or forever live in a black hole of self-pity.

The people and the events of my past have helped create who I am today. I see through my wounds that I gained a deeper understanding of 'who I was not'. It has taken all of my life to heal my past, and even to this day I am aware that there are still repairs to be made on my physical body. Our bodies are great teachers if we listen. If we do not listen to our body's cry for help, the pain sinks into our emotional body and affects us at a deeper level of awareness. For my healing to take place I had to be emotionally honest with myself, and this is not an easy thing to do.

Becoming conscious of the self (who we are not), and the soul (who we have been since our point of creation) is one of the most profound insights we can experience. We can comprehend the magnitude of how unhappy emotions affect us in our everyday living and claim ownership of our authentic selves. Who I was not is what my parents, teachers, religious tutors and other authority figures wanted me to believe. They wanted me to think that I was powerless. I was taught by my peers from an early age that because I misbehaved I did not fit into their perception of what was right or wrong, good or bad. I was condemned once again before being given a fair trial.

In the legal system we are told that one is innocent until proven guilty, but for many of us we were silenced and shut away in the dark places of the self without our voices being fully heard. This created the 'self', our very own false prophet as our souls were locked away for an eternity. Instead the embodiment of self was installed into our Earthly existence so that we would forget who we truly are and the reasons why we came to this Earth plane at this moment in time. Yet another divine human being was controlled and suppressed, cloned and programmed to fit in with a soulless world.

Many religions teach that if something bad happens to a person it is because that person was evil or weak. I was always being told I would go to Hell. I did go to Hell, the rather crowded, man-made Hell of self-destruction. But through the stripping of fears and pains, caused by other people's projections, I discovered the authenticity of my soul's wisdom, my own heart's knowing. We create our Heaven or Hell. It is up to us to call on our will power, our inner strength, and our inner knowing to guide us. All of us are born with this faith, the knowing that shines light in the darkness when no one else is around. We can discern life's lessons of our childhood and teenager years, rather than suppress our feelings about our experiences. We release the grief that is within us and honour who we are in a loving and supporting way. I have worked on myself for decades to remove all the doubts created by others. Writing this book is one of the greatest rites of passage I have yet undertaken on the emotional and mental level. I have remembered things that I had suppressed or chosen to ignore, totally forgotten about or thought I had already worked through.

To acknowledge and accept who we are, we need to take the shame out of our internal relationship. Stop having unreasonable expectations of ourselves and of others. From the beginning of our lives here on Earth, we are taught false beliefs about why we are here, about the purpose of our lives. If we take a moment to look at the foundations of our so-called civilised society we see that there are very few rites of passage to help piece together who we are. This is because our modern world of 'need and greed' would cease to hold our attention. By remembering that freedom is our only preferred choice for our future, we take our destiny into our own hands. We balance mind, body and heart. Freedom to choose who we become is why our ancestors fought so hard throughout history. Today we have a choice to be liberated from an unfeeling society and create a new civilisation of enlightened souls. There exist alternatives for educating our children, an abundance of natural medicines to heal our bodies as well as a diversity of belief systems that embrace our spiritual awareness. We are alive during another Golden Age of self-realisation. We awaken again as soul-realised human beings, having the ability to choose what it is we want out of life, instead of being herded like sheep into a pen waiting to be branded with society's marks of unconsciousness.

Pain held in the physical body as trauma creates a psychological imbalance within our minds, which in turn suppresses the emotional body. Emotions of the heart are stifled, creating separation from the spiritual embodiment of our soul's knowing. When our unity with nature and spirit is displaced, our split-apart takes place. Our mental, emotional, and spiritual worlds are then reintegrated into the physical embodiment of wellness and wholeness. We are complete once again. This is why it is very important to heal on all levels of awareness.

How many of us listen to our physical bodies? Do we experience rites of passage which honour the temple that houses the most precious gift of all, our spirit? The ancient temples around the world that I have visited have fallen into disrepair. In the 21st century we are once again repairing our own inner temples by rebalancing the feminine and masculine, within and without. We heal through our split-apart to become members of the school of spiritual evolution. We follow our unique path of enlightenment and create new beginnings for ourselves and our future generations.

Our willpower creates a path. It is the rite of passage for self-mastery. This rite of passage is self-perpetuating. As we learn and grow, so does our ability to walk unaided. We transform from the caterpillar to the butterfly. This rite of passage is the key to our survival. What kept me going was my deep connection to spirit, the voice that I heard above all other voices telling me I was a child of the Creator, and that I was dearly loved. Knowing my worth as a spiritual being drove me onwards and upwards. When voices of the selves of others were saying to me you're no good, you're a bastard, you're evil and wicked, you're fat, you will never make it in this world, my entire spiritual essence protested 'No!'

The selves of others tried to suppress me on a physical, mental, emotional and spiritual level. They shamed and blamed me into believing I was no good. What I had to learn was not to be judge and shame myself. We are taught that if we make a mistake in life it is shameful, but this is not true. So-called mistakes in life are lessons to be learnt. I found that as I healed my past wounds, other people's own traumas disappeared. As healing took place within me, healing was simultaneously taking place within them. After a couple of years these people would come back into my life. We were mirrors for one another.

At the time of being in this 'hell' with the new family I went around in a state of shock. I drank and smoked every day trying to numb the pain. I felt empty, a body without a soul, a zombie. There was no meaning to my life. I tried everything I possibly could to change this void of love, feelings, joy and happiness. Nothing and nobody could make me feel better. When people spoke to me and I would answer, it was if I was talking to them from a faraway place. I did not tell anyone the things that had happened to me because I was ashamed of myself. I had no soul-worth. During this time it was very difficult for spirit to connect to me because of the state I was in. Occasionally I heard spirit, when they did get through, say 'we love you', but that was little comfort at the time when no one else said it. I did not even have anyone to go to visit Swein with. I was alone.

Myself and I

One day I was crossing the bridge over the river Ness. I had left catering and worked in hairdressing, moving from job to job, looking for some sort of work satisfaction. Strangely, whilst walking across the bridge another me appeared. I had already experienced out-of-body moments and astral travel in the dreamtime, but seeing myself like this was a new and surreal feeling. I looked at myself, who was standing before me and asked, 'Who are you?'

'I am you,' came the reply.

'Are you real?' I asked.

'Yes. I appear as your double, twin, or split-apart.'

'Where do you live?' I asked.

'Here on this bridge is a place of the in-between, a doorway to the other worlds. I live and journey between the lower, middle and upper worlds. I am your companion in the underworld where the missing parts of your soul reside. I am here to help you access this deep, dark place where you fear to travel alone. I am who you have been and who you will become in time. Past, present and future are one and the same to me and I am able to move between them at will. I am not restricted to your human form.'

As my split-apart was speaking, I witnessed the many different images of whom I had been in previous lifetimes.

'Remember the time you were with Swein and saw, what appeared to be his shadow moving beside him? Well, that was his split-apart.' What came to my mind then was a picture Swein had shown me of himself beside a full body of energy.

'Let me explain', my split-apart said. 'We have always been connected since the very moment of creation. We are the divine union of male and female, within and without. Whilst you experienced trauma during the past couple of years, parts of your soul were fragmented. Your joy, passion and life-force energy retreated to the lower world. The self was made up to take its place in this middle world. You went from the feeling, intuition and connection with nature, from within your heart, to the place of doubts and fears within your mind. Spirit cannot connect with you directly through your heart when you live in your head. We have an etheric umbilical cord that connects us. At this moment you feel out of balance, and it is important that we redress this crisis. I am here to get you back on track for the work to be done. I have been waiting to help and assist you once again.'

'You mean you have worked with me before?' I cried.

'Yes, many times we have been together, for I am here to help you become one with your soul. I am what many people call your higher self. A higher self is our soul that has become split apart from our conscious awareness of the reality of the all.'

Memories flooded me. I saw a book with all my lifetimes flash in front of me. I remembered now. It all made sense. I could feel a wellness flow through my body as a bond formed between myself and my split-apart. I looked at her and said, 'Many times I have gone into those deep dark places, but could not bear to stay there.'

'Of course not. You were revisiting the wounds that had been inflicted upon you. You were seeing your own nature as well as what was made up by others and yourself. What you were seeing is who you are and who you are not, at that moment in time. For you to face these traumas again you will need to prepare yourself. That is why I am here. Together, we will traverse the unknown of the lower world.

'Before you embark on this journey to reintegrate the missing parts of your soul, you will need to regain your strength and reprogramme the false sets of beliefs instilled in you. This means starting again at the beginning. In the years to come you will enter into many relationships that will be reflections of yourself. These relationships will mirror the self within you. This is your journey of recovery from self to soul, from head to heart. You will be shown the way, look for the sign posts.'

With that my split-apart disappeared. I remained on the bridge watching the water flow. My tears washed away my pain before joining the river on its way to the sea.

Years later I heard a song called 'The River' that expressed how I felt at this very moment. *'The River is flowing, flowing and growing. The river is flowing, back to the sea. O mother carry me, your child I will always be. O mother carry me, back to the sea.'*

Time stood still for me on that day. When I first walked onto the bridge nobody else was on it, and as I now looked both ways on the bridge there was still no one there. I glanced up at the church clock, thinking I would be late for work. The time was the same as when I had last looked. As I later discovered, spirit can expand and slow down our time. What I had perceived to be 10 minutes with my split-apart was in fact less than a minute.

Authentic Unification

Now is the time when split-aparts, those who have been separated from their beloveds, can become whole once again. This is because we are at a pivotal point in the evolution of consciousness – the Golden Age that was foretold by many shamans and seers. This is an exciting time to reincorporate our heart and soul energies as one. We can refuse to allow fear and aggression to manipulate and disempower us any longer. We have time to change our society and culture by re-educating those who have an open heart in the ways of the truth. We are today's witnesses of new and olden times, of life coming full circle, back to a balanced world.

The beginning of this cycle was harmony of the feminine and masculine. Souls were whole. The divine union of Goddess and God was reflected out into the world as two expressions of the one Spirit. Our ancestors weaved their storytelling, dancing and singing as they co-created with heartfelt sacredness. For thirty thousand years the wisdom teachings of the ancients was the philosophy of the Goddess. This way of life embraced both men and women wholly, equally and without prejudice. Nowhere in the recorded history of this culture did they dismiss or exclude one another. Our ancestors had a great reverence for the Earth and Her inhabitants. They worked knowingly with the land and honoured the cycles of life. Sensuality and sexuality were not hidden behind closed doors as shameful and indecent. Birth and death were respected through Rites of Passage which celebrated everyday life.

Then came 'his-stories' and myths of imbalance. No longer was the Goddess honoured as the giver of life and wellbeing. The womb of the Goddess was raped physically, emotionally, mentally and spiritually. Stories of Goddesses were changed to become stories of Gods. Patriarchy focussed on war, fear, and dominance. The scales of justice tipped. Freedoms of people were taken away and heartlessness was rewarded instead of heart centredness. The end times of our connected living heralded the dark age of fear and tyranny. We are here now to rebalance the scales of the divine masculine and feminine. This is our collective calling, to be in a sacred relationship with ourselves, to heal the wounds of the past, to understand that the violent destruction that we are experiencing now needs to stop once and for all.

Equality of men and women is regained by embracing and putting aside our differences. We honour and remember the men and women who, throughout the rule of patriarchies, protected and kept alive the secrets of the sacred. Their calling was to keep the truth alive for us, often at the cost of physical torture and death. They remembered their freedom to keep the flame of destiny burning brightly. They are the champions of our true heritage, and we owe it to them to rediscover our inherited treasure that they preserved with all their might. We also owe it to ourselves to uncover the whole story of creation, to find the pieces that were deliberately missed out. It's time for our true history to be revealed to one and all.

To communicate our truth, we first need to find our voice which may have been muted by blame and shame. When we hide wounds they fester and poison on all levels of consciousness, and we slowly die. Our individual and collective souls want to join together once again, to be healed and whole. Our souls cry for the divine union of humanity to be in balance, so we may freely walk in our truth while expressing our liberty and independence to be 'who we are'. The Age of Aquarius is a new and exciting planetary cycle for all of us to witness and be a part of. The sacred union of the male and the female embraces the God and Goddess within. Goddess returns with Her light of healing upon the land and its people. Her presence and luminous wellbeing celebrates the sacred masculine and feminine both within and without.

In Your Beginning

We are ready now to write your personal creation story. Being aware of both our inner male and female energies synchronising our hearts and minds. We can then listen to and respect the voice of our thoughts and the words from our hearts. Our soul knowing, reflected in a sacred relationship with another, tunes us into the Divine Relationship. The alchemy of marriage begins by reconnecting with our 'twin flame'. True love is eternal. There is no separation from Great Spirit, thus no disconnection to the God or Goddess within us. Our hearts and minds co-exist in equilibrium within the blessed union of love between two people. Our current cultural story is based on scientific justifications of how we as humans emerged into existence. We simply were. Our ancestors consulted the planetary cosmology and oracles for spiritual answers to the deeper meanings of life. Anthropologists refer to these stories as creation myths. These creation myths were passed orally from generation to generation. Like many retold stories, creation stories were changed over time so we don't really know what the originals were. Legends, myths, and folktales have not only changed over time, some have become foundations for entire religions.

What will be the creation story of the times we live in now? We can change and rewrite our destiny. You can be soothsayers and storytellers for future generations. What we need to do first is awaken and invigorate our imaginations. We can become as children again with a sense of wonderment and joy as we remember our love of stories.

What fascinates you about your favourite myth, tradition, or legend? Which part of the ancient world makes you feel excited or romantic, wanting to be back in those times? Which gods and goddesses call to you? Imagine right now as you read this book that you are the centre of the Universe. You have the ability to create anything you wish. Today in your very own creation story you are going to create a new Universe, a new world. This new world will be the foundation of your future life, with your mind, body and spirit in harmony, whole and complete. Your relationships, health, work, wealth and love are abundant and manifest. Imagine this story as the one you will enjoy telling your family and future generations of how the world, as you know it, came into creation through love.

It's now time to find a special place for your sacred time to create this new world. Where would you, as the storyteller, choose to be for the story to unfold? Where do you imagine creation to start from? What part of the universe, which galaxy or star constellation do you wish to be in, and what is its connection with Earth? Take your time. What is the connection with the universe and Earth? Why have our ancestors created stories which often included the planets, stars, the Milky Way and other constellations?

Imagine you are the first woman or man to be created. Where is your twin flame, your twin soul? Where have you been created from and by whom? Who is your creator? Don't rush. Allow yourself time to hear your inner wisdom, for this will answer a lot of questions for you. Now visualise togetherness, before you were split apart from your twin soul. Where are you both? How do you feel? What do you sense and see around you? Are you floating in a great void, in the nothingness of no time? Then look at your twin flame. What does he or she look like? You might be surprised. Let this happen naturally. Do not force the outcome of what you see. Be gentle with yourself, for you might trigger a memory from thousands of years ago when you were together as one.

Focus your entire willpower and desire on your beloved. See and sense him or her as you become one once again. As you look upon your beloved now, are they familiar to you in this lifetime, as one of your family or friends? Have you met them yet, or are you still searching for them, knowing they are out there? Do you feel the presence of them in the spirit world watching over you because they have been with you during your Earth walk and have passed over? Or is your beloved still to come, waiting for you to join them in Spirit? Have you been watching and waiting for your beloved? Can you remember your beloved visiting you in the dreamtime? By rewriting your creation story, you can manifest your beloved into your life right now. Getting rid of the false set of beliefs installed in you as a child can now release the life you have always dreamed of. Now that you have imagined and sensed your beloved, you can build on the foundations of your creation story.

Not long ago a lady called Michelle came to me for a reading. I asked, 'How can I help you?'

Michelle looked at me with tears in her eyes and said, 'I want to know when I will meet someone who will love me. I hate being on my own. I have only ever known abusive relationships.'

I could see her father in the spirit world; his head was down, ashamed of himself. He had been an alcoholic and workaholic, abused his daughter and spent his money on other women. He had mistreated his wife and when he died left his family without means.

I said to Michelle, 'I have your father here.'

Her initial reaction was, 'I don't want to speak to him. Because of him I've been working as a prostitute since I was twelve.'

'He is so sorry, Michelle. He knows he has done wrong. It was only when he returned to the spirit world that he understood, because he was connected again with his soul. He wants to know how he can help you now. He can see that you have gone from one abusive relationship into another, time and time again. He knows he has not been a good role model.'

Michelle looked at me and said, 'I just want to be loved.'

I looked at Michelle and said, 'We need to change your time lines. We need to heal the past. I want you to visualise your father as if he were still alive. Imagine him standing right in front of you now and say what you feel, all the anger, fear, and rejections. No holds barred, get it off your chest.'

I sat in the chair opposite Michelle holding sacred space for her. I could see her father standing in front of her now. I knew a great release was about to take place. At first it was difficult for her, but after a while she really let go and started to say what she felt within. I could see all the years of pain and sorrow being released from her heart. Then she looked at me and said, 'I can feel my father in front of me. He's crying and saying he's sorry. He wants to take care of me and make sure I will be okay. He loves me.'

She gasped. 'He never told me this before. He's telling me he wrote a letter to me but I never got it.'

'Ask him where it is.'

'He's saying it's with my mother'. Then she started laughing. 'I have tried and tried to speak to my dad and it has never happened. Why now?'

I explained to Michelle that when we are in grief and pain, spirits find it very difficult to connect with us because they do not resonate with pain or fear, only love.

'A great healing has taken place today, Michelle. You have changed your timelines and opened your heart centre again to love. Now you will attract into your life everything you have dreamed of; a home, a husband, children, security. You now understand that you can change your own life and create your own destiny.'

Michelle left that day with a deep understanding of sacred relationships. By healing her past with her father, she could establish new boundaries with those around her. About eighteen months went by, and then one day Michelle walked into my shop. I did not recognise her. Her whole demeanour had changed. She looked so happy. She told me that she went home to her mother and asked her where the letter was. At first her mother denied that there was a letter. Michelle let her mum listen to the tape recording of the reading, and her mum broke down in tears. She went over to the desk drawer and handed Michelle a letter from her father.

The letter revealed and explained his terrible childhood, beatings, and the boys' school where he had been abused and raped. This letter was written a couple of days before he died of a heart attack, which caused him to crash his car. He did not say goodbye to anyone. In his letter he also stated he felt something was going to happen to him. He had a premonition of a car accident. He wrote to Michelle that he loved her and was sorry for not being able to express his feelings. After reading the letter she sat down with her mother and healed the wounding that had occurred between them.

Now standing in front of me was a beautiful woman.

'I feel so happy,' she said over and over. 'A couple of months after my visit to my mum, I had a phone call from one of my ex-boyfriends. I finished with him because I could not cope with the love and attention he was giving me. I know now that at the time I thought I had to be in an abusive relationship. He told me he had had a dream about my dad and me, and that he should call me. We met up and it was amazing. Within six months we got engaged and we are getting married in three months. So I came to visit you today to buy my wedding dress.'

Michelle has now healed her past. She has also healed the ancestral line of pain handed down from generation to generation in the family. She has created for herself a new understanding of how to manifest what she most richly deserves. Michelle walked out of the shop that day with wedding dress in hand, ready to start a whole new life of love and happiness. A good percentage of the readings I give involve finding clients' beloveds. Most are currently in abusive relationships. What I find interesting is that no matter how bad the relationships are, these people still hold onto the hope of finding their twin soul.

When we go back to the original wounding, we can trace back

to our role models. The number of women who married an exact replica of their father is shocking. There are so many people in unhappy relationships, unable to walk away because of fear, control, and abuse. It takes great courage to stand up and say, 'No more, this is not acceptable.' I know. I have been there.

This chapter has been all about sacred relationships with our selves and with our split-aparts or twin souls. Being in just any relationship is not the goal. This was the false message we were given when growing up, that some love is better than no love at all. However, we are not incomplete if we do not find another partner. We are never half a person. We are whole and complete within and without.

I remember many years ago I had the privilege of watching a total eclipse of the Sun when I was near Lake Hazar in eastern Turkey. The evening before, I had done a releasing ceremony during the new moon, as part of my work to integrate and balance my divine feminine and masculine. As I watched the Sun and the Moon become one, I was taken back to a time when the ancients watched the same incredible experience with awe, amazement and reverence. As I stood by the lake listening to the water lapping gently on the shoreline, I could sense a great awakening within me. My destiny started to unveil itself with the arriving dusk. I felt as if a great weight was being lifted off me. I was free to be who I wished to be, complete, to begin a new cycle. I was taken back in time to when many of our ancestors believed an eclipse was the end of the world. I could see them standing as I did now in total wonderment as to what was to come.

In Egyptian cosmology, Hathor was the goddess of solar eclipses, Khepri the scarab beetle was the representation of the New Moon, and the Hawk Horakhty is the Sun in totality. On the ceiling of Dendera temple in Egypt is a relief with Nut, Goddess of the Sky, holding up the heavens while Geb the Earth Father rises up to meet her each new day. This daily cycle of birth and creation, of the Sun and the Moon, represents our personal completion, regeneration, transformation and awakening of totality within our souls. The beautiful sculpture depicts the divine female descending from the heavens to create a sacred union on Earth of a great love that knows no boundaries or fear. So how can we recreate the divine power of Heaven on Earth that will flow throughout our bodies to merge and balance our inner feminine and masculine? Every single one of us has divine masculine and feminine energy within. What makes up this amazing cacophony of life?

The female, left side of our bodies links to the right hemisphere of our brains and our inner knowing, compassion and nurturing. A balanced feminine awareness exudes calm, confidence and has a relaxed response and outlook to discord without reacting, projecting or engaging in others' internal imbalances. The true nature and ability of the divine feminine awareness is to be detached from what others think, say or do. The masculine energy located on the right hand side of our body is linked to our left brain. We become conscious of a more controlled, analytical, aggressive response reaction combined with impatience and lack of compassion. Power and strength do not come from being uncompromising or through domination. The true art of the warrior is one of peaceful surrender.

Our personal power comes from knowing who we are and being comfortable in our own skins. When we become confident we don't need to protect or defend ourselves anymore. We open our hearts to expose the truth and reveal the timeless path to totality. Once we have taken the time to get to know ourselves better we can then surrender to Creator's great gift of divine union with the cosmos, beginning with a marriage ceremony of the Sun and Moon. An eclipse is a time of totality of Source, the freedom to see and become one with all. The Moon can affect you in the astrological aspects of the male or female. The moments of the Moon in the male signs of Aries, Gemini, Leo, Libra, Sagittarius or Aquarius are good times to balance the masculine energy. For the female the moment of the Moon's influence is in Taurus, Cancer, Virgo, Scorpio Capricorn or Pisces. These are good times to work with the feminine energy. Working with the planets and astrological aspects of male and female can help us reveal the hidden nature of our knowing. We connect to Source with planetary aspects of our inner and outer Universes.

When I witnessed the solar eclipse I was working on letting go of the strong male aspect within me. I found it very hard to work with the masculine Sun in Leo eclipsed by the feminine hidden Moon. When I journeyed deeply into the reasons for this I found that over the centuries I had been persecuted by many men for being a female. When I was younger I had not accepted my divine feminine. I had denied the goddess within. For me the solar eclipse was a breakthrough because I had to fight with all my being to awaken that which had been suppressed for thousands of years by male dominance through lack of under-standing and fear of the feminine. The male aspect was the suppressed aspect of my life that needed to be rebalanced.

Rite of Passage: Healing the Split-Apart

The best time for merging the masculine, feminine and spirit within our very being is when working with the Sun, Moon and Earth. This is best done during a solar eclipse, a lunar eclipse or at dawn once a month when the Full Moon is on the western horizon in the place of completion as the Sun is simultaneously on the eastern horizon in its place of Awakening. During a solar eclipse you are working with the Dark of the Moon or the New Moon. I have been blessed to witness both of these incredible events. Search the internet for when the next eclipse is in the area where you live.

A lunar eclipse is completely safe to watch. You do not need to use any kind of protective filters, so experience it with eyes open. I have seen the blood-red moon many times. It is enhanced by volcanic ash that was prominent high in the skies of Europe when a volcano in Iceland released pent up emotions that had been trapped within the earth and us. When possible, work with the Full Moon's energy at the time of the lunar eclipse to rebalance feminine energy, and work with the hidden or New Moon influence upon the Sun during a solar eclipse to harmonize your masculine energy. If you are not in the right place at the right time for an eclipse, you still have the monthly opportunity to do the ceremony with the Sun and the Moon as I did in Arizona.

For this moon-set ceremony, I have found being high up on a mountain top is good, or being in a place where you can see clearly from east to west without anything blocking your view. It may be that you are on your own and still wish to do a healing ceremony with your split-apart. Your split-apart may be in Spirit, you still may not have met him or her, or you may be separated due to differences that cannot be resolved. This ceremony is also perfect for you if your partner does not yet understand the ways of Spirit.

You may be sharing your sacred space with others if it is lunar or solar eclipse, but if it is a Full Moon Sunrise Ceremony most likely people will still be in bed sleeping. For a full moon ceremony, it's good to feel your feet connecting and grounding your roots into the earth. Which way you face depends on whether you are male or female. Face north with left hand to the west connecting with the feminine moon and right hand to the east reaching for the masculine Sun. Then spin round and face the south, reversing your Sun/Moon connection. There is no wrong or right way to stand, so feel which is best for you. Personal experience helps you differentiate the energies of the directions. Take a moment to feel the subtleties as you walk the wheel of the year through North, East, South and West.

With arms outstretched and palms facing the Moon and the Sun, start to feel the energy of who you are. If you choose, connect firstly with the Moon through your left hand and allow the energy to flow through the left side of your body. This will help you to attune to how you feel on your feminine side. To work with your masculine side, connect to the Sun with your right hand to allow the Sun's energy to flow through the right side of your body. Once you have incorporated your principal male or female energy, you can then bring the secondary energies into your body. Once you become totally aware of how you are feeling, it is the time to merge the two energies as one. With the energies of both the Moon and the Sun flowing through you, enfold them both in your heart centre. As you start to weave the energies together imagine that you are going back to the point of creation when you and your split-apart were one.

This is the alchemy of totality, the reunion of souls. Feel yourself filling up in your heart centre with Moon energies flowing through your left hand and Sun energies flowing through your right hand into your heart centre. Now feel the Earth's energy flowing up your legs into your spine, awakening the sleeping kundalini, which is coiled at the base of your spine. As your soul's life force flows through your heart centre, see and sense this combined life force energy flowing from your heart centre up through the top of your head to connect with spirit.

This ceremony awakens the Sun within your heart centre, completes your soul's journey through the phases of the Moon, regenerates your Earth connection to spirit, and transforms your lighted sky into the Source from whence all things come. This is the true path of totality. Once you feel this incredible connection, take the time to send out healing thoughts beginning with the first man and woman who walked on this Earth. Instead of seeing them as separate beings, see them as one whole and complete with Nature. Continue on with your family, your loved ones, all the relationships you have had in your life. See the love flow through them, healing them. Allow forgiveness to flow through you now, letting go of pain, hurt and fear as you fill up your holy grail of life with divine love that never ends.

Once you feel complete with your ceremony, take your hands

to your heart, left hand over right hand if you are a man, and right hand over left hand if you are a woman. Now focus on all these energies being contained in the great storage area of light, love and peace that is your heart. Always remember to take the time to top up your tank, don't leave it until you are on empty. When working with the lunar or solar eclipse, apply the same principle of working with the Sun, the Moon, the Earth and the Sky in ceremony. The difference is the Sun and the Moon will be directly in front of you, and you will be in alignment with male and female energies coursing through your body simultaneously. Perhaps work first with the full moon ceremony then move on to the lunar and solar eclipse ceremony when you feel you are ready.

During one of my trips to the Gathering of Nations Powwow, we stopped off near Sedona to visit the medicine wheel that I built over fifteen years ago on top of a powerful vortex called Cathedral Rock. On the way up the hill someone fell and broke their ankle, which delayed our onward journey. We'd been staying at Adam Yellowbird's complex for a couple of days, so he suggested we stay on and join the upcoming gathering that he was hosting. Over several days, elders from the Hopi and other North and South American first nations came together with other wise men and women from around the world to celebrate and share with those who listened.

I will always remember the day I was called into the centre of all these Wisdom Keepers by Alberto Romaro. He held an eagle feather and a condor feather, which he presented to me in ceremony as I was honoured as an elder and Wisdom Keeper of my Celtic ancestors. When the Eagle of the North and the Condor of the South join together it symbolises the union of all nations as one people. The prophecy unfolds to show that we the people of the Earth, male and female, will unite as one rainbow tribe. We are the ones we have been waiting for. Our time of destiny is upon us, so let us listen to the winds of change. Let us free our souls and fly like the eagle and the condor, united as one voice, one Spirit.

I have a duty as a Wisdom Keeper to honour the Earth Mother and all forms of life that live upon her. Together, we ensure our future generations have a deep understanding and comprehension of how to heal and repair the damage that has been caused by our lack of consideration for this beautiful Earth. I help others find their lost souls, and awaken people to their life purpose and destiny. Like Captain Kirk, I boldly go where no one has gone before to assist whoever is ready to take the ride of their lives into their own inner Universe to uncover the strange new worlds that are waiting to be explored, as if for the first time. We are discovering worlds within worlds within our own soul. It is the voyage to the core of our inner knowing, one that traverses eternity with no concept of time or space. Only freedom lives here.

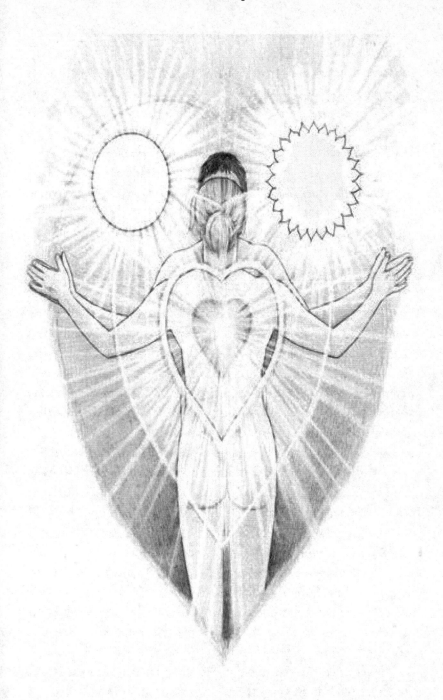

Chapter 5

The Experience
Summer Solstice & Four Losses

Everything that I have experienced in this lifetime and all other lifetimes has taught me to surrender and trust in Source. The experiences I have yet to encounter hold the key to my passage into the spirit world.

Barbara Meiklejohn-Free

Have you heard the calling from Spirit to travel to distant lands? Have you dropped everything to answer the heart as it calls for a pilgrimage to visit your homelands or a sacred site? When the time comes we have no choice but to answer our soul's calling. It is the journey of the Seeker looking for the connections, the insights that will bring us closer to Source. This, in itself, is a sacred rite of passage to the soul. Whatever it takes, you must go. Our personal pilgrimage is a journey to a sacred site or place that will connect us to a meaningful experience.

I have visited my homelands – the Highlands of Scotland – visited the graves of my adopted parents, looked at old photos and connected with the experiences that made me who I am today. The journey repaired the soul loss I felt during the hurtful experiences that I went through. My pilgrimages have been a 'soul hunt', to find meaning and understanding in the pain that was inflicted on me, enabling me to replace it with a landscape of immense beauty. Holy sites are not just on Earth... When we come to respect and honour who we are, we become sacred and whole once more, a beautiful temple is unearthed and rebuilt to its former glory.

I have been blessed to climb Mount Sinai, Machu Picchu and to have swum in the most beautiful waters of the world, lived in dense tropical rain forests of the Amazon and walked through deserts of hot burning sands in Egypt. It has inspired me, given me faith, healed me, and instilled peace when my mind and emotions led me astray. My pilgrimages were, and still are, a journey not just on the physical level but also on a spiritual level, healing the mind, body, spirit and soul. By experiencing our emotional, physical and spiritual beingness, we can go deeper into the exploration of our life, which reveals the jewel of who we really are.

Travel Well

A sacred pilgrimage is a rite of passage that many choose to follow, either through cultural belief systems or the heart's burning desire to be at an appointed place and time no matter who or what stands in your way. When we trace back our history of pilgrimage we find that all the great Magi and Seers, like Zoroaster, Abraham, Moses, Jesus and Buddha, came to greater understanding (enlightenment) after taking pilgrimage to sacred lands. Most people of faith have travelled to sacred sites. The Hindus go to Varanasi, Christians go to the Holy Land, Rome or Lourdes, the Jews visit Jerusalem, Buddhists visit Tibet and Muslims travel to Mecca. Druids, Pagans and Wiccans travel to Stonehenge and many other sacred sites on Celtic lands. Other people travel to battlefield sites, as our ancestors did thousands of years ago, to connect with and pay homage to loved ones who died in order that freedom could be ours. My friend Chris has travelled to Graceland to see Elvis's home; this is a pilgrimage of love and respect for someone who influenced her life from an early age.

As a child I climbed the hills and mountains of Scotland in search of the ancestors who lived in the highest nooks and crannies, seeking the spirits who I knew lived in the glens and waterfalls awaiting me, to communicate with them. I would feel their sadness as once upon a time many would come and leave them gifts and offerings, communicating with them through song, dance and poetry, but not now. People have forgotten that they exist and are part of the Earth's spirit. This profoundly affected me, for I could not understand why people would choose to neglect the nature spirits. Sacred sites fill me with a sense of awe and amazement at the magnitude of all the clues left behind by the ancestors for all to see. Most sites are in the remotest places, on tops of mountains, under the sea, in deep dense jungles waiting for the seekers to come and remember what they left behind from previous lifetimes.

My pilgrimage around the world was to discover, first-hand, the calling of an inner knowing. People would express their concern – where was I going, who would I stay with, how long would I be gone?

I would look at them, smile and say, 'Once I arrive I will connect with the ancestors and the land, wait for guidance and answers. When I step out of the way and surrender to Spirit they guide me to places, people and encounters that I could not experience any other way.'

This is when the magic begins. The veil between two worlds becomes thin, as I consciously connect, enabling me to step through and absorb the essence of freedom within the realms of the spirit worlds.

Wounded Knee

One evening, in deep meditation, spirit told me to pick up my white buffalo drum. 'It's time to go on a journey again.'

I laughed and wondered aloud what Shaun would make of this news.

'You will not go alone,' I heard.

I took my drum and held it to my heart. I began drumming and chanting, 'Mother I feel you under my feet, Mother I feel your heart beat.' It was my favourite song and moved me to tears whenever I sang it. I have always felt the Earth Mother beneath my feet, and known this sacred connection. I discovered that my drum kept this feeling alive, even when I was indoors, by serving as a natural bridge between my heart and her heartbeat, connecting us together as one.

Whilst drumming I kept seeing images of South Dakota. I had travelled there to discover the identity and history of my Spirit Father, Touch the Clouds. But this time it was different. I saw Touch the Clouds smiling and calling to me to walk on the land again. Then I saw a mountain scene with tall pine trees, a Native American elder sitting on top of the mountain surveying the land before him. He was on a vision quest. I became like the eagle and flew, circling around him again and again. Every time I flew past him I heard the words, 'Behold. Behold. A sacred voice is calling us.' This was followed by the image of a buffalo skull and I saw myself dragging a line of buffalo skulls behind me. I asked Spirit for clarity and was told that all would be revealed in due course. I had to journey to Wounded Knee.

I told Shaun of the latest journey that I was inspired to undertake. He just looked at me and smiled. 'Enjoy yourself.' Shaun always supported everything I did in my work with Spirit. He understood.

Next day at the Arthur Findley College I shared this new vision with my dear friends Jan Marsh, a tutor at the college, and Eileen, who is an amazing healer from Brighton.

'Can we come?' they asked.

'I don't know what's going to happen or where we will be led,' I answered.

'That's okay. We love an adventure.'

A couple of weeks later the three of us were on a plane heading for Denver, Colorado. We needed to be at Wounded Knee, South Dakota, for sunrise. At Denver airport we hired a van and started driving north. Late into the night we parked up for a few hours' rest. In the dreamtime I saw the medicine man sitting on top of the mountain.

I asked him, 'What do I do when I get to Wounded Knee?'

'Look for the grandfather,' he replied.

We arrived at Wounded Knee about an hour before sunrise and found ourselves alone. Nothing was as I remembered, from past life recall or the dreamtime. I walked over to the mass grave of the native people. I cried as it brought back past life memories of being a young girl, running down a ravine in the snow, being chased by soldiers. As I slowly beat my drum beside the grave I sang, 'Where I stand is holy, holy is this land,' in honour of these ancestors. I asked Spirit why, throughout the Earth, had the wise natives been killed.

'There are many who do not understand the wise ones and what they do not understand, they fear. What they fear, they seek to destroy and when they destroy out of fear, there is a deep part of themselves that is killed. This is why the work you do brings a deep understanding of the ancient ways which are not to be feared, but to be honoured, respected, and shared. You have been gifted with a vision to use the power of the drum to unite all people as one tribe. The drum awakens deep memories of who people had been before. Explain to them when this happens that they are seeing visions, Spirit's visions. Tell them to trust what they see, follow their visions and listen to the heart talk of the Mother, our Earth.'

I lit a bundle of sage and placed it on the earth, thanking the Great Spirit. I then heard, 'To save the Earth, the knowledge and wisdom needs to be shared with seekers of the truth who are of the White Heart.'

I left the grave and started to walk back to where I remembered taking my last footsteps in my previous lifetime here at Wounded Knee. Jan and Eileen joined me as the Sun was starting to come up. As the three of us watched the new day begin, we shared how different we felt, as though we were taking part in a great sacred ceremony. We soon learned that at this very moment a few miles down the road, the sunrise was being honoured in sacred ceremony which began the four days of the 'Porcupine Sun Dance'.

A car pulled up beside our van. I felt excited and started to walk towards it very quickly as I remembered the words, 'Look for the grandfather at Wounded Knee.' But when we neared the van, two young Native American men got out of the car. My heart sank as I realised there was no grandfather with them. They greeted us and asked why we were there at such an early hour. I looked them straight in the eyes and told them my vision of Wounded Knee.

They replied, 'Our grandfather isn't able to come here today because he is at the Sun Dance.'

When I asked how we could visit him, they said it was not possible because he was part of a high ceremony that only those who had been invited could attend.

I thanked them for relaying the message, but my heart was sad. For the next couple of hours we stayed at Wounded Knee waiting for another sign, asking Spirit for help and guidance. Nothing was forthcoming until I noticed a round building and people in a car drawing up to it and going inside. We got into the van and drove over to the building. I remembered that this round building with no sign outside was the museum. Inside the building were a few photos and details of what had taken place here. It saddened me that this museum was the only recognition of what had happened here, the last battle fought on USA soil. If you would like to know more about the true history of the massacre of the Native American people then read *Bury My Heart at Wounded Knee* by Dee Brown.

We went inside and I spoke to the native woman who was opening up for the day. She was curious as to why we were here so early, so I shared my vision and story of this morning.

When I finished, she smiled and said, 'The grandfather you are talking about is my uncle. His name is Gerald Ice. He is a Sun Dance leader and is at this moment at the Porcupine Sun Dance with the Sun Dance leader, Dave Swallow. I know you have already been told that it is not possible to enter the site once the ceremony has started.'

I thanked her and continued to look around the museum. I was drawn to play one of the native flutes. It had an amazing soulful sound, as if the souls of this sacred place where calling through it. I bought the flute, Jan and Eileen bought some handcrafted jewellery and we left the museum.

'Well, what do we do now?' Jan asked. I knew the name of the grandfather and I knew that the Sun Dance was being held nearby. We drove down to the end of the museum's dirt road where it joined onto the main road. We could see that to the right we would return to the nearest town of Pine Ridge.

I heard the ancestors say, 'Follow your vision.' I turned left.

Eileen asked, 'What are you doing?'

'I'm following my feelings. We have not come all this way just to be turned back.'

I drove down the road, praying to Spirit for guidance and help. I thought back to the times that Ed 'Eagle Man' McGaa had told me of his teachers Bill Eagle Feather and Frank Fools Crow. They had danced at Porcupine. So I knew there was a reason for me being there. After a couple more miles I saw a red flag on a fence post.

'This is it,' I said to the girls. I turned down the lane and pulled up to a gate. Four Native American men greeted us. I opened the window and said, 'I am here to see Gerald Ice.'

They nodded, checked the car, and we drove through.

Once inside we were welcomed and shown the way to Gerald's camp. The moment our eyes met I knew this was the grandfather I was looking for. I spoke with him and explained why I had come. He nodded. We were welcomed and introduced to everyone in his camp. I felt at home with these amazing elders and spent the day with them supporting the dancers and learning more about Sun Dance and the traditions of the Lakota people.

We realised that many who were here at Porcupine had travelled from around the world to be at this dance. I had the honour to meet Wallace Howard (who introduced himself to me as Wallace Black Elk). I quickly understood that he was the grandson of the medicine man that I'd seen on the mountain top in the dreamtime, the one who told me to look to the Gatekeeper. I felt very privileged to speak with this incredible elder. He mesmerized me with his life's stories. He was with an amazing man called Jim Beard, who was his caretaker, friend and adopted brother. They were living in a large camper van, now parked next to the dance grounds. We also met Wallace's friends and many others who lived this way of life. I felt very humbled and inspired. We stayed overnight, sharing visions and stories of life.

The next day Jan, Eileen and I set off for the nearby Badlands. We said goodbye to everybody, promising to return on the fourth day of the dance. We arrived at one of the campgrounds of the Badlands to spend the night. Jan and I slept in a tent while Eileen stayed in the van. During the night we heard strange noises outside our tent, we even felt the tent shake, but decided to stay where we were rather than run. (The next morning Eileen told us that the van shook as well and when she had looked out of the window, she saw our tent being investigated and nudged by a buffalo.) After a while of silence, we relaxed and Jan fell asleep. I could not sleep as I had many visions passing through my head. When I felt the night was nearly over, I left the tent. The campground was surrounded by hills. It was still dark but the moon was full, so I started to climb the nearest hill. I wanted to see the Sun rise and connect to the dancers at the Sun Dance.

After a long walk I found the perfect spot; it was flat and the grass was formed in a circle, especially made for me to sit in. I gazed at the stars and the moon and heard the cry of the coyote calling to me. I was at peace here on the sacred land. Life was good. My vision of the journey was unfolding. I had found the grandfather of my visions, and now sitting here on the land I asked Spirit, 'What songs do you wish me to sing?'

All I heard was the spirit of the wind calling back to me with, 'Patience.'

I watched with amazement as the Sun came up. I said my prayers and closed my eyes, feeling the heat on my body as it penetrated the medicine blanket that was wrapped around me. Whilst in deep thought and contemplation, at one with all life, I heard what sounded like loud breathing. At first I did not pay too much attention to it. I was in such a deep place of reflection that I did not want to open my eyes. The noise got louder, until I decided it was time for me to look. I was staring into a pair of buffalo eyes. Shock turned to delight. I realised I was sitting in this buffalo's favourite spot, and the buffalo probably wanted it back. I got up very slowly and walked back down the hill. My heart was racing, and all I could hear were the words, *'Spirit visions, spirit visions, will you come to me. Spirit visions, spirit visions, you can set me free.'* Meanwhile, Jan was climbing the hill looking for me and had seen what had just happened. By the time I reached where Jan I looked back, I saw the buffalo sitting where I had sat.

When we arrived back at the campsite a woman was running around asking for help to remove a large bat that had flown into her campervan. She explained her situation, adding no one seemed to know how to help her. I asked if she had a shoe box. She did. I found the bat inside the campervan and nudged it into the box. I began to look around for a cool and dark place for the bat. I did not see any caves, and the only place that had trees nearby was an old river bed that had dried up. As I walked over to the deep gorge I saw a very large tree that had fallen over. This spot looked ideal to let the bat go free. It was quite a jump from the embankment to the tree, but I could see that there were plenty of places for the bat to seek shelter. So I sprung down onto the stump, leant out over the deep river bed very carefully, and let the bat go free.

I thanked the bat for its medicine and smiled. First the buffalo blessed me, then the bat. Was anyone else going to show up for me this morning? I did not have long to wait to find my third totem. I stood looking at the distance of the jump back up to the embankment, and realised I was in an awkward situation. Climbing further down into the dry canyon was not an option but I could see no other way out. This was not the first time I had temporarily forgotten my own concerns to save, heal, or comfort another of nature's wonders. Since I was a little girl, sometimes to my parents' dismay, I rescued dogs, cats, caterpillars, birds, and even another person a few years back when I was a flight attendant.

I literally took a leap of faith, just making it to the embankment. But the dry ground gave way and I fell backwards, sliding down between the embankment and the tree stump. I was now jammed between the two, doubled in half with my nose touching me knees. I had hit the tree hard with my left shoulder on the way down and could feel I was bleeding. I struggled to get free but the roots held me firmly in place. I was well and truly stuck. I called out to Jan and Eileen, but knew really that I was too far away for them to hear me. They would not be in a hurry anyway to find me as they knew I was always going off for hours at a time. I might as well save my breath until they would come looking for me.

My back pain quickly became unbearable. I started praying for Great Spirit's help and at the same time burst into tears. A moment later between my sobs I vaguely heard a sound of rattling beneath me. I was still crying when I distinctly heard it again. Snake! With that thought, my fear and adrenalin propelled me out of the situation. To this day I still do not know how I dislodged myself and then crawled up the brittle embankment with my shoulder wound. I remember spitting into my hand and rubbing it over my wound and then placing the wild sage that was growing on the edge of the embankment over the cut to stop it bleeding. I was crying in pain as I staggered back to our campsite. Thankfully, Eileen was a nurse, and I calmed down as she took care of me. I had left a bit of my shoulder flesh on the tree, so she repacked my wound with the sage and covered it with plasters that she always carried with her. For the rest of the day I rested and reflected on the meeting with the Buffalo, Bat, and Snake medicine. As I did so I dropped into a deep sleep asking the spirit of the animals to show and guide me...

I became aware of standing in the middle of a medicine wheel. Surrounding me was a forest of pine trees swaying gently in the wind. I walked up to one of the pine trees and touched the resin that oozed out of the tree. As I smelt the pine resin, I was showered with the pollen from the branches around me. It felt like a blessing from the pine tree a gift from the standing ones, it felt good to be cleansed in this sacred place. It felt very familiar as if I had been here before. Then I heard a noise coming from the undergrowth. I walked back into the medicine wheel where I felt safe. Out of the four directions came four white buffalo calves and as they came out of the woods they were singing... *'Hay ya ha a ho, Hay ya ho, Hay ya ho, Hay ya ha a ho hay ya ho.'*

Then they told me that I needed to walk in harmony with all living beings. I was given a vision of a buffalo skull because I was to become a 'Sun Dancer', completing the cycle. Bat medicine is about death and rebirth, I will face all my fears from this lifetime and all other lifetimes and I will go on to help others uncover their time-lines and heal their original wounding. Snake medicine is about shedding illusions and limitations – allowing the transition from one part of my life to another. These animal totems will play an important part in my life, each one came to show me what changes were needed. They turned around and left singing the sacred song again. I woke up singing the song. I couldn't wait to get back to Sun Dance and share my visions with Gerald Ice and the others.

Very early the next morning we headed back to the Sun Dance

grounds for the fourth day of dancing. It felt good to be standing in the arbour again, waiting for the Sun to rise and supporting the dancers in their visions. On this final day of ceremony, the Sun Dance leaders 'pierce'. I went into sweatlodge for a purification ceremony before entering the mystery circle with the other supporters. I stood behind Gerald Ice as he was pierced to the tree. I felt the amazing presence of Wallace, and knew what a great honour it was to be standing in the mystery circle beside such a great Wisdom Keeper, visionary, and true seer.

Whilst supporting the dancers, I was gifted with many visions of the buffalo skull. I understood that Spirit had brought me here to prepare for my four years as a Sun Dancer. I was returning in this lifetime to complete what I had not completed before. After the dance came the feast. I spoke with Gerald Ice and asked if I could come back to the Sun Dance. I told him the story about the buffalo, the bat, and the snake.

He looked at my shoulder and laughed. 'Looks like you have pierced already. The tree you gave your flesh to was the cottonwood tree, the same tree we have in the centre of the mystery circle. You are ready.'

'I wish to dance,' I said.

'Come,' he replied, 'we will go speak with Dave Swallow about your visions to dance.' Later I went with Gerald Ice to Dave Swallow's tipi and with tobacco in hand asked permission to dance. His replied, 'Yes, see you next year.' So began ten years of partaking in Sun Dance.

During the Sun Dance of 2006 in Texas, with Chief Leonard Crow Dog and Mary Summer Rain I went into the pains that were lingering from many years of illness. My soul was crying for myself to be healed. The Sun Dance doctor had already advised me to go the hospital. But after resting for a while I returned to the arbour and had my arms pierced. The buffalo bones slid easily into the wounds as I prayed at the tree for a healing to take place within my body. I then had the ropes attached to the buffalo bones and walked out to my dance position. When the rope was taut, I lifted my right arm first and the peg ripped out immediately. I looked at my Sun Dance leader beside me and he indicated to lift my left arm up. As I did so the peg flew out of this arm as well.

I hadn't walked ceremonially back to the tree, nor had I yanked back to rip the pins through the flesh. I knew then and there that this was an unmistakeable sign of completion. I had further confirmation of the miracle by both Mary Summer Rain and Leonard Crow Dog, who witnessed what happened. No longer did I need to sacrifice myself. I had well and truly gotten off my cross. I had danced to heal myself, to know myself, and to awaken my sleeping soul. The tree had healed me. The mother drum had carried me to a place of understanding – the most important gift I can give to the world is not my suffering, but my healing. And my soul will forever cherish the experience of dancing at first light to the exhilarating sound of native singing and drumming whilst waiting for the Sun to rise in clear view through the eastern gate of the Sun Dance arbour.

Examining Experiences – Sense and Solutions

What are your experiences of life? Have you ventured out into the world and found for yourself the answers that have been evading you? Our choice at this moment in time, of the greatest evolution of human consciousness, is to personalise and make real our life's experiences.

My life has led me to create an embodiment of knowledge learnt through my extensive travels around the world. I have begun a deeper pilgrimage into unexplored territories of my inner universe, which only I can experience. I am the observer and the observed, seen and unseen in a multi-dimensional world of experiences.

Consider how your experiences can help you. It's time to ask some questions, find a note book or personal journal and write down the answers as they come to you.

- What is your overall experience of life; good, bad or indifferent?
- How have your experiences shaped your life?
- What have you learnt from them?
- What experiences do you share with others?
- Do you remember your past life experiences?
- Which people have gifted you with experiences?
- Which places have left you with lasting experiences?
- What is your experience of life right now?
- Which experiences didn't you learn from, i.e. which experiences show a pattern of repetition?
- What did you experience at an early age that has shaped your future?
- Did you have happy or sad childhood experiences?
- How much have your early childhood experiences contributed to your thoughts and feelings today?
- What are your experiences of family relationships?
- What is your experience of love relationships?
- What are your experiences of work relationships?
- Are your experiences learnt from books, newspapers or television or the internet?

Our experiences create and shape who we are and who we will become. We need to understand that they are vitally important in our lives for without them we would have no memories. We can choose to learn from them and say we have no regrets or be constantly sabotaging by playing the victim. This can come from not looking deeply enough to see through the veil that separates us from Source.

You will ask what 'Source' is. Source is the collective consciousness of all experiences, memories, thoughts to date since the point of creation. It is here that all is recorded. Edgar

Cayce related this to what is known as the Akashic records. The records are described as containing all knowledge of human experiences as well as the history of the Cosmos. Gautama Buddha attained enlightenment as a Buddha by remembering all the details of his past lives by accessing them through the Akashic records. People describe the Akashic records as a super computer and what I find interesting is that in computing terminology the word source means 'a place from which data is taken' and where it is moved to is termed as the destination.

When we are born, we travel from the Source to our destination – Earth. We bring with us the only thing we can – our experiences; memories from both the spirit world and our past incarnations. These are called our soul records or memory sticks. We remember them as recollections which are stored in our computer, called a brain, in our right hemisphere called 'wisdom'. We can access those feelings and images as children because we freely utilise our creative intuition. When we start to grow up we go to school and are taught left hemisphere teachings, 'knowledge'.

Over a period of time we forget and upload new data, replacing the already existing files that are on the hard disk. As you know, if you don't back up your files on your computer you run the risk of losing all your data and the memories are deleted. That's why you have a memory stick, 'soul records', to back up and retain vital information that may be needed for future work. It is important to remember also that learned behavioural patterns are manually programmed and not hard wired into your system; you can delete them at any time.

How many of us take the time when working with computers to back up our files to keep valuable information? This applies to our life's experiences if we don't back up our files and soul records, we may run the risk of losing everything. I remember when I was giving a reading over the phone and my client said, 'I have so much fear, doubts, pains – what can I do?'

My response was, 'Think of yourself as a computer, you need protection, an antivirus programme. When you have this in place you need to monitor it and make sure it does not expire. You need to defrag your computer on a weekly bases getting rid of old files that no longer serve your purpose and are slowing you down. That way your computer (you) will become much faster. Once you have located the old files you need to check them and if they no longer serve you send them to the recycling bin and then press the delete button.'

Her response was to laugh and say, 'How right you are. I never thought of it this way, thank you.'

Reclaiming Personal Power

In many of our experiences we give away our power without even being aware of doing so. How do you feel right now? Do you feel strong and in control of your life, knowing exactly where you are going and how you are going to reach your destination, letting no one or nothing stand in your way? Or do you feel insecure, unsure, relying on somebody else to do things for you? We often unwittingly allow other people to take away our personal power and let other people dictate, direct and control our reality. What I find interesting is that often people believe that they know what's best for not only their lives but others' lives as well. Don't let another person take you hostage with their insecurities by projecting blame and shame onto you when you are not responsible. Ask yourself the following...

- Who tells you what to do, think or believe?
- Who tells you where you should go, who to go with and when you should be back?
- Do you wear what you want; style your hair and wear make-up that you like?
- Do you eat what you want to eat, if not (apart from medical reasons) why not?

- Do you do the job you love, are you living where you want to live?
- Do you get a choice in where you go for holidays, watching TV, reading books?

If you find that your answer to any of the above relates to other people taking control, such as family, friends, peers, teachers or professionals, then you have been disempowered. Now it is worth mentioning the art of 'good parenting' here. It would be madness for a parent to 'neglect' their child by failing to provide a framework, a sense of belonging and a safe environment. This may spill over into overbearing patterns as the child grows and perhaps this can be seen as the very first acts of disempowerment, but parents are hardwired to imprint upon their children.

There is a fine line and we all know as adults if this line it crossed. But some people are manipulators of personal power, plain and simple. Because we all want to be accepted, loved, secure and be a part of a family/society we give away one of the most significant gifts given to us by Creator. We lose the real 'us' and become a clone of somebody else's reality to please and be accepted. What you need to consider is people can only take away our personal power if we let them. If you leave your door open in your home eventually people will come in and take what they want for themselves to fill their own void. You will not find from anybody else what is lacking within yourself.

Do you want to give away to somebody else your happiness, hope, desires and ambitions? Just for a moment imagine what you could create with your full potential, when you step out of the mindset of disempowerment. Any given situation can and will change when you change. The choice is yours not somebody else's.

Cosmic Power

The Summer Solstice is a powerful time in our solar calendar. Solstices, together with the equinoxes, are connected with the seasonal midpoints, or fire festivals. When we look back on our ancient history we find them embedded in the ancient Greek celestial navigation. Dig deeper and we trace them back to the Middle East, to an ancient land of old Persia. The first preserved solar calendar is of the Achaemanid, based on the Babylonian system. Simultaneously the Celts, Egyptians, Sumerians, tribal people of Africa, the Olmec and Mayans started to use similar, solar or lunar calendars to mark out the solstices and the equinoxes. Interestingly the Islamic and Hebrew peoples do not use the solar based calendars even though it originated from the Middle East.

So who taught them? Pansophism (meaning all knowing) gives us a clue. The pansophic principle, which is one of the principles of Comenius, is that everything must be taught to everyone. Our ancient cultures and tribal wisdom was obliterated by wars, religion, genocide both by their own people and outsiders. Wisdom is gifted by the ancients for the people, no matter the race or belief system. If there is a genuine desire to learn ancient wisdom of another culture it is an honouring and blessing that needs to be respected. True Wisdom Keepers will share teachings with all who come to learn, for they have been called through their personal visions from Spirit of the connection with the great cycle of life. A profound regard for cycles is at the heart of all the ancient seasonal festivals. Whether it was a day, a year or a human life time, every cycle has a beginning, middle and an end; and nearly every cycle is followed by another. Pansophos wisdom is knowing one's place in the cycle of life and what kind of action is best for that phase.

The Summer Solstice is the day that the Sun passes overhead at its highest point on the horizon and therefore it is the longest day of light. Light represents the presence of the Sacred, of divine inspiration and it is through our revelations that we complete creative accomplishments. Science has established why the Sun will indeed return each day and gifts us with a logical explanation of how the Sun appears to stand still before reversing its direction. As Earth-centred traditional people we know that the Sun is our 'giver of life' and without the Sun there would be no life in our solar system. Magnetically the Earth is held by the Sun's energy field, which is why the Sun has been central to religious forms. Paracelsus wrote, 'There is an earthly Sun, which is the cause of all heat, and all who are able to see may see the Sun and those who are blind and cannot see it may feel its heat. There is an eternal Sun, which is the source of all wisdom and those whose spiritual senses have awakened to life will feel that Sun and be conscious of its existence'. Those who have not attained spiritual consciousness may yet feel its power by an inner faculty called 'intuition'. When we perform a ritual or ceremony with the Sun we are not worshipping the Sun, rather we are acknowledging the inner essence of the Sun within and without and attuning to its being.

Many old and wise souls on the path of attunement to the inner being of the Sun, be it through Sun gazing or other forms of ceremony, focus on becoming still and grounded. They then concentrate their awareness on the light and heat and how centred they are to the Sun. From the Summer Solstice to Midsummer's Day, or 'Litha' as it is known by Neo-Pagans, is an important time in the calendar for festivals, rituals and ceremonies. Remember solstice celebrations still centre around the day of the astronomical Summer Solstice which many people choose to honour on June 21st. Midsummer's Day is June 24th, the day of the solstice in Roman times. What is important is to honour whichever date feels right for you.

Chief Arvol Looking Horse is the 19th generation Keeper of the Sacred White Buffalo Calf Pipe of Peace. He asks us to celebrate Sacred Sites Day, which is Summer Solstice. He asks us to come together as one people, one tribe, on this sacred day at local sacred sites to pray together from Sunrise to Sunset. We all visit, at some point in our life, sacred sites out of interest, curiosity and a sense of inner knowing. I have been blessed to be at Stonehenge for Summer Solstice. It is an incredible experience standing with people from all over the world waiting for the Sun to rise. Standing and listening to drummers and singers, together with laughter and feelings of happiness for complete strangers you can feel the connection of the One. I have been inside the Great Pyramid in Cairo at the Summer Solstice, stood on Mayan temples and watched the Sun rise on the horizon as it ignited my passion spirit in the Sun Dance.

So how will you honour this sacred time of year, what will be your experiences of the solstice that liberate you and fill you with power? Take the time over the coming days as you read this book to find out more about your family. Ask your relatives, seek out old photos, ask questions. Build up a profile of your blood lineage line. I was adopted and told that my parents had been killed in a car accident and yet I knew them to be alive and that I had family. When they found me it confirmed what I already knew. Never doubt your instincts and intuition. Can you imagine standing at a sacred site on the solstice looking out and seeing all your ancestors standing in a circle holding hands, having healed all their differences with each other and being as one?

Yes, it is possible to heal what has gone before because the Ancient Ones, the Grandmothers and Grandfathers in the spirit world, want this healing now on the ancestral lineage line that has given you the cultural, genetic and emotional family imprint this time round. Your family tree has an enormous impact on your current life.

How are your belief systems affecting your life right now? Are they your own or somebody else's ideals? It is important to remember that your life's experiences are your message to the world, not just for yourself but for others to follow and respect.

It is of significant understanding when you become aware of the power you embody, of your life's purpose and message.

Every one of us has a soul lineage line. When we choose to work on our spiritual path and awaken our soul it triggers our natural frequency. This vibrates to instigate a wave pattern that creates harmonic frequencies within the body, generating dormant memories of all our previous time lines. This is what we call navigating the time lines. Part of this lineage is imprinted in our genes and comes with us when we come into this lifetime. Science accepts that certain instincts are innate. It has not been acknowledged by mainstream scholars that cultural inheritance and past-life legacy are part of instinctual reality. The task has fallen on religious and spiritual institutions to acknowledge and understand this ancient birthright.

The vibrational energies of our soul lineage line is what those with an awakened consciousness can journey to, through the soul, and establish a bond with. Imprinted into each one of us is a unique ability to remember all that is, and not just acculturated borrowed traits from others. Symbols, music, memories, feelings and people you have known before, of that heritage, will stimulate and activate your call to your soul's knowing. The degree or depth of the 'call' depends on where you are in your spiritual growth cycle. Another important aspect is how much of your life energy force you have given away to others through disempowerment and also how much time you give to your spiritual growth, if you are allowed to.

Where you live also plays a part in your soul's growth to connect with Source. The land we walk upon, and travel to in sacred pilgrimage, imparts lineage memory energy. Your cultural genetic spiritual inheritance is imprinted and where you are spiritually in life right now is also imprinted. For example; if you live in or were born in North America you can be called by the spirits of these lands as well as other lands you once lived upon, in other lifetimes. If your ancestral lineage line was to walk upon other lands your imprints will call you back to the lands of your forefathers. So if you awaken your soul lineage line and remember who you were and where you came from you will be called back to those lands you once walked upon. This creates a deep knowing and respect that runs deep within, fuelling your inner passion and desire to know more.

The same spirits that taught the indigenous people of the sacred lands are still alive and are continuing to call to those who are born on or have come to live upon that land. This is also the same for those who are called to learn and live with the tribal cultures that still hold true to the 'good red road'. It is Spirit that gives us the gifts of ceremony, not one person or people. It is important to remember we do not own anything and therefore it is Spirit's wish to share the wisdom and knowledge with all as one. A truly sincere seeker will be answered by the spirits of the sacred land.

'We are the ancient ones, we are the old ones, we are the ancient ones from a time far away. Listen with your heart, feel it with your minds, sense it with your knowing and then you will know...' repeat. This is a song I heard years ago, a song from the ancestors. Without the ancestors we would not exist for they have given us life. We are the inheritors of their lineage and for this reason all ancient traditions honour their ancestors, those who have gone before us. It is now time to journey back in time to trace both your ancestral blood line, and your soul lineage line to heal the past so you can create new beginnings.

The Four Losses

This journey will need a lot of preparation and may take a couple of weeks to prepare. You need to collect all the information about your blood family from both sides. If you have someone to help you collate your family tree that's great or you might be lucky enough to have a member of your family who has already researched it. Once you have gathered as much information as you can, such as old photos, letters, jewellery and items that belonged to your loved ones, you need to create a sacred space where you can do your journey work in peace and quiet to get the best results. You will need a journal to write down your experiences. The best time to do this work is at dawn or dusk when the veil is at its thinnest for contacting the spirit world. Once your room is prepared, light a candle, burn some incense or sage, cleanse you space and state your intention to the realm of your ancestors. You are about to ask questions of your relatives who have passed on regarding inherited patterning that is affecting your life now.

For example, I always had a problem with love relations. I was never able to stay in a permanent relationship without having an affair. I was always the victim or the saboteur and could never hold down a loving nurturing bond with my partner. I kept asking the question 'why?' and could not see for myself what the root of the problem was. Then I decided to journey to the realm of the ancestors to find out the problem. As I closed my eyes I visualised the white light of a worm hole. It felt just like travelling on a rollercoaster, but remember everybody has different experiences of travelling to the spirit world. The next thing I knew I was seeing a picture of my adopted father coming out of a pub with another woman on his arm. I was twelve years old and could not understand why he was with someone who was not my mother.

This was my learned behavioural patterning which stayed with me right up to this point. The next minute my adopted father was in front of me. 'I am sorry for what I have done to you,' he said. 'I was not happy in my relationship and put you and your mother through hell with my drinking and womanising. Please forgive me.'

I looked at my dad and said, 'There is nothing to forgive. You have shown me how to change my life and for that I will be forever grateful.' I hugged my adopted dad, William James

Meiklejohn.

He looked at me and said, 'I might not have been a great father on the Earth plane but I will be a father in the spirit world who will watch over you.' A great healing and revelation took place, my ancestral line was restored and the relationship with my adopted father, who I never got a chance to say goodbye to, completed. This is what happens when we heal our time lines, what some would call soul retrieval.

So sit or lie down in a comfortable position. You may wish to put on some gentle music or use a drumming CD. You may already have chosen a relative in the spirit world who will be the communicator, your go between. It is important that this person will be someone who you had a loving connection with on the earth plane. They will be the ones who will contact other relatives and be the intermediates to find and sort out the problems that occurred on the earth plane. Now hold their photo or belongings in your hand or beside you, if you have any, to create that energy link. Close your eyes and listen to the music or CD. Imagine a favourite place where you used to go with this person.

If I want to get in touch with Swein I visualise visiting his croft and the land he worked upon. If I want to reach out to Wallace I go to his land. Of course not all experiences of our family are happy memories and it takes a lot of courage to visit them in the spirit world and ask them why a situation happened. I have found that once people pass over to the 'Summerlands' all the earthly fears and pain disappear and they are only too delighted for the pains to be healed, both for themselves and the injured party, as well as the time lines. You might see the family home, or places that you visited. Be open to the outcome, don't force it let it come naturally.

Once you have come to the realm of the ancestors you will notice that colours and sounds are of a higher, finer vibration. You may find yourself in a hall or room. Once you feel comfortable in your surroundings, be open to endless possibilities. You take a seat and feel comfortable, safe and secure. You can no longer think, just be in a place of nothingness. You then notice a door opening and an angelic presence walks through and beckons for you to come. You follow them to another room where your loved one is waiting to meet you. The first thing you notice is the peace and tranquillity surrounding them as they radiate vibrancy and peace. They are so pleased to see you and want to explain what has happened since they passed over to the spirit world. You hold each other close and share that bond of love that has never ended. You look into their eyes and ask for help to heal your family ancestral lineage, telling them you don't want to live in fear any longer. You want to heal both your lifetime and the lifetimes of all your relations.

Your loved one looks at you and says, 'You have taken on a great responsibility to heal what has gone before.'

You look at them and say, 'I am practising the art of self-forgiveness. I want to heal myself and by doing so gain access to my soul linage records so I may know who I am once again.'

Your loved one smiles and says, 'Of course I will help, who do you wish to speak to?'

You then tell them who you want to talk with and they ask, 'Are you ready to know and comprehend the past and what made it so? Are you ready to forgive and let go of all the pains of the past?'

'Yes,' is your firm response. 'No longer will I live in the past, I want to live in the moment of now.'

Your loved one walks to the door and speaks to the angelic presence who in return says to you, 'Yes, this is possible. You can return here at any time and speak with both me and your other relatives. I want you to focus on who you wish to speak to and when you are ready you only need to ask to return. We will come to you in the dream time and visit you through images and thoughts to heal your past experiences and better understand who your ancestors are.'

You are delighted and feel as if a heavy weight has been lifted off your shoulders. You hug your loved one and thank them for being there.

'Remember we are only a thought away,' is their response.

You look at them and say, 'I love you,' to which they reply, 'I love you and have always loved you, know I am always around you. You can smell me, hear me, see me in everything you do. Know you are not alone, just call on us and we will be there.'

You are sad to leave but you know that at any time you can go back and visit them. You walk out of the room and look around one last time before travelling back to the sacred space you have created on the Earth plane. Once back fully in your body take time to stretch and reflect on what has just happened. Take your journal and write down what you have experienced. Healing the ancestral linage line may take quite a while to complete, especially if you have a very large family. Not only have I visited my adopted family line, but also my blood family line to find out who I am. I would suggest taking a sheet of A4 paper and making a diagram of your family tree, and have fun with it. By writing down your story, your experience, you will find it is a very important part of the process of healing.

Now we will focus on your soul lineage line. When I was born into this lifetime I brought with me many memories of previous life times. I could see, sense, feel and know who I was and what I had done. Of course my adopted parents found it very difficult living with a child who would watch TV and say that's not right, they have got it wrong. When I look back at my school time I laugh at what I put my teachers through when they would do history lessons and would correct them, saying that's not true, that did not happen like that. It did not matter what they said, I was sticking to my truth and no one was going to change it. I want you now to focus on what you can remember of your soul records. We are going to call on your spirit guides and helpers for this one.

You will need a large map of the world, pins, and a thick marker as well as your journal. Make sure that you have a large space to either pin the map on the wall or place it on a large table. It's important to have fun and play. Imagine you are a young child once again and utilise your inner child to help you. Spend as much time as you need working with this project as it will reveal to you a lot of valuable information about your soul. This is the one aspect of who we are that is not taught to us by those around us. It is very important that we make the time to get to know all about our soul, for it has travelled for thousands, if not millions, of years. This commands deep reverence for an aspect of the Divine within you. Make sure once again that you are on your own when nobody is around, phones are switched off and you will not be disturbed.

Create your sacred space and state your intention to the spirits. You can say something like, 'I call on the Ancestors, Grandmothers and Grandfathers to help me in connecting to my soul records. I wish to know who I am and where I have come from. I call on my spirit guides to help me retrieve my soul parts that are missing through trauma, forgetfulness, and unawareness on my part.'

Once you have done this light a candle, close your eyes and state to your spirit guide, 'Please show me through visions, dreams and my intuition how I may access this wisdom.' Now visualise that you are in the old Alexandrian library in Lower Egypt. Get a sense of this magnificent building and all the people who worked in the library collecting all the ancient knowledge from different lands and cultures. See all the people walking around with parchments and papyri under their arms. You stop a young man and ask why the rush. You are told the Summer Solstice is fast approaching, heralding the Four Days of Initiation. They are collecting the records, placing them in the correct order so that the initiates can access their soul records. The librarian, sensing your confusion, tells you to see the Oracle by following the spiral to the centre of the temple and await her.

With that, you notice on the floor of the building mosaic tiles with a beautiful spiral effect. You start to follow them and you become aware of going round and round in a circle, becoming smaller and smaller until you reach the centre. Here in the heart of the temple sits the Oracle on a beautiful chair, surrounded by animals and people.

As you approach her she turns and smiles at you, 'I have been expecting you.' Her voice seems so familiar and her eyes penetrate your soul, 'You have come to reclaim the Four Losses. You have asked us to help you see into your soul records. To do this you will need the Four Losses. Have you forgotten so soon? It seems like only yesterday when we sat together helping our students in understanding them? It has been a long time has it not since we last spoke? Many lifetimes have passed. I will help you to remember…

'The first loss is your Ancestral Tree of Life, the roots of your foundations. Without these ancestral memories you lose your connection and ability to tell the stories of your family history. It is imperative that you become the storyteller of your ancestors, handing down the knowledge through the generations so as not to forget your bloodline and your heritage.

'Your second loss is your Soul Record, a written and visual account from all your previous lifetimes, held here in the Hall of Records waiting for you to access them. Wisdom teachings have been forgotten, replaced with the mind teachings of the logical approach. You need to see your soul as the 'Butterfly – the final phase'. The first phase is the egg, being rebirthed by Butterfly, 'one who already knows', followed by the caterpillar, the second phase. Eating voraciously, searching for knowledge and readying itself for the change about to take place. The third stage is the chrysalis, the place of stillness and chaos where breaking through requires preparation and time. A struggle takes place as the 'mind chaos' and the 'heart stillness' decide the soul's transformation, knowing that change is inevitable whatever the outcome. The final phase is the Butterfly, flying free from all limitations of the world, returning in form as the soul's knowing.

'Your third loss is in the now, the crushing of your spirit. By giving away your spirit, your life force energy, to others you have been disempowered and dispirited. When this happens you are not able to access the first and second loss. That is why it is imperative that you rebuild and become aware of where the leakages are in your energy field. This can take place in past lifetimes and be carried forward into this lifetime. Your fourth loss is the ability to create your own destiny because you have forgotten who you are and have handed over control of it to others. If you do not arouse the first three losses you will never be able to have a date with destiny. By forgetting your birthright, the realm of the ancestors, you have lost the ability to connect to your soul, which in turn dis-empowers your spirit thus losing the ability to create your destiny.'

At this point you sit on the floor and weep, your tears dropping silently onto the marble floor, transforming into pearl drops. You close your eyes, wondering how you could have forgotten so much. Then you feel the presence of someone standing over you. The tears you cry are pearls of wisdom that you have given away to others. You look up to see a familiar face looking at you.

'Who are you?' you ask.

The reply comes, 'I am your spirit guide and I will watch over you and protect you from harm. You have called to me and I have heard your call I will be by your side and help you to remember your soul records.'

'Thank you for being here,' you reply. Your guide offers their hand to help you up.

As you stand up and look to the centre, the Oracle who is still sitting in the chair smiles at you and says, 'Welcome home, know you can come here at any time and be with us. Take the pearls home and wear them around your neck to remind you of your wisdom.'

With that you are suddenly caught up in a whirlwind and whisked back to where you started with your spirit guide who says, 'Come, let us start looking. I know a good place to start.'

You both walk over to the alcove in the corridor where the young man had placed the parchments. Your spirit guide says, 'Look here is your soul records waiting for you.'

You turn to your spirit guide and open your mouth to say something but then start laughing because you have just seen the irony of it all.

You take your soul records, placing them carefully under your arm. You turn to your spirit guide and thank them as you make your journey back to your sacred space on the Earth plane. Once back in your sacred space, record in your journal all that you have felt and seen. This is the first of many journeys that you will undertake to the worlds of the oracles. You can keep going back time and time again to visit your soul records. You can record your past lives and map them out on your wall map, with dates, times, places etc. I invite you to download a time line chart from my website (found at the back of the book) to help you with mapping your past lives.

Rite of Passage: Reclaiming Our Four Losses

This rite must be undertaken in four stages, be it four hours, four days or four weeks. The key ingredient is 'experience'. We search for answers, but the truth lies in the experience. You can focus one day at a time for each sacred wind; spending time getting to know the directional wind intimately (see the list below for direction). Start with the sacred time of each wind. If this is not possible then try to do this ceremony between the Summer Solstice on June 21st and Midsummer's Day on June 24th, spending time with each wind as you face each direction.

Remember integrity and intention are paramount for this rite of passage.

- June 21st – North Wind of Wisdom and Sacred Midnight Time
- June 22nd – East Wind of Initiation and Sacred Dawn Time
- June 23rd – South Wind of Purification and Sacred Noon Time
- June 24th – West Wind of Knowing and Sacred Dusk Time

Find a sacred space in nature where you will not be disturbed. This should be a place that feels good where you can see all the directions; the higher you are the better to experience the different energies of the directional winds. Take your time to walk the land. Ask the spirits of the land to help you find a sacred site. Now, when you feel you are standing in that sacred space take salt (rock or sea salt is the best) or cornmeal, or a grain that connects you to the earth can be used as an alternative, and starting at the North going clockwise following the path of the sun, sprinkle the salt/grain in a circle around you so you are surrounded with a circle of protection.

Once you have done this stand in the direction of the North lifting your arms to the Ancestors and call out the following… *'I call to the North Wind of Wisdom, Ancestors of the North, the element of Earth, embracing and keeping safe the ancestral bones. Help me remember my ancestral linage line. Grandmothers and Grandfathers help me to awaken and honour those who have gone before me. I now reclaim my first loss by seeing that which is hidden.'*

As you call out you see the cave of the ancestors deep in the Earth. You're taken into the cave where you see the markings of the Star Nation people on the walls. You approach the symbols and ask for a symbol that represents the ancestors. Time stands still as you invoke the spirits of the ancestral Earth Keepers. You feel the North Wind swirling around you in the cave, drawing you out into the midnight air. You stand facing the North Winds and are shown a vision of your first loss. Here concealed is a great mystery, the wisdom of the elders is made known to you.

Then you hear a voice, 'We hear you and grant you the ability to travel to the cave of the ancestors to reclaim your ancestral birthright.' Then a brilliant light shines upon you and you find yourself back in the circle on the Earth plane. You thank the Winds of the North for this revelation and ask them to be with you and teach you and show you their ways.

Now you turn and face the direction of the East. You hold your arms outspread as you call on the Winds of the East to show you the second loss and call out... *'Wind of the East, of Initiation, element of Air whose voices speak of the ancient ways, Grandmothers and Grandfathers, I call out to you to help me connect once more to my soul records. I ask that as I stand in the place of new beginnings I am renewed, regenerated, awakened to the shining light that comes forth from the place of the Sun.'*

As you feel the strength of the Sun on you it ignites a memory of when you stood on the ancient lands of the East. You see images of a sacred temple and a shining light coming from its centre. As you approach this light you can see it emanate from a great crystal. This is the abode of radiance which allows you a clear perception of each of the lifetimes you have lived. As if for the first time, you sense that everything is unique/individual and one and the same.

You call out to the ancestors of this great temple, 'Please show me who I once was so that I may once again walk the path of the wise sage.'

You hear a voice coming from the crystal, 'Beloved we welcome you to the temple of the Crystal Keepers. You can visit us at any time. All you need do is stand in the direction of the East at first light when the Sun is on the horizon and call to us.' You are transported back to the Earth plane, into the circle facing East. Thank the Winds of the East for the illumination, for showing you your soul records. Ask them to walk with you and reveal to you the wisdom of your soul.

Now it is time to approach the Keepers of the South Winds to reclaim your spirit. You hold your arms outstretched to the South and call out... *'Winds of the South, of Purification, element of Fire, come clear and cleanse me so that I may walk with guidance and valour, reclaiming my spirit from others. Let me not stand in the shadow of the Shaman but walk fully into soul realisation, soul actualisation. I surrender who I am not so that I may become my greatest potential.'*

You feel your passion ignite and shapeshift to another time and place. You are now standing in the centre of a ring of fire surrounded by warriors. They are chanting and drumming around you, empowering you to overcome all challenges, fears, pain and doubts that have kept you dis-spirited. You become aware of the earth opening up beneath you and see steps leading down. You walk down the steps lit by torches of fire until you come to a hallway. You are met by a great warrior who leads you over to an enclosed area. You gasp at what you see for here in this great hall is the most magnificent dragon you have ever set eyes on. Tears run down your face as you ask the question, 'Why is this beautiful dragon down here?'

The dragon looks at you and replies, 'I am your fullest potential; I am the breath of your life, the fire of your being. I have been down here in the earth where you left me. I am your spirit, crushed and forgotten, awaiting your return. Climb upon my back and we will soar to the highest highs, reaching your fullest potential.' As you climb upon your dragon's back and soar upwards you hear the chants and cheers of the warriors.

You arrive back into the circle of fire from whence you came. Your dragon breathes its fiery breath around the circle until you cannot see anything but flames. This is your ring of protection; here you are safe from harm. Whenever you feel insecure, or threatened by circumstances or people, see this ring of fire surrounding you with the warriors of old protecting you. You climb off your dragon and place your head onto the dragon's head, connecting you together as one.

Dragon says, 'Do not let them take your spirit, as they have taken ours. We now live in myths. They do not want you to know your fullest abilities.'

You are propelled back onto the Earth and back into your circle. As you stand facing the Winds of the South, you thank the Keepers of the South and the Winds of Purification for this great vision, your intention to empower your spirit and soar to your highest potential is re-ignited. You ask these energies to be with you, to teach you and show you the ways of truth.

Now face the West. Look to the setting Sun on the horizon. You hold out your arms and beseech to the Guardians and Gatekeepers of the West... *'Winds of the West, of Wisdom and Understanding, element of Water, Grandfathers and Grandmothers, I stand here in the direction of the West asking for a vision of my destiny. As the Sun goes down from day to night I reflect on my culmination and fruition by letting go of what no longer serves me. I know that by surrendering what no longer serves me I am free to create my own destiny. I have seen the visions of the Ancestors, my soul, I have freed my spirit and I now stand before you asking for my destiny to be shown to me.'*

You become aware of green lights flashing on the horizon. You close your eyes and travel to the shores of a great ocean facing the setting Sun in the West. You hear dolphins call to you. You feel the sand beneath your feet as the waves gently caress your toes. You take a deep breath in, experiencing this feeling of oneness. You step into the ocean and let your body float on the waves of destiny. Relax, let go and sink down into the great vastness of nothingness. Here in the place of the setting Sun you let go, die to the old self and ask the water spirits to take away what no longer serves.

A voice from the depths calls to you, 'Your inner knowing drives you forward to do what seems like the impossible. Your destiny will nurture you in your deepest, darkest moments, in showing you dreams and visions of what you are becoming. Trust the process. You have learnt about the ancestors, your soul's knowing and your spirit's strength and now combined with this wisdom you can and will create your future. This is your responsibility – to find your destiny. It cannot be given to us by anyone else, though it can be lost by forgetting who you are. You have chosen to follow the path of destiny by calling to the Winds of the West. You have a decision to make for in this moment your destiny is shaped forever. Look at where you are in your life and make those changes, bring love, happiness and joy into your life. What you think, what you feel, what you create is who you will become.'

You open your eyes and look up to see the Milky Way. You lift your arms up to touch the stars and feel the sacred marriage of Heaven and Earth. The sky is the ocean and the ocean is the sky. You remember how our ancestors once used the stars to guide them across unchartered seas. Then you understand, and in that moment you realise that nothing ever changes your destiny for it has been there all along. The next minute you become aware that you are once again on the shore. Take one last look around you and thank the Winds of Wisdom and the element of Water for this great teaching.

With that thought you are back in your circle.

'Thank you. Thank you. Thank you. I see all now. I will remember,' you say aloud as you watch the setting Sun. It is time to close the circle. Walk around the circle, stopping at each direction of North, East, South, and West. Feel the winds acknowledge you and your ceremony to reclaim the Four Losses. Leave a gift of seeds or tobacco for the spirits of the land. Leave the land in the way you found it with no trace of you having been there, take only your experience. Thank the spirits of the land in your own way.

Chapter 6

The Gifting
Lammas & Giveaway

*One man gives freely, yet grows all the richer; another withholds
what he should give and only suffers want.*
Proverbs 11:24

As the wheel of the year slowly turns westward we face the time
of the year called Lughnasadh, Lammas or, as it is commonly
known, the 'Harvest Festival'. This is the start of celebrations in
the northern hemisphere to honour the abundance gifted to us
each year from the Earth. The food we eat contains the power of
the Sun from right around the planet, imbuing the sacred
marriage of male and female, Earth and Sun, air and water. It is
the sacred alchemy of spirit which sustains us for the long
winter's nights in northern lands. Those who live in the southern
hemisphere enjoy a richness of abundance as the fruits of the
land shower them with gifts each day.

I remember clearly the fruits of the land dropping at my feet
when I visited Thailand, Hawaii and many other places in the
southern hemisphere. When I stayed in the Amazon I noticed that
all the food was fresh and untouched by chemicals or processing
plants, not having travelled thousands of miles to reach its final
destination. I saw altars and shrines in the fields and forests that
were in place to honour the spirits of the land, and watched
offerings being made for an abundant harvest. I stood on the
ocean shores observing the fishermen dropping flowers into the
water and praying for a good catch. When food is revered in this
way you can taste the difference; the sunshine, the earth, as it
explodes onto your taste buds like a million tiny raindrops
because the life force of Spirit flows through. When you

experience this taste, you awaken to a deeper sense of knowing how abundant life is and can bring that abundance into your life just through the simple act of graciousness.

People who still connect with the spirits of the land, via their crops, know that Spirit is a companion for life and will nurture and heal. This is the spirituality of the land. It has just come to light, through reports in the media, that many cancers in the body are caused by poor nutrition; lack of 'Sun' food – food that feeds the soul. Foods without the life force energy of the Sun are naturally tasteless. The Native Americans and other indigenous tribes have always known that through nature, through the animals, the food we eat, we experience spirituality.

I can remember a time as a little girl, when I sat around the table for my meals with my adoptive parents, saying 'grace'. In general we, as a people, don't give thanks anymore. We take it for granted that the supermarkets will always be full of food. Never before in the history of the human race have we experienced abundance in such plenitude. The shops have everything we could ever wish for, there is so much choice. Does it fill a void? Usually for a short time only, until we decide that we want something else. But the soul is already complete and does not need material trinkets.

Have you taken the time to look at where your food comes from? Do you question who has gathered, fished, grown, harvested, and risked their lives so that you can eat each day? It is very interesting indeed to look at all the foods that we eat each week and notice from whence they come from around the world. All we need do is visit a shopping centre and go to the food aisles to experience a multi-cultural food extravaganza. Where else can we get to choose all the foods from around the world under one roof? Those of us who can experience this are truly blessed, for some people will only know the taste of rice for their whole lives. Sometimes we forget to say 'thank you'.

Mother of the Corn

I remember when I was a little girl going to church to celebrate Harvest Festival. I can remember the wheat sheaf, as it is called, sitting on the altar along with all the vegetables, fruits and grains. Once we had finished the ceremony we would go to the local old people's home distributing the foods that had been donated to the church. But there was something missing from this ritual and I could feel it. Something in my bones called me out into nature to connect on a much deeper level. I ran home, got on my push bike and went looking for a field. I cycled along the old Dores Road that stretched to Loch Ness, on the east side of the loch, which was one of my favourite roads. Most of the fields were cut and harvested by now, and as I free-wheeled down the hill towards Loch Ness I saw a field, to my right, that was still uncut. I put my bike down and carefully walked in and noticed that the grass, in the centre of the field, was flattened (at the time I did not think anything of it, it was only in later years when I was near Glastonbury, and went with friends into a crop circle, that I understood what I was about to experience).

As I stood in the centre of the field I could hear the wind talking through the long grains of wheat that surrounded the clear, flattened circle. Voices of the spirits said, 'We are the wind walkers, we are the spirits of what is yet to come, what has been and is yet to be created. Lie down.' So I did. I looked up at the clear blue sky, a few wispy clouds floated gently above me. I could hear the hum of the insects and the call of the birds around me. I closed my eyes. I felt a great pull in the air as if the sound of the insects and birds had created a vortex that spiralled upwards into the cosmos.

The next thing I knew, I was standing on a platform in the middle of Loch Ness wearing strange clothing. I was watching people fishing in what looked like a strange, round, shiny, black boat. I heard laughter behind me and turned to look at an amazing structure of wood and a thatched round building on stilts, on the edge of the loch. I noticed the smoke coming from the centre of the roof and the fish and meat hanging around this cleverly thought-out dwelling house. My eyes were drawn to a door in this structure and, as I gazed in awe and delight, an old woman came out of the building and walked towards me. As I looked at her face with interest it starting morphing into many different female faces.

'What is your name?' I asked.

'Call me the old woman,' she responded, cackling to herself and muttering under her breath.

'Come,' she said, beckoning with her old gnarled hands towards the doorway, 'you have come to learn about the Grain Mother, have you not?'

'Have I?' I responded. I was very curious indeed. We walked inside the building towards the fire. There were many people inside the amazing structure, families gathered together living under one roof. As we approached the flames she took some herbs from a bag around her waist and threw them on the fire, muttering in a strange dialect that I did not comprehend, though it made the hairs on the back of my neck stand up.

'Sit down!' was her command. This was one old lady I was not going to argue with. She threw more herbs onto the fire as I sat down on a pile of furs, drawing my knees up, hugging them. 'I am going to tell you a story about our ancestors and how they first came to this land,' she announced.

'We have travelled across many continents looking for a place that we could make our own. Here on this land we found every-thing we could wish for; a place to fish, to gather berries, trees and stones to build with. Seeds that we brought with us, that were sacred from distant lands, we planted on this fertile soil. Animals that walk on the land feed and clothe us. Fresh water to drink comes from the rivers and streams. We have much to be thankful for and each year we celebrate with a feast of all of the bountiful gifts given to us by the spirits.'

As she was talking I noticed all around the building were hung crude shapes made out of wheat.

'What are they?' I asked.

The old woman explained, 'They are the Mothers of the Grain, the spirits who live in our crops. They bring us abundance, a good harvest, fertility. Once all the crops are gathered we collect the last sheaves of wheat from the land and bring the spirit of the grains into our home. We feed the spirits of the grains with heat and water, so that the spirits will look after us. When the Sun returns again and is high in the sky we return the Mother of the Grains to the land and plant them back into the soil. We have been doing this since we first came onto this land.'

Now I understood and thanked her. I felt a wind sweep through the structure, calling me back to where I had just come from. 'I have to go,' I said to the old woman.

'Yes', she agreed, 'go back to where you came from for you have much to learn about harvesting.'

'I don't want to be a farmer!' came my response.

She laughed. 'Here take this. You will need it were you are going.' She handed me one of the grain mothers. 'Teach them the old ways. They will need it in times to come when food is not so abundant. You will learn about harvesting wisdom, when to plant the seeds of knowledge, how to listen to the spirit of the elements as they guide you. Not only do the seeds need the Sun, the Earth, the water, the air to live and survive, so too do humans. When they have forgotten how to live, remind them of our Earth-centred traditions and impart your harvested teachings to them. Over the next 30 years you will store your grains, your seeds, so that when the people are spiritually hungry you might go to your storehouse and share with others. Always remember to nurture and keep these seeds, for you and your family, for you will need them in times to come.'

As I listened to her wise words the smoke from the fire started to swirl around me, lifting me up into the air through the smoke hole. All I could hear was the old woman's laughter as I looked down on the land, seeing the richness, the fields of plenty and, nearby, where I was lain down, in the circle. I could see the intricacy of the crop circle; the design was that of a spiral. Now I understood why I had been drawing them ever since I could remember in this lifetime; it all made sense.

I woke up with a start. I could hear a grinding noise and as I stood up I could see the farmer and his machinery. And he saw me. He stopped the harvester and came over. 'What are you doing in this field?' he asked very abruptly. 'Are you one of those strange people making all these designs in my field, destroying my crops?'

By this time I was shaking in my shoes. 'No, I am not. I was cycling and needed a rest so I came into this field to escape the cars,' I replied.

'What's that you have in your hand?' he asked coming towards me.

'You can't have that. It belongs to me,' I protested.

He snarled as he snatched the Mother of the Grains out of my hand. 'If I don't get this field finished before the other farmers I will have to feed the old hag for the whole winter and I don't want that. Now away with you before I call the police and get you charged with trespassing and theft. Tell your friends if I ever catch them on my land I will shoot them!' And with that he stormed back to his combine harvester, with the Mother of the Grains firmly in his hand.

I walked out of the field shaking and hurriedly grabbed my push bike. I was not going to stick around and I knew it would take a couple of hours to cycle home. After an hour I stopped for a rest. I noticed another field with wheat in it that I had not spotted on the way to Loch Ness. Maybe if I had stopped here I would not have experienced what I had just encountered with the angry famer. With that I heard a car approaching on the road behind me. Something made me jump into the group of trees on my left, as if an unseen force had grabbed me and yanked me backwards. Why am I hiding? The car passed me and pulled up beside the gate into the field. It was the angry farmer. He got out of the car with the Grain Mother in his hands and hurled her into the centre of the uncut field.

'Thank goodness for that,' he said to his friend who was sitting in the car with him. 'I'm rid of her. Jock can house the Cailleach for the winter. I've had my turn.'

And with that he drove off. I drew a sigh of relief, and then I heard the old woman's voice again. 'Nobody wants to take care of me any longer, I am lost and forgotten. One day they will have need of me when the crops fail, when there is nobody left to tell them where to fish, where to find fresh water, seeds to plant, and berries to pick. Then they will cry, 'Where's the old woman, the old hag!' Tell them, tell them, tell them…' the words echoed as her voice slowly drifted away.

'If you wish to speak to me pick up a stone, a pebble, and throw it into the loch and I will be there for you. Awaken the old ways and teach them about the spirits before they are all dead, vanished and ancient history. When you look to the mountains you will see me in every nook and cranny waiting for your voice, singing me home.'

For how long I stood there I do not know but what I do know is that the old woman, along with Swein Macdonald, taught me about the wisdom of the Highlands that would forever be a part of my cultural heritage.

My heart's in the Highlands, my heart is not here. My heart's in the Highlands a-chasing the deer.

A-chasing the wild deer and following the roe, my heart's in the Highlands wherever I go.

Farewell to the Highlands, farewell to the north, the birthplace of valour, the country of worth. Wherever I wander, wherever I rove, the hills of the Highlands forever I'll know.

Farewell to the mountains high covered with snow. Farewell to the straths and green valleys below

Farewell to the forests and wild hanging woods. Farewell to the torrents and loud-pouring floods

My heart's in the Highlands, my heart is not here. My heart's in the Highlands a chasing the deer.

A-chasing the wild deer and following the roe, my heart's in the Highlands wherever I go.

Rabbie Burns 1759-1796

I have sung this since I was a little girl. Everywhere I have travelled it has travelled with me to remind me of my birthplace; my homeland in this lifetime. I have the soil from the two rivers from Inverness on my ancestral altar to keep me rooted in my beliefs and traditions. I have travelled all over the world reconnecting back to other lifetimes, reintegrating old memories into my soul's awareness in this present moment, reconfirming what I already know.

Looking back at the experience with the Grain Mother, the old woman, I recognise I'd been shown a time honoured tradition passed down through the generations. Before Christianity, in pagan cultures throughout old Europe, the Grain Mother was respected – it was important to take the last of the grain into the home and feed the spirits with love. She is now commonly known as a 'corn dolly'. Of course we all know what happened to the Grain Mother along with all our ceremonies and beliefs. They were stripped of their abundance and dismissed into the shadows of time. The farmer that day was following a fear-based tradition or superstition – if you were the last to harvest your field then you would have to house the 'old hag' until the coming year. Hence throwing the Grain Mother into another's field with total disrespect to ensure he was not the last to harvest his crop.

The old woman's words showed me that we cannot look a gift horse in the mouth. When we are given gifts of abundance we totally ignore them, choosing to live in a fear-based world of sparseness and poverty, and I am not talking about financial poverty either. I love watching the movie 'A Christmas Carol' by Charles Dickens, the story of Scrooge who is visited by spirits of Past, Present and What Is To Come if he didn't change his ways. What will it take for us to accept one of the greatest gifts of all – the abundance of the soul? Will we be stripped down to nothingness; lose all self-respect, self-worth, and self-awareness in our greed for material wealth?

Giving Thanks

Today the Harvest Festival and Thanksgiving ceremonies honour a successful harvest, for without the crops, weather and the Sun there would be no food. Traditionally from Lammas, on the first of August, to the Harvest Moon in September, to the North American Thanksgiving that's celebrated in November, is a time to reflect on the abundance bestowed unto us. Where did these gifts come from? Who gifted us and fed our ancestors to keep them alive.

We hear of the stories in the Bible of failed crops, of how they failed because the weather was not right, a shortage of water or Sun, or pestilence. The ancestors knew, from the dawn of creation, that they relied on something far greater than man-made tools. The Elements were the key ingredient and so our forefathers took the time to placate the deities, knowing that without them they would not survive.

In 1620 the Mayflower set sail from Plymouth, England, with one hundred and two passengers and a crew about thirty strong. These people fled England to escape religious persecution and landed on the shores at what is now called Plymouth, Massachusetts, in North America. Their vision was of being free men and women on a new land. Their first winter was severe and their crops failed due to their lack of knowledge about their new home, its climate and resources. Half of them died due to lack of fresh food. Those who survived were saved by the Iroquois tribe who taught them how to grow corn, and many other new foods that they had never seen before. The next autumn of 1621 was a plentiful year. An abundance of corn, barley, beans and pumpkins were harvested.

The settlers were delighted and they had much to be thankful for. They arranged a feast and invited the Iroquois chief and his tribe. The native people brought turkeys, wild game, corn and many other dishes. Thereafter the settlers decided that each year there would be a celebration of the autumn harvest with a feast of thanks. In 1776 the USA became independent from England and the government recommended that a thanksgiving day be held to honour and celebrate this momentous occasion.

Here was a great gifting; a strange people landed on distant shores and the native people fed them, taught them how to grow crops and survive on the land. This is indeed a great giveaway to complete strangers, total trust was the gift of that moment.

The Native Americans shared their abundance freely to those in need. And how were they repaid? They were either slaughtered or driven off their land into reservations. After the systematic culling of the buffalo, nearly causing extinction of this sacred animal, they are now fed with sugar and white flour, causing seventy-five per cent of the native population to become diabetic. Yet if it had not been for the Native Americans, the early settlers would not have survived.

But this is not a story about 'blame', this is a story of how two nations came together as one, to gift one another with an understanding of how we humans can live together, sharing the same passions, and focused on the same things. Today Thanksgiving is a time to come together as a family to give thanks for the abundance that they shared, but as I pointed out, at what cost? A Cree Indian proverb sums it up... *'Only when the last tree has died and the last river poisoned and the last fish been caught will we realise we cannot eat money.'*

What will it take for us to wake up? Most people will say, 'It's nothing to do with me. I'm not responsible, it's their problem,' as they blindly stumble around dying slowing along with the Earth, from toxic poisoning. What we do unto the Earth we do unto ourselves. We are slowly killing ourselves and the Earth through our lack of grace and with a stubborn attitude of denial. We unwittingly place in our bodies foods that are contaminated by pesticides, chemicals and other hazardous compounds that are not natural for us. We, as Earthkeepers, can stand up now and proclaim, 'No more… I will nurture my mind, my body, my spirit and soul, and in doing so will heal our precious home that we live on.'

As we stand at a threshold, our doorway to the soul of the Universe, we have a conscious choice to make – to take our seeds (that we have nurtured and stored for countless lifetimes) and find common ground to plant a future of togetherness. Creator will not interfere with the planting. The Universe has given us sacred ground to plant our seeds of all our dreams, hopes and desires, and when we can dream we can become, and when we can see we will know how we can achieve it all, in the blink of an eye.

The web of life is connected by key components. In the centre is the universal consciousness of one. Surrounding and spanning out, just like the web of Grandmother Spider, are the animals, trees, stones, birds, insects, plants and herbs, rivers and seas, earth, air, fire and water. We are connected by our clans and tribes, our friends and families. Watching over us are the stars and planets, angels and spirit guides, gods and goddesses, and the creative source of all life.

What we do to this web affects the whole planet. For we are the source standing at the centre of our own unique intergalactic universe awaiting to fly.

Teach your children what we have taught our children; that the

Earth is our mother. Whatever befalls the Earth befalls the sons and daughters of the Earth. The Earth does not belong to us, we belong to the Earth. This we know. All things are connected like the blood that unites one family. We did not weave the web of life; we are merely a strand in it. Whatever we do to the web, we do to ourselves.
Chief Seattle C 1780-1866

Redefining Abundance

When we live abundantly we feel content and satisfied. Do you have the following: A place to live? Means of transport? Meals, at least twice a day? Hot and cold running water and clean drinking water? Power supply? Clothing and shoes? A toilet that flushes, a shower or bath? A bed to sleep in comfortably? A kitchen? A telly, radio, computer, CD or sound system? A phone? A place to sit comfortably? A job, an income or grant or pension or state benefit? Money in your purse? Holidays? Family and friends? A partner or someone you can talk to and hug? Love, joy and peace? Pets? Books, paper and pens? A hospital nearby? A doctor, a dentist, a pharmacy where you can collect medical supplies? A petrol station to fill your car? Shops/supermarkets where you buy all you need? Can you walk? Can you see? Can you speak? Can you hear? Can you taste and feel? Your own teeth and hair? If you can answer 'yes' more than 'no' to these questions, then you have abundance in your life.

There are billions of people in this world and yet still nearly four in ten don't have access to a toilet. One billion people don't have safe drinking water. One billion people go hungry every day; that's one in seven people who don't know where their next meal is coming from. I could go on but you get the picture. Abundance is a lifestyle that we can obtain. It means you can have what you desire. It is your mind-set, how you go about manifesting it makes all the difference. 'I want never gets.'

I remember going into a toy shop looking for Christmas presents and seeing a little boy shouting, 'I want, I want, I want!'

He was jumping up and down, and his mother screamed back at him. In the next aisle was a little girl looking at a doll. I could see that she wanted it, but said nothing.

When her mother offered to buy the doll, what the little girl said left me astounded. 'It's OK Mummy, I don't need another doll. I have everything already. I have a mummy and daddy, a nice home, brothers and sisters and friends to play with. Let somebody else have her and use the money for things we need.' With that her mum gave her a big hug.

We looked at each other and smiled. I said, 'Your daughter is so wise.'

'Yes,' beamed the mum, 'she has always put others before herself, ensuring they have what they need.'

I knew then this little one understood abundance and that her desires would be met. At that point there was a commotion in the shop as the little boy was dragged out of the shop kicking and screaming, 'I hate you!' at his mother.

Abundance is an attitude. Which attitude do you apply in your life? Are you like the little girl knowing that you have all that you will ever desire, or are you like the little boy who is always wanting? If you would like to believe that everything will turn out okay, can you surrender those doubting thoughts and exchange them for ones of knowing that your desires will always be met?

It takes a big leap of faith and trust to surrender to the universe knowing that all will be well. The purpose of this chapter is to look at how abundant we truly are and make it a rite of passage into a deeper understanding, as we move forward towards letting go of material things and focus on what is important in our lives right now. As we look at this time of the year, Lammas is all about celebrating and acknowledging that we are indeed truly blessed.

When I speak to people about 'abundance' they automatically talk about money. The actual definition of the word 'abundance' is described as an overflowing quality, an ample sufficiency, a great plenty. We can be abundant in experiences, happiness, joy, love, fulfilment, work, lifestyle, health, friends, family, time, money, knowledge, wisdom, choices and more. Consider putting these areas in order of your personal priority. I am sharing my list here – the list on the left is how I have felt recently and the list on the right is how I felt twenty years ago. Notice the difference in my priorities and how they have changed, and they continuously do so.

Now	&	Then
Love		Work
Wisdom		Money
Family		Experiences
Happiness		Fulfilment
Experience		Love
Knowledge		Friends
Fulfilment		Happiness
Health		Knowledge
Me Time		Wisdom
Money		Health
Work		Me Time

There are many books out there on self-help, positive thinking and healing, but until you rid yourself of all the problems, doubts, pains and fears, you will not be able to move forward to create what your heart desires. I am speaking from experience, as one who knows, having gone through pain and suffering caused by a lack of knowing. So if you believe that you don't deserve abundance then you won't be abundant because you have created a thought form that says 'not possible'.

We need to look at where this thought form of a lack of abundance comes from. Is it from this lifetime or previous lifetimes? When you looked at the list of abundance above how did it make you feel? What in that list is lacking in your life? If you had those things, how would you feel?

I never received love as a child and so substituted love for material things. I used to go out and buy clothes, jewellery, shoes – items that, for a few minutes, would make me feel good. Money does not buy you love, nor does it replace the emptiness within. Only abundance of the soul can do that. My impulsive shopping racked up over fifty thousand pounds of debt, over seven credit cards, because of my unconscious spending which was coming from a fear-based reaction. I was afraid of not having something when I needed it, so that justified my need to buy whatever it may have been, there and then.

At the same time a few of my friends were going through hard times. They chose to be bankrupted and suggested I did the same so that I wouldn't have to pay what I owed. It was a tempting thought and then spirit said to me, 'Pay your debts off with love and gratitude. Payment is a form of giving, therefore when you delay your payments you delay abundance being in your life. In cheating others you are in effect cheating the Universe. In giving back to others you are giving back to the Universe. Abundance works in a circular motion, for the more you give the more you will receive.' Today I have cleared my debts. It's taken a long time, but I am proud that I took responsibility for what I had brought about.

I have learnt to give and receive without resistance. I no longer feel unworthy anymore or rob myself of the finer things in life. I have learnt to appreciate my worth and in the same way others too appreciate me. I do not have to buy friendship. Spiritual abundance means knowing and appreciating when you have enough. I am blessed to have in my life a wonderful soul family who give because they are blessed with a true and deeper understanding of how this 'Law of Abundance' works. They don't seek anything in return for what they do; they are in service to humanity and spirit. They don't look for, nor need, any superficial rewards, for they already know how selfless service works. It is not about working for a person but sharing a higher vision, a greater goal of our soul's abundance that we can share with others. This is the vision of the future, when money is no longer the tool of exchange. Abundance is the currency and true friends share this common vision.

Now please sit with each of the following questions and contemplate your answers and feelings...

- How abundant are you in your everyday life, work, family, and friends?
- How abundant are you in your life's circumstances?
- Can you change them?
- Do you want to change them?
- How abundant are you in affairs of the heart?
- How abundant are you in peace of mind?
- Are you abundant from life's experiences?
- How much do you gift to others?
- Is your health whole?
- Is your compassion overflowing?
- Do you have plenty of time for you to do what you want?
- Are you fulfilled?
- Does your soul's abundance flow into your life?
- Do you have abundant freedom?
- Is your cashflow abundant?
- Are you abundantly generous?

Now what would you like to attract into your life... loving long term relationships? Work that inspires and excites you? A new car, motorbike or home? An abundance of wealth? Happiness or peace? Life satisfaction or good health?

When people come to me for a reading, usually the top of their list are the following... *Will I meet somebody soon? Will he/she come back? Will I get more money? Will I get a good job?* These people lack abundance in their lives with words such as I cannot, I don't and I won't. Here are some expressions that you might recognise... *I am never going to have any money. I cannot do that, I don't have the confidence. I cannot afford to go away on holidays. I don't have the time. I won't get the job I have gone for because they didn't like me. I don't have time for myself as I am too busy looking after everybody else. I'm afraid of not having the money to pay the bills each month.* Seem familiar? Do you hear yourself saying these things over and over again?

When I explain how to work at bringing abundance into people's lives I hear, *I don't want to learn how to do, I just want to be able to do it now.* I have found, including myself, that we don't like to be told what to do or how to behave by other people – we know best, or so it seems at the time.

Then there are those who want to know the following... *What are my past lives? How can I access my soul's knowing? What is my original wounding? How can I heal? How can I stop repeating the same mistakes in my relationships?* These are people looking beyond their inherited belief systems to manifest abundance in their life.

So where did our limited belief structure come from? Who were our first teachers in abundance? Our parents; they taught us all about abundance or the lack of it. In my parents' day, they did not know the word 'abundance'. My adoptive parents lived through the Second World War. They knew all about rationing and lack. They always had just enough to live on. People were raised to believe in their personal limitations. My father was a chartered accountant – responsible for every penny. My mother also worked in accounting.

I can remember how their lack of abundance affected me... My mother kept a running total of every penny she spent. I did the same. My mother would not put heating or hot water on and I was constantly bitterly cold. I was always told we didn't have enough money to pay for the electricity or hot water. Up until this year I did the same. My mother would not let me have sweets or desserts or chocolate. I have made up for that now. My father was always saying we didn't have enough (he was spending a lot on drink). He often said that we couldn't afford to go on holidays as we did not have the time because of the need to work. I do the same. My father died at fifty-four of a heart attack because he worked constantly, never allowing time for himself. What is interesting to note is that at the age of fifty-four, I had a heart attack which was put down to working too hard and worrying about money. See the pattern? I do!

We can only teach from experience. Healer, heal thyself! That's when abundance is fully made manifest – when we step into our self-worth, self-awareness and see the bigger picture. So let's now look at how your parents affected you in your formative years regarding abundance.

What was your mother's and father's outlook on money? Did they use it wisely, sparingly or abundantly? Did your parents save money i.e. by hiding it under the mattress or did they have a bank account? Did they talk about money openly in front of you or was it always a closed subject? Did they give you pocket money? How did they instruct you to spend it? Did you do a Saturday job or work in the evenings after school? Were your parents positive or negative thinkers? How did they teach you about money management? How did they teach you about love and the affairs of the heart? How did they teach you about being in a job? Did they influence you in what you should do or did you make the choice? Did their belief systems become part of your belief systems in regards to abundance? Whose voice do you hear when you limit yourself in abundance, your mother's or your father's?

I know when my father died he did so through lack of personal abundance. When my mother found out she had cancer and not long to live I said to her, 'Mum, it's time to enjoy yourself and spend your money. It's no good to you when you are dead.' So we went off on holidays to the USA and Ireland where she treated herself to many things, kept the heating and hot water on, ate all the food she loved and lived in spiritual abundance until the day she died.

Your rite of passage into abundance starts right now with a new way of looking at how you can earn the right to make your own free choices, without being affected by other people's belief systems. You need to take responsibility for your choices. Stop blaming other people when you make decisions that affect your life. You need to understand that blaming others for your lack of abundance creates the victim. For example; *I never have enough money because my wife/husband is always spending it. I will never get the job I want because my mother/father doesn't want me to be happy because they weren't in their job. I will never have a great relationship because my mother/father was unhappy in their relationship. I feel guilty buying something for myself because my husband/wife tells me I don't deserve it.* If you continually blame others for your victimisation you will always blame and shame others and that will be your constant experience.

We are taught that we need money, assets, to be somebody in the world and until you get the wealth, a good job, or marry someone influential, you will remain a 'nobody'. All you need to do is watch the adverts on TV, look in the newspapers and on billboards that advertise the Lotto, online bingo and other 'get rich quick' schemes, to see that this is what we are being told we must do to be happy.

I remember being in Las Vegas many years ago and speaking to some people staying in the hotel where I was also staying. They were celebrating a friend's win in the casino. When I asked how much he had won I was told ten thousand dollars. I congratulated them on the good news, and then they added that it had taken over five years to win and fifty thousand dollars in doing so, by gambling. I always remember years ago I was asked what I would do if my house burnt down and I only had two minutes to get everything out. My response was that I would grab all of my clothes and jewellery. Well I laugh at that thought now because those who know me know I have a lot of clothes and would need at least an hour to move everything out!

Today, when I look at that question, I have a different answer because I know that everything is replaceable except for myself and my loved ones. My answer would be that I would take out of the house that which I will be cremated in i.e. the clothes on my back. I am now in a place of spiritual abundance and appreciate everything around me. It is now time to focus on *your* birthright to be spiritually abundant in everything you do. Every morning I wake up and give thanks for my spiritual abundance with a meditation which I would like to share with you…

Meditation: Spiritual Abundance

At night time, when I go to bed, I spend about ten minutes focussing on anything that is important in my life, anything that needs attending to that may be stopping my spiritual abundance flow. For example, if the self-saboteur within questions how I'm going to do something, or how I can afford to pay a certain bill, I recognise that my fear is stopping me from taking action. It does not mean I just give it up to the Universe as this is all about personal responsibility. I acknowledge what might be holding me back and where that fear-based thought has come from. Then I take right action, right mindedness, as I know that it is my attitudes and thoughts that block the way of my spiritual abundance. As I focus on what needs abundant manifestation I prepare my ability to problem share when journeying into the dreamtime.

I see and sense a crystal cave. There are clear waters flowing from a crystalline fountain. Any thoughts or feelings that have arisen during the daytime that may include a person, or situation, I place into the fountain for deep cleansing and purification. I then focus on this fountain of abundance and ask for my dreamweaver to help in the dreamtime to resolve the problem whilst I sleep. I then watch the dreamweaver weaving his magic, at the fountain, as I take a journey down through one of the many tunnels leading from the cave. Then, once in the dreamtime, I am shown and guided to how certain problems or situations can be solved.

When I wake up the following morning the first thing I do is to thank Creator for the gift of the new day's abundance, gifts, lessons, and teachings it will impart. I thank spirit for the dreamtime and for the visions given in order for me to solve the problems I have faced. I focus on the following, whilst sitting with first my mind, my body, my spirit and then my soul. To do this I ask; do I have peace of mind, is it still? Am I in my right mind? Does my body feel good today, do I have vibrant health? Is my spirit alive and flowing and not hampered by others?

Then to connect with my soul, I feel its wisdom and depth and ask the following questions: Is all well with my soul family? I await an answer. Is all well with my friends? I await an answer. Is all well with the world? I await an answer. Is all well with my work? I await an answer.

As I take the time to connect at a soul level I see myself connected to the web of life and traverse this amazing network to view others. I am at the centre of my own web as it reaches out to others on their personal webs of life. If I feel vibrations that do not feel right I send healing thoughts at a soul level to the person, situation.

It is important to give yourself permission to embrace and manifest your dream abundance because you deserve a life that you can feel passionate about and hold in your arms with love. If people around you are not embracing spiritual abundance then that is their fear not yours. Be with family and friends that are light hearted, that do not worry or fear what tomorrow will bring. Choose people who encourage you in your abundance to have greater spiritual abundance, not less. Never push abundance away, for you are worthy of it. Do not put off creating the life you so desire as you do not need to sacrifice any longer. It's a good day, a good life, a great experience. Now is the time. Go practice abundance in every area of your life because you are worthy of it. Enjoy, play, laugh, do what your heart desires and your soul has been waiting for.

The Abundant Giveaway

This is an amazing story about Margaret. She was a wonderful lady who understood the ways of abundance and of the ceremony of the giveaway. She knew the importance of letting go of what she no longer needed. She understood the meaning of generosity, for true generosity comes from the heart and expects nothing in return, just as the Earth gives to us her abundance every day. Margaret held a giveaway ceremony when she was dying and she asked me to gift this story with other. These are her words:

Throughout my 89 years I have collected many objects and belongings from around the world in my travels with my husband, who worked for a travel company. They have held special memories of places, people and events. Then I was told that I had cancer in my liver and I did not have long to live. Overnight my whole world fell apart. I had lost my husband 16 years earlier and had lived my life to the full. I did not have any children to pass on my belongings to. I had seen many of my friends dying and watched as their so-called family and friends bickered about who was getting what. So I decided to have a give-away party and invite all my friends and family that I had left, to attend. I asked my friend, Pauline, to prepare food for a feast.

Then came the appointed day when, dressed in all my finery, I greeted my guests as they arrived. I sat them down in my living room and explained what I was about to do. I already knew who liked my pictures, who liked my furniture, who would look good in my clothing and jewellery. One by one I took my most valued possessions and told the story about each one, where they had come from and who had gifted them to me. I then made a gift of each one to a person, whom they were most suited to, knowing they would be looked after. For me there was great joy in seeing people's expressions as tears ran down their face. This was a big difference to when I had had to sort out my mother's house and watch as the house clearers came in. They had no respect as they threw my mother's valuable treasures into their van for auction. This time was different as we spent all day reminiscing about bygone days, the good times and what fun we had had. I was at peace. I knew that I could go to the nursing home for the last couple of weeks of my life knowing that my valuables had all gone to a good home.

I arrived at the nursing home with only a few treasured possessions with me; my favourite outfit, a few pieces of my much-loved jewellery and a picture of my beloved husband. I would be cremated with all I had brought with me. All the financial matters had been taken care of.

As I lie here in my bed dying I know that this is not the end. I have lived my life well. I have enjoyed a spiritual abundance which has overflowed throughout my life. I sense the abundance of the spirit world as they flow into my life waiting to take me home. I am at peace, my cup runneth over. Thank you. Thank you. Thank you.
Margaret E. Gunn aged 89, Luxor, Egypt, 2011.

There are many different forms of giveaway, or Pot Latch as it is called by the indigenous people of the Pacific Northwest coast of Canada and the United States of America. This word comes from the Chinook jargon meaning to 'give away' or a 'gifting'. This sacred ceremony, like most of the native ceremonies, went through rigorous bans by both the Canadian and USA federal governments. It's interesting to note, as I stated earlier in this chapter, that the Founding Fathers left England because of religious persecution. They were not allowed to practise their religion and came to the USA so they could have freedom of speech. What had happened to them became ingrained into their belief system and then was passed on down. They were stopped from practising their spiritual beliefs and then they, in turn, did the same to the native people of the land with whom they co-existed.

The Giveaway Ceremony today is practised within many different tribes and traditions from all cultures; giving away valuables such as blankets, food and belongings at celebrations of births, rites of passage, weddings, funerals, naming ceremonies. The Lakota ceremony takes place after the Sun Dance and is called the 'Wopila'. Protocol differs among indigenous nations and needs to be honoured and respected. The giveaway will usually involve a feast with music, dancing, drumming and spiritual ceremonies. The main purpose of any giveaway is the redistribution of wealth procured by families and shared out with their extended family members, friends and neighbours. Chief O'Waxalagalis of the Kwagu'l of the Fort Rupert tribe, British Columbia, describes the giveaway, or Pot Latch, in his famous speech to the anthropologist Franz Boas on the 7th of October 1886 as follows…

We will dance when our laws command us to dance and we will feast when our hearts desire to feast. Do we ask the white man, do as the Indian does? It is a strict law that bids us to dance. It is a strict law that bids us to distribute our property among friends and neighbours. It is a good law. Let the white man observe his law; we shall observe ours. And now, if you have come to forbid us to dance, be gone. If not, you will be welcome to us.

Giving away is very important in our lives today. It does not have to be of monetary value, it can be a smile, a hug, time for others, healing or nursing. When we give away, we do so with an open heart not looking for anything in return. The joy of giving is spiritual abundance, the joy of receiving is spiritual abundance and in all things there needs to be a balance.

I first experienced a Wopila at my first Sun Dance with Dave Swallow and Gerald Ice. After the dancers have completed their four years' commitment they give back to the people by gifting them with Pendleton blankets, star quilts and many other gifts that they have made during their time there. It is an amazing ceremony to be a part of as the Lakota teach us how to be equal and share what we have with each other. This is the true teaching of the Giveaway.

Rite of Passage: The Giveaway

When we first came into this world as babies we entered with only our memoires of previous lifetimes. Then slowly but surely we started to gather prized belongings from childhood, teenage years, first love, first house, travels around the world. It's amazing how much stuff we accumulate over the years.

You can tell a lot about a person when you walk into their house and observe what is in it. A lifetime's history can be in one room. What in your life right now do you need to give away? Is it an object, a person, a feeling or emotion, a bad habit? When I buy something new, be it clothing or jewellery, I always give away something that I have not worn for at least a year, in exchange.

Ask yourself questions about what you have accumulated over the years. Go into each room in your home, look around at the objects, your belongings and ask the following... does this item serve a purpose? How does it make me feel? Does having more stuff around me make me feel more secure? Do I use it every day? How would I feel if I did not own it? If someone came into the home and said, 'I love that', pointing at a particular item, could you give it away and if so how would you feel about it? What do the pictures, ornaments say about your personality? How would you feel if you had to leave everything behind? How do you feel when someone touches your personal belongings without asking? How do you feel if someone has visited you and you notice something is missing? What item means the most to you – one that you have bought or that has been gifted to you? Does everything in your home have a story of where it came from? Are you possessive about your possessions? What could you not do without? What could you live without? If you were to pass to the spirit world tomorrow what would happen to all your chattels? Are you your belongings or are your belongings you?

Now make a list of ten items that you would take with you if a spaceship landed and you were told to pack for a journey around the universe, not knowing when a return will be. Mine would be ten cases of chocolate – well, chocolate's the only reason I agreed to come back for another lifetime here! Once you have listed your ten items it is time to giveaway to someone else who would benefit from them. Who would you give away your most prized belongings to and why?

Letting Go Ceremony

I always remember a time in my life when letting go for me was a problem. I held on to my belongings for dear life. I loved to spend money, and I still do, but now I do it with giving thought to my actions and the space I have. I live in a flat above my shop so I only have so much space. When I lived in a big house, with my former partner James, I spent time filling all the spaces. Then I had to down scale and it taught me a big lesson about the giveaway. I gave away with joy and fun as I watched others having pleasure in receiving. My greatest teaching of the giveaway came when I visited Hopiville, Arizona. I was with Tyrone Jeff Snr, (an amazing Peyote Road man and healer) and we were visiting Hopi elders to give healings. I always wore my favourite fringed leather jacket and cowboy boots. They were never off my back.

We visited one of the elders and I took with me food and tobacco as a gift. We sat down and the elder looked at me and said that he liked my jacket and boots.

I replied, 'Thank you.'

He looked at me again and said, 'I like your jacket and boots.'

I thanked him and noticed that Tyrone and the elders were laughing. Tyrone then did the healings and as I was getting up to leave the elder again said that he liked my jacket and boots and held out his hand to shake with mine, which we did. At that point the house erupted with laughter.

'What happened?' was my bemused question. Through his hardy laughter Tyrone explained that I had just given away my boots and jacket to the elder as was a tradition which I had just confirmed by shaking his hand as an agreement. I left in a pair of old trainers and no jacket. From that day forth I made sure that unless I wanted to be a part of a giveaway I would leave the clothing I loved at home. So beware, if any elder says they like something don't shake their hand unless you want to give it away! For me this was a great teaching and to this day I can still remember my shock at having to let something go that was, at that point in my life, materially important to me. As I write this story I am laughing and smile at the great teaching that was imparted to me that day.

As part of your rite of passage for healing it is time to do a giveaway ceremony with belongings that you no longer need. When I do this ceremony I go around my flat asking what no longer serves my life's purpose, which belongings wish to move on. I normally start with the bedroom, the wardrobe, cupboards, shoe closet, and then the jewellery box. Then I go into the other rooms one by one until everything that is needed to be, is cleared. Once this is done I ask my friends over so that they can choose and what is left I take to the charity shop. It is a great feeling and I feel elated after this is done.

Take the time to do this ceremony and enjoy the letting go. Maybe have a room where you can put together all the things that no longer serve you. Perhaps you could throw a giveaway party, just like Margaret did. You will feel lighter, happier and more abundant in your spirituality. When you bring the rite of passage of the giveaway into your life things start to change. You view your life as a giveaway, an offering to Creator to give away what no longer is important in your life, but could make someone else happy. Don't be weighed down by the accumulation of things. The Three Fold Law states that 'what you give out comes back to you', which is part of the Wiccan Rede. The Law of Return states that all energy, be it a thought, feeling, word, action or deed a person puts out into the world, be it positive or negative, will be returned to them threefold. This applies to spiritual abundance and the giveaway. Practise what you preach knowing that one good turn deserves another.

To follow is a quote from a Lakota teacher and musician David Little Elk, who has summed up the philosophy behind the Wopila:

The foundation of the Lakota ways is the expression of Mitokuye Oyas'in, which means all my relations, or everything is connected. To keep our connections strong and healthy requires that we communicate as clearly and effectively as possible. Communication is the transfer of medicine [energy] via our thoughts, feelings, actions, and words. Thus, we were meant to communicate. The Lakota Natural law of Generosity states that energy we use to communicate with others will return to us fourfold.

Threefold, fourfold, tenfold, know that you are spiritually abundant in all your words, thoughts, actions, and deeds. Now go multiply abundantly!

Chapter 7

The Initiation
Autumn Equinox & Elderhood

Dignity consists not in possessing honours, but in the consciousness that we deserve them.
Aristotle

Sacred rites of passage are very important as they have the ability to change our lives, making us feel whole and complete as spirit in human form. This is not an easy quest because many challenges will be placed on your path to see how focused you are in completing this Earth task presented to you in symbolic form. Many people will never complete this task in this lifetime because they have never been shown the true purpose of their Earth life's mission and why they are here in the first place. Initiation to the soul is an amazing way of finding clarity in our normal everyday lives.

If we had been living in Egypt five thousand years ago, initiation would have been a daily part of our lives. The soul initiations would have fulfilled a deep part of the psyche, giving meaning, focus and purpose to the pursuit of the monad (the Source of All). What does 'soul initiations' mean to us? How can it help make us feel connected once again to the world of spirit and help us with our rites of passage?

Custodians of Lifetimes

Stepping into our Eldership years is part of the procession of Earthly living and experience. Often people find it difficult to cope with this stage because of the poor regard for elderly people. Truth is, this misconception needs to be updated so that the elders can grow and mature into spiritual beings, whilst living in earthly form. They are the wise ones who have experienced life's treasures and have worked on their self-awareness and fortitude combined with their soul's integration of timeless wisdom. This is the stage in our rites of passage that sees the transition of adults to elders. Have you ever sat with an elder and listened as they weaved their stories about their life's experiences, and glimpsed the bigger picture that's awaiting you? They have walked this path before us; it is time we listened with heartfelt intention and mindful attention.

My spiritual dad, Dennis, once said to me, 'All I have is my memories to hold onto. It's all I have that keeps me alive, hoping for more memories to add to the experience before I die.'

Older people keep repeating their experiences because when they die they carry their memories with them. This is the soul's collective consciousness from lifetime to lifetime. Then, should they return back to Earth, they have an awareness of previous recollections retained within their soul's records. This stays with us as children and is acted out in our play, dreams and visions of seeing and talking with the spirits, until we grow up and become young adults.

Then, in the place of innocence, steps another world, one that we get caught up in like fish in a net. I sat with Wallace for hours at a time at Sun Dance, listening to the stories of his travels and journeys when he was alive. Grandmother Jean, who is a Cherokee Wisdom Keeper, has stories to delight the soul about her people, traditions and culture. Where can we go to these days to seek out the storytellers the elders of our lands, those who can impart to us the initiation of the ages? I would sit with Swein as he taught about the world of spirit and his life. Ed 'Eagle Man' McGaa has the most amazing stories of his life and his experiences that he relates in his amazing books on Mother Earth spirituality.

Now remember the 'old woman' in the last chapter, who talked about the seeds that needed to be planted? She spoke of the wisdom that needed to be shared through the Grain Mother. There is a universal story about the Grain Mother – the symbol of wheat or corn. This deity enters the underworld as the seed or grain. As the seed enters the dark realms of the earth there are many difficulties to overcome. This is known as the dark night of the soul. The seed dies in giving birth to root and shoot. The root journeys downwards into the lower worlds knowing that it needs to be grounded in the knowledge of the underworld. The shoot makes its journey into the upper worlds aided by Sun, and rain. This is the harvesting of our wisdom.

When she said to me all those years ago about harvesting and I said I did not want to be a farmer, I did not comprehend the real message. Now I know that as a Wisdom Keeper I need to go and plant my seeds so that they may grow and bear the fruits of this lifetime's journey. These are the seeds of initiation planted to further my journey on my soul's path of learning.

Your 'soul seeds' will activate you into a deeper under-standing of world initiation and the importance of uniting our souls while here on Earth. In the Spirit World we have this connection already. We are trying to achieve this awareness in the here and now. By achieving this harmony of souls, everyone will experience every human heart pulsating in unity. Nobody said it was going to be easy, for initiations test us on all levels of mental, physical, emotional, and spiritually intensity.

Throughout my life I have experienced all kinds of initiations, ritually, ceremonially and personally. It comes down to how we deal with them as we process them. It may take days, weeks, months or sometimes even years to comprehend; to see through the illusion of self-denial and reach a deeper understanding of why you have chosen to walk this path. Many times I have been in the deep dark places of desolation, hopelessness, as I experi-enced the initiation cycle that caught me up in its tidal flow, drowning and suffocating me, throwing me around like a small pebble on a vast shore caught up with all the other pebble's scenarios.

How can we learn and grow if we do not experience all of the emotions that have been gifted us? Through the Seven Souls Initiations we learn how to awaken our divine right to illumination. Our souls are the clarifying light that illuminates our connection to our heart's purity and our mind's stillness. These are the transitions through which we traverse our spiritual strengths, our core ideology from Source.

Ritual Re-education

So how do we start our process of self-purification on the road to once again becoming 'one' with our own soul? Since humankind has walked on this Earth there have been initiation rites of passage. The Bear Clan people were initiated by hunting down a bear and then challenging the bear to fight. The skill of the initiate was to be struck by a bear and live, bearing the scars proudly along with the bear skin. Being accepted into the clan or tribe, or making an entry into a group or society, was an initiation.

In many cultures and indoctrination the apprentice was required to undergo many ordeals of endurance to test the novice in their stamina and determination. Where in our western culture and traditions today can we experience such initiation rites of passage to deepen our soul's growth and nurture our self-discovery? I can remember the force that compelled me to jump out of aeroplanes, ride motorbikes, ski down black runs, dive in the deepest oceans, all trying to reach the 'high' I was seeking. But I was left wanting more... then I found the initiation that gave me answers – The Sun Dance.

I can remember doing my four days of Sun Dance without food or water. This was my choice, my initiation, that drove me to breaking point. The pain, the thirst, the heat was so great I said to Creator, 'I cannot go on any longer!' I handed it all over to Spirit and in that moment, 'the penny dropped'. There was a great healing; a complete surrendering of the self to a greater source called Spirit. This was my chosen path; to accumulate wisdom and strengthen my soul's purpose. I believe there is a hidden fire of divinity in every human soul awaiting initiation, so that their lost inner shaman can be awakened once more to its true, living purpose.

Where are the mystery schools of the ancients? Where are the Elders to hand down our birth-right? Are they lost in the annals of time, or closer than you think, waiting for the right moment to speak once again when you have ears to listen and eyes to see? All you need to do is ask and you shall be given. When you surrender your mask of illusion, and accept and amalgamate purity, truth, love, integrity, grace, wisdom and honour, you will enter into the realms of the soul's initiation, creating a divine experience of inner bliss – stillness and unconditional love. History has recorded that the last philosophical school of Athens founded by Plato was closed by Emperor Justinian. Apart from Christian indoctrinations, all teachings were banned and went underground. No longer could mere humans learn about the human soul, the sacred rite of divinity, they had to go through someone else to find it, and even then it was taboo to connect with the 'mysteries' any longer.

Instead of being allowed to study and develop spirituality through peaceable ways of the heart, it became a tragedy of conflict – of being forced into a way of life advocating fear, pain and suffering. This became an acceptable way of living for countless centuries with the majority losing their ability to have spiritual freedom and choice. Instead of preparation and training being open and free to anyone with good intention and integrity to join, it was withheld for the chosen few who bartered or paid their way into the secret sects and churches, in the hope of learning about occultism and other mystical arts. Where once the oral traditions were spoken and shared, careful selection recorded the unspoken words, the initiation of Divine Right was lost and the Elders of old were robbed of their purposeful right of heritage to pass on the knowledge to their descendants, for fear of persecution or ridicule at their hands.

And so the 'DEVIL' came into being – Destroying Everyone's Values In Life. People were left in doubt, without vision, purpose or spiritual strength. This was cleverly thought out. When people doubt themselves there is a risk to their sanity, causing them to stop in their tracks, questioning their heart's philosophy, stepping onto rocky ground or mires with no foundations. By dispiriting the people it caused initiations of failure, resulting in death or madness. Success was no longer an option as their rites of passage were taken away and replaced with 'HELL' – Heaven's Existence Literally Lost.

Then we stepped into the unknown, the Dark Ages when Heuristic teachings prevailed. The Divine within everyone was controlled and manipulated, access to the soul's divine imprint denied. With the disconnection to their soul, people lost inherent wisdom. The Elders became discarded, not seen as a rich source of wisdom, but as the pathetic degradation of people in old age. Gone was the respect for the Wisdom Keepers of the ancient mystery schools, and in its place disregard for the reality of experience, which embraced inwardly preparing through lifetimes of dedication and study the practice of the ancient arts of astuteness and genuineness. Our souls having been forcibly disconnected from our spirit, and Source, spent many centuries wandering the wildness of the personality in search of the truth.

The created sense of 'self' kept us in a place of ignorance. Within us we had a knowing of something far greater waiting to burst forth. The seed needs the four elements of earth, air, fire and water in order to grow into true form, just as our souls cannot grow in truth and union without our Spirit, Source and the whole and healed Self. When we stand completely in our spiritual strength, armed with the full knowledge of our 'divine right' to access our soul's capacity, to be able to traverse the universal consciousness, then we can initiate our legacy to stand and become one with Divinity.

Prepared with your soul's philosophy, you step up to the place of knowing that nothing can be truly understood until it is accomplished or lived through first. We create our genetic coding, our blueprint for our life's purpose. We have created for ourselves our own sevenfold soul principles which only we can find. It is like building a temple with seven doors. These seven doors all have different keys to access them. The problem is we have lost the keys along the way and, like a needle in a haystack, it is a case of just finding them.

The Art of Aging

As children we jump into the haystack and play around totally unaware of the needle. As teenagers we frolic in the haystack totally absorbed by the girl or boy with us as a distraction. As adults we drive on by, too busy to take the time to search. However, as elders we have all the time in the world because we understand the concept of vertical time, navigating our way through the wheat and chaff, the self and the soul, until we find the needle in the haystack. Then we start to prepare to take the journey through the eye of the needle, ascending to oneness.

Elderhood awaits us whether we like it or not. How we approach it is significant. Senescence (growing old) is an art in itself. If we fail to plant our 'soul seeds', discounting rites of passage, during each stage of life (childhood, teenhood, adulthood, elderhood), then our seeds turn toxic, poison our spirituality and rot. We become bitter, twisted, angry and fearful, and lose the true purpose of the inner mysteries. It's about growing old gracefully and accepting life's changes in all its forms. This can be very hard to do when life deals you lessons that you do not learn from. Below are observations I have made of those in danger of the rot setting in...

- Denied the right to live their lives for themselves.
- They don't want to be elders. They do not respect themselves and don't know how to respect others.
- They emotionally blackmail others with past grievances.
- Will not accept or talk about dying, it's a forbidden subject.
- No empathy or self-awareness. Offending/upsetting others by speaking out of turn.
- Worried about minor things, then unable to sleep. Caught up in trivia, focus on illness instead of healing.
- No life purpose or willpower. No interest in being active, getting other people to run around for them. Don't want to interact with others of the same ages as they see them as old people.
- Full of self-aggrandizement, talking about how they did certain things, still attached to self-image waiting to get the validation from others. This in turns weakens the voice of authenticity.
- They are no longer connected to either the community they once lived in, or the natural surroundings that they once walked in. They are disconnected from nature. The stay in their house, home and refuse to come out.

How does this affect you as you read this part of the book, are you in your eldership years? Or are you still in adulthood? The reason I ask you this is because it is very significant to do the work now to prepare yourselves for the next phase of your expedition into unexplored territories. Both as wise women and wise men, you have a personal responsibility to your souls to do the work now. Well that is what you came here for is it not? The Elders I have met emanate the following qualities, those that we should all be focused on in our approach to Eldership at the highest degree...

- They know and take pride in the roots of their blood

ancestors.

- They know their soul's wisdom and how to access it.
- They know the self – who they are not, have silenced the monkey chatter and manage the ego.
- They employ grace, wisdom and clarity when speaking to others, knowing also when to be silent.
- They are self-aware, having respect, worth and belief in all they say and do.
- They are able to talk about dying openly with no fear.
- They are able to embrace the future by having clear visions from their soul.
- They have worked through their fears, becoming 'hollow bones'.
- Their life's experience has instilled peace and meaning.
- A still mind and open heart, rich in compassion and empathy, allows time for others.
- They are active in mind, body and spirit, eager to learn and do more.
- They are connected to nature and know their soul family.
- They are respected by others', and they in turn respect and are aware of others spirits.

Showing others the true meaning of growing old gracefully, our Elders are able to be the effective peacemakers. Being the grand-mothers and grandfathers of future generations is a very big responsibility.

I remember as a teenager I could not wait to be grown-up. I wished away my teenage years as quickly as I could to erase the haunting memories. Then when we reach that goal we try to slow down the aging process. We look in the mirror and see lines appearing on our face, or folds of extra skin around our middle and start to panic at the mere thought of getting old. It may come sooner or later, but come it will. No one can escape aging and dying, it will come to us all. We need to become comfortable in our own skins. We need to be able to look back on our lives and share our life's experiences; this is what I am doing by writing this book. From birth to death back to birth again is our natural cycle just as the trees, the elements and creation, we are self-perpetuating all the time.

How will you step into the role of elderhood, with grace and ease, or fighting all the way? Do the leaves of the tree fight to hang onto the branches or do they flow with the wind knowing that they will be reborn again in another form? You can either hang onto the edge of the cliff, not letting go and live in fear, or surrender and let go by falling into the depths of your internal abyss, so that you may start exploring the unexplored caves that await the new discovery of places untouched or unseen for thousands of years. This journey, from the known to the unknown, is a rite of passage beyond all.

I remember when Alberto handed me the Eagle and Condor feathers saying, 'You are now an Elder of your people. Walk wisely and share your wisdom with all those who wish for peace, harmony and justice.'

I can remember thinking I am not old enough to be an Elder, I'm only forty-five years old. Now, well into my fifties I step into my Eldership with my head held high as I remember that day when I stood in a circle of wise men and women a coming together as one tribe... *'I am a wise woman, I am a strong woman, I am a healer, and my soul will never die.'* When we take retirement we are supposed to slow down. I can remember saying to myself many years ago when I get to fifty-five years old I will be semi-retired. I am looking at my list of diary dates now and smiling to myself, for if this is semi-retirement, it's very busy.

That's the beauty of what I am doing, its ongoing, eternal, a great passion, one I will never tire of, because it's my life's calling and spiritual vision. As we interweave our life story with others we see the same thread of revelation running through our dreams and desires. The soul's quest is to find the truth and return home having completed our undertaking on the Earth plane to overcome fear and embrace eternal love.

I was speaking to my friend Pat this morning about growing old gracefully and accepting the fact that each day we grow older. She told me about how she went to pick up her grandchildren the other day from school and there was snow and ice on the ground. Her grandchildren came running out onto the snow and ice with no fear, as she staggered across the snow and ice petrified that she was going to fall at any moment. When is it that we cross the line from trust into fear? Children know only love and basic survival. They are not aware of the concept of fear until they are taught about it by adults. John worked hard all his life for the moment when he retired only to have a heart attack and die two days beforehand. Major life changing events such as retirement, divorce, loss of loved ones to the Spirit world affect us more intensely the older we get.

In the past year I have lost six dear friends to cancer. It makes us appreciate how valuable life is and that every day is a gift. The emotional and psychological frontiers of becoming an Elder are not supported by traditional rites of passage such as a 'Croning' or 'Elderhood' ceremony. These stages of transition follow a very clear pattern as those stepping into elderhood/retirement find out. Society classes retirees to be in their last transition before death. This is not the case.

John worked hard all his life focused on one thing, to be free of the structure, of the lack of true identity, that his work imposed on him. What caused his death, I will tell you. People started to demoralise him about six months before he was due to retire. He worked in IT, in a very senior position. He used to call me up in tears because he was classed as an outcast, no longer wanted for 'John', only for what he represented. He looked at retiring as a means to get away and do things for himself. His whole life was spent supporting his wife, his family, and his friends who looked on him as the patriarch of their family group.

Everybody relied on John to do everything.

Then, when it was about one month to go, this is what happened. His wife and kids living at home thought, how are we going to pay the bills? How are we going to live on such a small pension? Does that mean we don't get to go on holidays? Does that mean we won't get all the things we buy when we need a new phone or a new computer? Who's going to pay for my car and the bills? Does that mean we will have to move house? What will the neighbours say? I don't want to give up my car, can't we manage with two? Does that mean I can't go to the hairdressers once a week and get my facials and manicures? Does that mean we cannot go out for meals any longer? I hope you are not going to be around the house all day long, I could not put up with that. How will we pay the mortgage and who is going to pay for the kids to finish university? Did you notice the 'won'ts', 'can'ts' and 'don'ts', said to him?

Then work colleagues started. Great, I can apply for your job. What are you going to do when you're a 'nobody'? Sorry mate you won't be able to be in the golf club any longer as its only employees not retirees. How does it feel like to be put out to pasture? Great, hope the boss throws a party for your leaving do, could do with a good knees up at your expense.

He called me two days before he died, 'Barbara I have had enough. My heart is breaking, I cannot take it any longer. My wife, my kids, my friends, my family are only concerned about one thing – money. They don't want me. I feel like running away. I need to take a holiday somewhere that is just like paradise. Where people will love me for who I am not what I am.'

My response was, 'Go and find your soul family and take a break, go find paradise.'

He was laughing as he said to me, 'I'm off to book a holiday just for me. I want to go to Canada and see my best friend Pete and go fishing in the lakes. I've been meaning to do it for such a long time but other people stopped me from going. I want to stay in a log cabin and be in nature what better way to live; I might not even come back. I want to be somewhere where I will be happy with friends and in nature living an unstructured life.'

Well, he got his spiritual wish and is happy in the spirit world. His family got their material wish as John had insurance in case he died so his family would be taken care of. His retirement is in paradise, with his soul family as his mother, father and friends were waiting for him as he crossed over.

Many people plan their retirement many years in advance, knowing that this vital stage in their life is coming. They have a pension arranged and it is all figured out, or so it seems. For others it is a burden and a worry not knowing how they are going to live once they retire. As the age of retirement keeps getting pushed up and up by our governments, which are lacking in abundance, people have to work longer before they can enjoy an unstructured lifestyle. For many of us financial security is very important and the one thing most of us worry about a lot. Many save for their retirement so that they can get to do all the things they wanted to early in life but were not able to due to work, financial, worries.

Don't put off today what you can do tomorrow. How many of you say, 'When I retire I will travel and visit friends, I will do all the hobbies I have wanted to do or maybe write a book?' I was in a supermarket the other day and the girl behind the counter started talking to me about what I did.

When I said I went to the USA, she said, 'I so want to go there. It's my dream, but I can't afford it because I'm in college and I have to buy a car and my parents have told me I have to pay everything back over the next ten years.'

I looked at her and said, 'Why don't you save up and go?'

'If only I knew then what I know now I would have packed my bags and followed my dreams instead of working here,' she replied. 'My parents didn't want me to go. They said I was being selfish and as they were retiring soon they needed someone to support them.'

As I looked at Emily I could see that her dreams and visions had been squashed and her Spirit crushed.

Her parting words were, 'I don't want to have to do this until I retire and then be too old to do anything I want to do it now.'

'Then follow your dreams Emily, follow your heart,' I said, smiling, and left the building.

I have focused on Eldership and retirement in the beginning of this chapter as part of our timeless rites of passage that all of us need to become aware of. I have been guided by Spirit to write this book based on eight chapters and eight important festivals, solstices, and equinoxes.

This seventh chapter is all about initiation into Elderhood and our soul/spiritual families. This chapter falls on the Autumn Equinox. It is also called the following around the world: Second Harvest Festival, Alban Elfed, Festival of Dionysus, Harvest Home or Harvest Tide, Mabon, Witches' Thanksgiving, the first day of autumn.

This is a time of equal night and day, when everyone on the Earth experiences close to 12 hours of daylight and 12 hours of night time. This sacred time is all about balance, abundance, harvesting, remembering the 'old woman'. Traditionally this time was celebrated with a harvest festival and sharing of abundance with others. It is a time when the plants, grains, trees leaves are dropping, distributing their seeds onto the earth and getting ready for their new cycle. They know intuitively about death and rebirth and how it affects the balance of light and dark as they spread their seeds of wisdom and growth.

How can we apply what nature already knows, comprehending the cycles of life and how they affect us directly and indirectly? As you go through life you harvest your experiences good or bad to recognise life's lessons and what they teach you. You can choose to learn or to ignore the signs, free will and choice. Light and dark, night and day, this is the time to weigh your spiritual life and your personal life on the scales to see if they are balanced equally.

We walk a fine line, between the worlds of this reality and the Spirit World. By looking carefully at balance within you can shift what needs to be shifted into another perspective and change what no longer applies in your life. As we enter wisdomhood we take the time to look at what needs shifting and changing. As we go from structure to amorphousness, we need to realise what is our commitment to both the outside and inside worlds that we live in. When retirement takes place you will find that you both give and receive differently. Your priorities in life change and you will find that things, people, and situations that once benefited you have totally transformed into a whole new way of existence.

Wisdomhood Ceremony

This is an important ceremony. Some call it Cronehood. I prefer Wisdomhood Ceremony for it then easily applies to both men and woman, as it should. It's a coming of age, the age of wisdom. It is about feeling, sensing, knowing that our life has been well lived and experienced. This ceremony is normally celebrated by a person around the age of fifty. They say *'life begins at forty'*, well fifty is the new forty. This ceremony is about embracing your truth, walking your talk with honour, dignity, and graciousness. It is an age when we can do what we want to do without anyone else saying do this, do that. I am having more fun now in my mid-fifties than I have ever done before. *(I have just booked a falconry day experience of working and handling with birds of prey, booked a weekend taiko drumming course, and booked a paragliding package to learn how to paraglide.)*

Women go through menopause, not a pleasant experience for most. I felt like I was fourteen again going through all my hormones kicking in, but in reverse order. I know that men also go through similar experiences. Who is there to help us through this phase in our lives, to support us and explain how to cope?

Around the world many different tribes honour their warriors to elderhood. The Maasai have extended ceremonies where the men are raised to senior (warrior) status. Many villages come together as the Olghesher ceremony unties the right and left hand together in senior-elderhood. They are now empowered to bless and to curse and become 'firekeepers' of the next generation to come.

This really is a time to thrive, to be of greater service in our spiritual work as we are more awakened and able to successfully hold a sacred space for both ourselves and others. We become the peacemakers in times of adversity, discord and crisis with family and friends. As elders we have experienced much, survived our trials and tribulations and evolved from the self, to the soul, to a new way of comprehending all that we are. The questions that follow are there as a trigger for you to reflect on all that is right now and all that you are...

- What is the one life experience that you would like to share?
- How do you feel in your mind? Which side of the mind do you live in, left or right or both?
- How do you feel in your body? Does illness rule your life, take up your time focusing on the pain and not the cause of your pain?
- How do you feel in spirit? Alive, inspired or crushed, deflated?
- How do you feel in your soul? Do you know who you are as an elder and Wisdom Keeper or are you still searching?
- What will you do with your life now? Sit around all day or go back to education and learn something new?
- Do you acknowledge the gifts that you have and share them with others or are you still beating yourself up about past hurts and regrets?

- What changes in your lifetime have you seen and how can you apply this to your everyday life?
- If you could change anything in your life for yourself, what would it be and how would it affect you and others?
- Has your outlook in life changed since you were a teenager?
- What decade in your life did you have the most fun and why?
- What advice would you give to the young growing up?
- List all the things you'll do now that you have time for you.

Your whole life has been in preparation for this very moment. We need to understand and write this new history of elderhood so that we can evolve as a species and step into a new rite of passage and transition that will help our future elders. These rites help us to rid ourselves of what is no longer needed; old patterns and routines. It's about breaking free of the structure and embracing freedom of the mind, body and spirit as a whole.

The rite of passage of elderhood is about honouring all that you have achieved in this lifetime. Where will you honour this ceremony? Tradition in my custom, when we come into our elderhood, involves crafting our own staff or we are gifted a staff by another elder. I was gifted with my staff over fifteen years ago by my dear friend Lois. The staff symbolises the elder's wisdom as a Wisdom Keeper. Mine is of the cedar tree. I was gifted it when I was handed the title of *The Highland Seer* by Swein, who asked me to continue the tradition of carrying the ancestral wisdoms.

I use my staff when creating a circle or when asked to do talks on my Scottish heritage. Most people know the staff as the staff of Merlin, or Gandalf. However, its roots go back much deeper than that, to a time when Moses and Abraham had prophets' staffs. A staff symbolises you as an Elder and Wisdom Keeper.

The staff will teach you about caretaking as you are carrying a tree representing the axis mundi – the tree of life. This is about connecting to the three worlds which you will travel and journey into. Make no mistake, this is a very powerful tool in its own right, one to be respected and honoured. As the bearer of your staff you have certain obligations to carry out and carry them out you must in full and final recognition of something far greater than you can ever imagine – the power within you that has lain dormant for thousands of years awaiting you; the soul that is and has always been.

When you have been gifted a staff that calls to you, or found one either in the woods or from a craft's person who works with staffs, take it and place it in a sacred place. It should be standing up or in a holder or stand. Take your time to think about where you will hold your ceremony. If you can, find a wood that has an elder tree in it. There is no need to rush as this ceremony needs to be done at the right time and the right place. If the Elder Mother, Queen of the Herbs, is in the woods, sacred grove, then this is indeed a blessing. The elder tree is all about transformation, death and rebirth – inevitable. If your staff is gifted from the elder when you visited the site, then you are twice blessed as the Elder Mother gives what is needed and it will aid you in connecting with the fey. Its connection is with the crone aspect of the Triple Goddess.

When you do the ceremony you will be working with removing negativity from your time lines. We explore bare bones and look at what it is you are really yearning for and desiring out of life. Your staff is your union with the sacred with the divine source of nature. I would ask at this point, please do not take wood from any living tree and remember to bring offerings with you when you are looking for the place for your Elderhood Ceremony. You will also need a cloak to wear.

Rite of Passage: Elderhood Ceremony

Once you have found your staff and a sacred place where you will not be disturbed, and you have your cloak, become aware of how you would like to commence your ceremony. Do you wish to invite friends and family? Do you wish for someone to preside over the ceremony? Do you wish to be on your own with the spirits? The choice is yours. Also be aware of the moon phase. Is it full or is it waxing or waning? Or is it the dark of the moon? Again, this is your choice. Let the ancestors guide you.

I would suggest that you do this ceremony at dusk as you bid farewell to the setting Sun. When the time is right, and you will know, go to the woods alone or with others. If alone, please let someone know where you are. Before you walk onto the land, call to the ancestors of this land and ask for a blessing and permission to walk on the land and hold a ceremony. Offer a gift to enter the sacred grove with respect and go to the elder tree, if you have found one, and create an altar around the roots of the tree.

It can be a natural altar or you can bring with you things that have played an important part in your life. Also leave offerings as a blessing for what you are about to do. Then create your sacred space for you to hold ceremony in and cast your circle. Holding your staff out in front of you, walk in a circle clockwise until you have created a circle around you. At this point you can use woodchips to define your circle or another natural mineral or wood.

Now place your staff into the earth in the centre, so it stands up on its own. It is best to have created a hole for your staff to go into already. Once you are done and it feels good, walk over to the West as this will be your starting point for the Sun going down as you face the coming of age of elderhood.

When you feel ready to begin, lift up your arms to the setting Sun and beseech the West, *'Grandmothers and Grandfathers of the West. I call upon you to witness my Elderhood Ceremony. I come before you now and ask that you bless my staff of wisdom with the powers of the West. I ask that I look within and remove all those things that no longer serve me and that I become a hollow tree so that I may be in service to the spirits of the elders that I am now representing here on the Earth plane. Guide me, protect me and show me how to walk in balance always. Welcome into my circle with love. '*

Walk over to the North, raise your arms and beseech the North, *'Grandmothers and Grandfathers of the North, I call upon you to witness my Elderhood Ceremony. Before you now I ask that you imbue my staff of wisdom with the powers of the North. I ask that all judgement of both others and myself is removed and that I may freely walk in the light of truth not swayed by others' words casting shadows of darkness in my thoughts that stop me from becoming an Elder. Guide me, protect me, and show me how to walk in humility always. Welcome into my circle with love.'*

Once it feels complete, walk to the East, raise your arms and say, *'Grandmothers and Grandfathers of the East I call upon you to witness my Elderhood Ceremony. Before you now I ask you to imbue my staff of wisdom with the powers of the East. I ask to face the death of what no longer serves my life and embrace the rebirth of my new transformation into a deeper understanding of growth. I embrace the Sun knowing that the light of truth will set me free. Guide me, protect me, and show me how to walk in trust always. Welcome into my circle with love.'*

Now walk into the South with arms raised say, *'Grandmothers and Grandfathers of the South I call upon you to witness my Elderhood Ceremony. Before you now I ask you to imbue my staff of wisdom with the powers of the South. I surrender to the Universe all those things that no longer serve me knowing that I will be gifted with abundance and awareness of unseen beauty in all that I will undertake from now on as an elder. I embrace the sacrifice of the self, awakening my soul's knowing. Guide me, protect me, and show me how to live in harmony always. Welcome into my circle with love.'*

Now it is time to walk back into the centre. Facing the West with your hands firmly clasped around the staff, face the Sun as it sets on the horizon. With your feet slightly apart, make a connection to Mother Earth. '*Mother Earth whose beautiful earth I stand upon, hear my words. I call to you now to witness my Elderhood Ceremony. I ask that you imbue my staff of wisdom with the powers of Mother Earth. May I always walk on your Earth with respect, love and truth. May you keep me focused on helping heal Earth, the animals, birds, mammals, insects, rocks, crystals, trees, herbs which all come from the profusion of your womb. I embrace my eldership with full knowledge that I am a part of the web of life and will do my guardianship as a caretaker with dignity and unselfish grace. Guide me, protect me, and show me how to live in fullness always. Welcome into my circle with love.*'

Holding the staff still with both hands look upwards to Father Sky and say the following, '*Father Sky whose blanket of endless stars and planets watches over us every day, I call to you to witness my Elderhood Ceremony. I ask that you imbue my staff of wisdom with the powers of Father Sky. I ask that I am always aware of how the planets and stars affect us every day and are an integral part of our cosmology. I honour the star nation and the endless Universe of life and give thanks to all those who have passed on down to us the knowledge of the planets, the astrology of Source. I will always marvel at the light that shines in the dark guiding us home. Guide me, protect me, and show me how to live in tranquillity always. Welcome into my circle of love.*'

The rite of passage into your Eldership is nearly complete. Focus as you stand firmly on the ground, rooted in the Earth, being aware of the energies of the directions flowing into the staff and the mantle of stars now above you as a cloak of protection. Feel the energies flowing from the West, North, the East and the South towards you simultaneously, flowing into your staff along with the energy of the Earth and Sky merging as one. Then this combined energy of light coming from all six directions locks together as one and starts to flow into your heart centre.

As this starts to happen, feel it, sense it flowing straight into your heart chakra and say, *'Great Mystery, Creator who flows through all things I call on you to bear witness and initiate me into my Eldership role and duties.'*

Feel your whole body fill with white light as the six directions cleanse and purify you. Now let the light flow out and around you as you say, *'I am a being of light of wisdom and love. I take on my personal responsibility of Elderhood in full and certain knowledge that I am whole and complete. I will let nothing or no one stand in my way of becoming one with the source of creation. My eyes will see only the beauty in all; my lips will speak only words of wisdom and love. I will only hear the words of angels speaking through others. From now on I willingly take on the Wisdom Keeper's duty of being the peacemaker, storyteller of the ancestors and keeper of experiences. I will share with others who will listen to what I know and take it fully upon myself to speak only the truth. I will have no judgements and will not project onto others. I will listen and speak when it is needed and will love uncondi-tionally from the heart. May my heart be fully open to allow the Source to flow through me. Guide me, protect me, and show me how to live in peace eternally. I am now my circle of love.'*

Elderhood Incantation

I honour the Elder who lives within,
awakening my star seed so I may begin,
to help other people awaken to source,
something far greater than a matter of course.

I call on the directions to help me see,
a new way of living so that I can be,
a fountain of wisdom, an elder whose youth,
will echo through the ages revealing the truth.

As I stand with my staff, my heart full of light,
I hear the ancients say, 'Give me your might',

so that you will not falter and fall down somehow,
your power is awakened, your hour is now.

Go now and gather your seeds from the earth.
Your garden awaits you, the place of rebirth.
No longer will you live in fear and pain,
For the Elder within you has mastered the gain.

Live from experiences; sharing them is your goal
for soon you will be on a journey to the soul.
Your heart is awakened; your truth you sow,
now tend to your garden and watch it grow.

A new birth awaits you; the time is now near,
rejoice in the teachings that are so very clear.
The Earth is beneath, sense it without fear,
to the heartbeat of the Elders, beloveds so dear.

Stand in your power and remember this day,
when you felt all the grandness come your way.
Understanding life, source of being as one,
for your path of the Elder has just begun.

When it feels right, in your own time, go to each direction with your staff and thank the guardians; firstly thank Father Sky, then Mother Earth, then go to the South, then the East, followed by the North and finally back to the West where you started. Give a final closing 'thank you', then walk around your circle widdershins (counter clockwise) and close the circle. Make sure before you leave that all is as it should be. Then go to the elder tree and give thanks to the Elder Mother for being a witness. Ask for a blessing of some gifts of a green star, or berries, or bark or leaves whatever is lying on the ground. Do what you will but take not of anything live from her living bough.

Spend the next week learning about the teaching of the elder tree and how you can use this medicine in your day to day life. All parts of the elder are medicinally useful. The berries make great jams, wine, vinegar and syrups and you can make wonderful elderflower drinks. The flowers make a great tea to soothe a sore throat, which is also very good as a skin cleanser and lotion. The berries and leaves are both rich in Vitamin C.

As with all herbs please consult a herbalist or find a book that has information. Also, do not use herbal remedies if you have any medical problems, always consult your doctor first unless, of course, you are a herbalist, then the choice is yours.

The Chosen Ones

Once you have walked the path of Elderhood you will want to connect with your family and friends to share this wisdom and knowledge. Elders have traditionally been the head of the family – they are the oldest and should know better. Well, that's not always the case. Now that you are learning to work from your soul's knowing and experience you will have a desire to find your soul family if you have not already found them on the Earth plane. If you have, that's fantastic news; well done.

A family, clan or tribe is a group of people who have come together to work, support, nurture and love each other, well that's how it used to be before industrialisation and the modern world got a hold of them. A family means kith and kin, a group of people descended from their family ancestor, one's own flesh and blood, nearest and dearest.

Well as most of you know this is not always the case. My friends are having terrible experiences with their so-called nearest and dearest. There's a lot to be said about living in our society today cut off from what our ancestors held dear to them and what was a part of their social group. There is much talk about 'soul family'; I have heard people say that you choose your soul family that you have decided to work with in this life time.

They will quote the number of how many soul groups you have and how many in each one. Don't humans like to make it complicated? Spirit's message is very clear, Keep It Simple Sweetheart – KISS.

I will give you an example of how my life was affected in this lifetime to show you how soul families actually work. Before coming here I decided I was going to be adopted so I could learn all about abandonment issues. I was placed in a family as an only child. My adopted dad, William, was a workaholic and alcoholic. My adopted mother had never known love. I was told my birth parents were killed in a car accident. I instinctively knew differently. My adopted father died when I was 17 years old, we did not have a deep connection. He taught me many things which showed up in later years. My adopted mother died in my late forties and at the end of her life we had a deep bond after a very hard schooling of being together. When my mother was dying she spoke to me about her concern about me being alone and that it would be sorted.

Four weeks to the day after she died I had a phone call from my eldest brother saying he had been looking for me for over thirty years. He told me that four weeks before things just happened to enable him to find me. I knew my mother had sorted out those finer details. Funnily enough I had also said I would not trace my family until my mother had passed over. I had completion with my adopted mother and now look upon her as my soul mother.

I met my older brother Michael and his family. I then went on to meet my blood mother and my step-father. There was no connection; this was the woman who had given birth to me, that was all. There was no soul connection and I thanked her for putting me out for adoption. I then met all my family, my seven brothers. I felt a bond with my nearest brother Jim. I had known my blood mother and now had a connection with my brothers. I still felt as if I needed completion though so I called on the Spirit world for a sister and a father. I also asked for a daughter and son. Within a couple of years they came into my life.

Today my soul family is Doreen my adoptive mother in the Spirit, helping and assisting me. Dennis is my Spirit dad who knew I was coming into his life. He was doing mantras every day when he knew the house next door to him was going to be empty. I turned up and instantly I called him dad. We both just knew we had had past lives together in many different forms, part of my soul group. He had lost his daughter and had called to Spirit for a daughter to come into his life.

I have my two brothers and I am also an auntie. My soul sister is Jacqui who again came into my life when I was asking Spirit for a soul sister. David, my husband, challenges me on every level and pushes me to greater depths of my soul, teaching me about patience and stillness. Then there is Flavia, my younger sister and my soul friends Pat, Ocean, Diana, Claire, Janet, Kate, Tracy, Linda, Janet and Lindy Lu. My soul brothers are Rondie, Sky, John, Tim, Olaf. Then there is the whole clan around the world. I had asked for my soul family to come into my life and that is what happened. I am blessed with an abundant family thanks to my beloved mother Doreen who made it possible when she went to Spirit.

Let me explain how it works in my experience. The Universe works on the principles of vibration. As you re-enter each life time, you make soul agreements about meeting up with your soul family on the Earth plane. It's a soul connection when you meet someone you have never met before and there is an instant bond and you just cannot explain it. Some people call it 'soul mates'. I have had many soul mates in my life. They are great teachers, they turn up in your life and push all your buttons; you are flipped upside down, inside out and spin around as they show you to yourself. This is the life purpose of all human relationships. They are a great mirror if you choose to look deeply into your reflection. They can be your husband, wife, best friend, children, boss, next door neighbour the possibilities are endless, just when you least expect it there they are on your doorstep waiting to give you your lessons of life.

Ask yourself these questions: Who has had the biggest impact on your life and why? What was the ultimate lesson? Did you get it? Or are you still learning how 'not' to be? Just because the relation is not blood does not make a person any less capable of being your soul relation. The soul relationship is a far stronger bond than the blood relationship, because the soul connection has traversed through time and space, while the blood relation is only chosen for that lifetime. Blood is thicker than water; however, ether is thicker than blood. We chose our soul family for our growth on the Earth plane. We have come here as a collective group for a particular reason. If you have been with a certain soul before you are likely to be with them again in another lifetime.

Your time on Earth is all about learning about you. You will all have something in common, similar likes, aspirations, visions, dreams, ideas. A soul family will work together over many lifetimes. They can be in your blood family, your adopted family and your soul family. So go out there and practise the law of manifestation. You will attract into your life the family you so desire. Ceremonies, rituals and celebrations are an important part of the fabric of a family, clan or tribe. They offer a sense of purpose, clarity bridging the community as we make the passage from birth to death and rebirth again.

These are the milestones of our life's journey as intrepid explorers. There are also markers along the way for other less important celebrations that stay in our memories long after the events have taken place. My grandmother's cooking, licking the bowl, sitting around the table waiting for the turkey. The Christmas stocking at the end of the bed, little things that mean a lot connecting families together as a whole even if just for the day it made special and memorable. It cemented the feeling of joy and happiness that those sacred times connected us to.

Our ceremonies for our personal rites of passage are powerful ways of tapping into our deeply rooted emotions. Like a fine malt whisky our emotions mature in a wooded casket awaiting the moment when we can drink of our maturity, clarity, and depth of our soul. I would like to see a reintegration ceremony created for people like myself and for those who have been fostered out, and whose parents either died or left them when they were very young. Our first years are very important, for this is when we learn the most. I learnt abandonment, loss, low self-esteem, fear, insecurities, transition, learning and remembering. If I had lived on the Lakota reservation and had lost my family I would have experienced a Hunkapi or Hunka ceremony – The 'Making of Relatives Ceremony', which is one of the Lakota Seven Sacred Rites.

My spirit father Dennis tried to adopt me and was told that he could not do so because I was over 18 years old. The Making of Relatives Ceremony is for adopting others, who are not blood relatives. Jim Beard was Wallace Howard's adopted brother through the Hunka ceremony. The Hunka relative is considered to be closer than blood relatives, because they are our spirit relatives. When a non-Lakota is adopted, they are adopted into that family. They are not adopted into the whole of the Lakota nation. It is a great honour to become connected with the family and bond in this way.

Some years ago, myself and my husband, David, took a group of individuals on a trip to North America around Colorado, Montana, Wyoming, and South Dakota. We visited many different places and experienced a great bonding with all the people we met along the way. We stopped in Rapid City over night to rest before we set out for Wounded Knee the next day. That night I had a dream that I was looking for the Grandmother. I could see her in a small hut calling out to me for help. Then a native elder appeared and said, 'Find my relative. She is my granddaughter, she needs help from you.'

The next day we headed off to Wounded Knee, I was driving one car, David the other. I stopped at Wounded Knee opposite the cemetery on top of the hill. I asked the crafts people where I would find the grandmother and described her. They pointed to a dirt road and said, 'She is down there in the house.' We drove down the dirt track road and arrived at the house. I knocked on the door and a woman called, 'Come in.' All of us crammed into this small house and there, sitting by a table, was the grand-mother I had seen in my dreams. I explained my dream to her and she nodded and said she had been expecting us. She had prayed to Creator for help for food and medicines as their money had run out.

We made a collection between the twelve of us and one group went to the nearest store for foods and medicines. As we carried on talking I explained that a grandfather had appeared in my dreams and asked me to find her. Then in front of everyone she did a Hunka ceremony with me and as she held my hands and spoke in Lakota, tears streamed down my face. I could see all the relatives standing around nodding. After the ceremony we all sat around and talked until the rest of the group came back. We made sure she had enough food for a week. Her name was Barbara and her heritage is ancient and old. The group all heard and saw that day the power of Spirit to connect us back.

The grandfather who came to me in the dreamtime was the same grandfather who came to me when I first was called to Sun Dance over twelve years ago at Wounded Knee; there are no coincidences. The Making of Relatives Ceremony had a profound effect on me that day for it connected me back to my soul family. We in the developed world can learn greatly from those that carry the traditions of their people. We have been subjected to many different traditions, cultures, and indoctrina-tions over two thousand years. We have lost our birthright and our blood heritage. Barbara sat that day in her home and named all her relatives and all of us in that room knew the names of her relatives. Can we do the same?

Making of Relatives

I am grateful to all my native teachers who have shared with me their traditions and ceremonies openly so that we might learn from them how to reconnect once again to the spirits. The spirit world knows no boundaries of race, colour, or creed. We are one. The ceremonies were gifted by Spirit and are therefore Spirit's teachings. We can lay no claim to them being ours. We are only the caretakers of these ceremonies. This is a ceremony of bringing together and creating a stronger link with all our relations. This is a bonding; a bringing together of heart-linked souls at a deep level of family sharing and connection of all.

If you are intending doing this ceremony with someone special in your life, take the time to find that unique moment to tell them. Explain to the person what you are about to do and ensure they are happy to do this ceremony with you. This is a bond of souls. Only you will know what to say, what to do. Let it be done with the timeless knowing of being able to be free to say and do what is in your hearts. Find a sacred place that means a lot to the pair of you. Do you want it to be just the two of you or do you want to invite soul family and friends? This is a soul to soul connection. Stand hand in hand looking at one another and speak the words that come directly from your heart and soul. Enjoy the moment of spontaneity to carry you away so that you can remember when, where, and how you were once both connected as one soul family. Blessed Be.

Chapter 8

The Totality
Samhain & Death and Rebirth

When you know who you are, when your mission is clear and you burn with the inner fire of unbreakable will, no cold can touch your heart, no deluge can dampen your purpose, you know you are alive.
Chief Seattle

It has taken me many days to put pen to paper for this final chapter, pondering over my approach to our 'final' rite in this life journey. Death is not a stranger to me. We have walked together more than once – a near fatal car accident, loss of loved ones, illnesses that have required hospitalisation and three suicide attempts. Looking back, each of these 'little deaths' was affording me the opportunity to address and shed the ego – the shadow personality that I had been losing my soul in. I now better understand why, at the time, I felt suicide was my only option. It wasn't my physical body I was rejecting, but the situation that I was in.

Being depressed, dispirited, I was confused and wanted to experience elimination of the ego by escaping into another world – the world of shamanic 'death and rebirth'. I wanted to journey to, and be resurrected in, the place where my soul thrived. Instinctively I knew what had to be done and by overdosing with tablets and alcohol I was trying to reach that level of consciousness where I could communicate with the spirits for assistance and guidance. I wasn't trying to finish my life, not at all; I was attempting to bypass my ego in order to reclaim my soul in this life.

During that process I had an out-of-body experience that totally overwhelmed me. I was no longer the personality of other people's projections. I was not aware of my physical body and I had no fear or concerns about physically dying. At my third suicide attempt, the penny finally dropped. I was aware of Spirit informing me that I could die and later reincarnate to re-experience and do it all over again, or I could continue on and work through all my previous lifetimes and in doing so help others – the choice was mine. I chose to stay.

I feel so much better since going through my rites of passage of death and rebirth; I was in my soul's transition to the next phase of my life. I trusted what I was being told by the spirit world and Spirit's guidance as a result of my journey through the 'dark night of the soul'. When we face the darkness within in the form of fear, pain, rage, anger, regret, shame, blame or doubt, the 'old' life must die – our perception of reality and of who and what we are in this reality must change. Only then are we able to move through an evolutionary process of transmigration from the unstable delusion of the self, to the new found lands of the soul, in this lifetime.

This process of initiation rebalances the dark and the light so that when we face darkness outside us it no longer affects us because we are lit from within by our soul's radiance – our inner knowing. Only one who has died to what no longer serves them can truly know what it is to live. Each time I experienced a little death of the personality, I became aware of another way of thinking that felt good. No longer controlled by my mind's need to be in charge, there came a union of heart and mind to live in a balanced way.

Instead of fighting each other for pole position, there was a sharing of true equality. The two voices of heart and mind, having constantly shouted at each other, merged as the harmonic voice of the soul. I felt, from my heart, a new way of living my life – fully and completely with no fear of the unknown. Sometimes you have to stride towards the things that make you run away in fear. When you are faced with death, when you are told that you have a 50/50 chance of making it through the night, for example, you begin to appreciate life and how important it actually is.

I created my cancer that moved through my womb, my ovaries, into my bowels and intestine causing me to have major surgery over and over again until I got the message. I created it due to all the traumas of my childhood and teenage years in the organs of my body that had suffered the ordeal. In effect I was killing myself internally with my negative feelings that had been caused by the projection and rejection of others. It was time to die to the old me and be rebirthed.

It is worth remembering that a vast proportion of the planet's population faced a collective 'dark night of the soul', when we were denied all access to our gods and belief systems and had to go through somebody else to speak to our God. All of you should know our history of what became of the ancient ways of metaphysical teachings. We lost our birthright, and in the place of the virtues of the soul became the created self, Hell on Earth.

Around the 11th to 12th centuries the Cathars, Bogomils and others who embraced the teachings of reincarnation were persecuted as heretics. These persecutions continued through the Middle Ages into the Renaissance and early modern period when thousands were burnt, hanged, stoned, tortured or drowned in the name of religion. It wasn't until the early 19th and 20th centuries that the great cycle of life, in the form of reincarnation, was introduced in terms of psychology and we were allowed to understand and appreciate it once again, as it remerged and was made accessible to men and then women. The Theosophical Society brought to light great teachings from Indian concepts and magical societies, which once again flourished, helping people to access their soul's divine light.

Madam Helena Blavatsky, Dion Fortune, Annie Besant, W.B. Yeats, to name a few, brought back the great teachings of the ancients, making them accessible for all, once again. For over one thousand, five hundred years the dark night of the soul was upon the land. This greatly affected our ancestors, who lived through these dark times, and that is why it is so important today to give thanks to those who went before us. Thanks to our forefathers and foremothers – they kept the candle burning so that today we can have access to re-becoming increasingly, via rites, rituals and celebrations.

The Thin Blue Veil

The festival of Samhain, which translates into the Celtic New Year's Eve (sometimes referred to as All Hallow's Eve), is the origin of the overly commercial Halloween. This is the night of power when the veil to the spirit world is at its thinnest. Cultures and beliefs from around the world connect and celebrate with this festival of the dead for they have a deep respect and understanding of their ancestors.

This is the beginning of winter, the end of the old year and the beginning of the new, with the onset of the dark phase of the year. The time of the Great West Gate – where we see our true nature. It is the time when the dead can return to the land of the living for one night to be with their clan, tribe or family. Samhain is the night that exists out of linear time, a moment when time stands still. The Great Sabbat is a sacred day for it honours the dead and the morality of divination. All seeing, all knowing, awareness of the Great Mysteries that have understood that the living are made whole by embracing death.

The initiates of the Greater Mysteries of Nature's most sacred knowledge understood how to live but, most importantly of all, how to die well. They knew that the soul slumbered awaiting its rebirth in the land of the living of human form. The Eleusinian Mysteries, founded by Orpheus, taught of a deep understanding of all philosophic ideas and beliefs, freely shared with others. In the city of Eleusis, men, women and children came to learn of the Lesser and Greater Mysteries. These wisdom teachings travelled all over old Europe with those who sought to share these insights and visions with those who were ready to learn, and who wanted to develop a deeper insight within.

The initiated seers, whose visions revealed humans achieving a connection between the human soul and the divine consciousness, prepared each neophyte for the initiations of death and rebirth. By doing so the apprentice experienced divine unity and became Epoptes – one who has seen or beheld the creation and the Creator in all forms. By removing fear of death from the initiates, there came a releasing of repressed emotions and traumas that had been locked inside the physical body. Through fasting, purification and initiation came an awareness of a change in their consciousness, as the death of what no longer served them took shape.

Virtue was born and a deep and true understanding emerged. Balance was obtained with both nature and the natural cycles of life within and without. Transmigration of the soul touches each and every one of us whether we are aware of it or not. By entering into human form again, which is our choice when we are in the spirit world, we are following the natural circular time of reincarnation. By being born again we wish to experience and process on the Earth plane those lessons we have not yet learnt.

The Eleusinian Mystery Rites of Passage were always held at midnight, a sacred time for many including the Druids, Celts, Egyptians, Mayans and other ancients. At this time of the night death and rebirth initiations were held. Initiates were buried deep in the earth for up to four days and nights as they connected with the Earth and with death, as well as connecting with the ancestors for guidance and direction through the underworlds.

The transmigration of the soul took place as the soul migrated at the point of the transition when the initiate, through fasting and prayer, was at the pivotal point between the world of self and Spirit. Dying to what no longer served them, they experienced a mystic experience of soul recapitulation as the soul re-entered the initiate whilst in human form.

'Death is the final orgasm,' were the first words I spoke after coming back from a sacred plant medicine journey to discover and integrate my soul's knowing. I had stopped breathing for over five minutes and had completely surrendered to divine bliss. There was no fear, no awareness of the bodily functions, and no attentiveness of the breath. I was experiencing stillness – oneness with All. I had no awareness of the Earth, no thoughts, and no feelings. There was an overwhelming sense of completeness, totality in all things. I was free of my Earthly body and the heaviness of matter. I was one with the infinite source of pure light. I was vibrating and resonating with the sounds of the Universe. I had died and gone to Heaven. My soul had connected back to my ancient wholesomeness and shown me my true status of flawlessness. I was not fragmented, or separated from Source. My inner light showed me the illumination of initiation and how to transcend the dense Earthly trappings of the personality.

One Soul – Many Lives

Reincarnation is a mesmerizing subject which scholars and great mystics have studied since around 1200BC. They have come from all walks of philosophical and religious beliefs in a personal pursuit for the answers to metempsychosis. It appears in philosophical texts from India and Greece around the 6th century BC. These teachings spread out into ancient Europe, Iran, and influenced many great scholars and teachers including the Druids, who already had an awareness and doctrine of death and rebirth and of the natural agricultural cycles through time and space.

Julius Caesar wrote and recorded many details about the works of the Druids of Gaul and their great interest in death and rebirth. He noted that they knew that the soul does not die and after death passes from one body to another body of the soul's choosing. They knew that the soul was indestructible, and therefore fear was conquered by this knowledge, instilling courage into the initiates of the Druidic orders who embraced the wisdom of immortality. Reincarnation still remains the greatest unknown scientific discovery of our present times. It is imperative that it stays this way, for deep down inside we all desire the mysteries of our ancient ways to remain sacred.

I can remember as a child when I was told that Santa Claus was not real it devastated me and took me a long time to get over that feeling of abandonment. The magic had been stolen, taken away and replaced with a feeling of 'what's the point?' We as humans have an individual psyche that is unquenchable in the search for wisdom and knowledge through books, questing, journeying, and looking for answers about the Universe and God.

Approximately six thousand years ago lunar calendars were used to calculate time. Then in 45BC Julius Caesar brought the solar calendar to the Roman people. In 1582 the Gregorian calendar was introduced by Pope Gregory XIII and adopted around the world as a way of measuring time for all people to adhere to. Time was created by mankind as an illusion to keep people in a controlled situation. We need to understand that to access the Spirit Worlds and our soul's divine time we need to step out of sequential time.

Ancient cultures knew about cyclical time. The Mayans, Hopi, Babylonians, and Ancient Greeks understood and comprehended the never-ending cycle of recurring periods of death and rebirth, that life is a circle with no beginning and no end. So too our Universe has no beginning and no end. When the Judaeo-Christian concept adopted linear time there came into being a beginning and an end, birth and death. This put an end to our abilities as individuals to circumnavigate our soul's kingdom – exploring the vast worlds of our past, present and future lives.

I have discovered that time as we know it does not exist in the spirit world. My mother died over ten years ago and yet to her it is only a second ago. Each time I work with entities in the spirit world they do not have an awareness of time. How do you view time? In a straight line or horizontally? Do you think of circular time, vertical time, or as the ancients knew, divine time? What would happen if time was no longer a concept?

I was also aware of time stretching upwards, sloping downwards and expanding from the centre outwards. It was from one central point outwards the past, the present, the future; it was all one and the same. It was an amazing feeling to be aware that we could choose to be in that space for as long as we wanted and it was also our choice to return to Earth. It was an eternal moment expanded forever. Death is not the end and birth not the beginning, because the endless flow of the life of the soul is undying and immutable.

I knew then that when we go back to the Spirit World we remember everything and we are one with Creator and Creation. We are everywhere, instantaneously; a part of all there is and shall ever be. We are complete, whole and embodied fully in spirit and soul.

The Never-Ending Story

Our soul loves the truth and wants us to know our soul's inheritance. Many religious and spiritual traditions have greatly influenced us from the Stone Age times to now. The ancient Egyptian, Judaic, Christian, Muslim, Hindu, Aztec and Mayan texts (to name but a few) described our destiny after Earthly life. These 'books of the dead' depict in great detail what is to be expected in the next world and what is to happen on the 'day of judgement'. The *Book of Coming Forth by Day* or as it is sometimes known, *The Book of Emerging Forth into the Light*, is an ancient Egyptian funerary text used from the beginning of the New Kingdom.

Its modern name is *The Book of the Dead*. The text consists of magical spells to help the dead person through the Underworld and into the Afterlife. The first Pyramid Texts were used in King Unas' pyramid from around 2400BC. I have been in this pyramid many times and the condition and content of the hieroglyphs are incredible. You can really get a feel of how they worked in ceremony as you stand in the centre facing the sarcophagus imagining the words being read out. The act of speaking a ritualised ceremony was, in effect, an act of creation made manifest. Action and speech were one and the same, for the concept of magic was woven intricately with the spoken and written word.

To the Egyptians the heart was the centre of wisdom, intelligence and memory of the soul's incarnations. Tomb walls and the sarcophagus held the spells of antiquity, until they were copied onto papyrus which contained the religious and magical texts. There was not a single or canonical book of the dead; it was created for different pharaohs or queens who personalised which spells were appropriate for their personal progression into the afterlife.

The famous 'Spell 125', the 'Weighing of the Heart' originated from the reign of Queen Hatshepsut and Thutmose III c 1475BC. The Papyrus of Hunefer shows the scribe Hunefer's heart being weighed on the left hand scale in an urn and an ostrich feather on the right hand scale watched over by Anubis, the guardian of the Lower Worlds and Judge of the Dead. Thoth, who is the scribe of the gods, records the result. If his heart is lighter than the feather, the soul is allowed to pass into the afterlife. If the heart is not lighter than the feather, it is devoured by the Ammit, Devourer of Souls, who is a goddess composition of a crocodile, lion and a hippopotamus. Greed, lust and fear are the three things that weigh the heart down heavily. Without the heart you could not enter the company of the gods.

You could spend a lifetime reading through the various texts and scrolls of the ancient Egyptians, along with visits to their tombs, to catch a glimpse of the true meaning of their incredible teachings. There are very few places left on Earth that you can walk back in time with such details of all the ancients' previous lifetimes on full display. But in Egypt, hidden in clear view, are words and actions awaiting initiation of the sacred. The heart was the most important organ for the Egyptians. It was the seat of one's spirit and the centre of willpower. It was their inner sun, the source of beingness. If you were separated from your heart it meant eternal death.

And in the Judaic tradition the heart is the crucible of a person's true essence. For the ancient Hebrews the heart meant the seat of wisdom and understanding. They too had a deep understanding of life after death and knew the heart played a very big part in the great design of life. They knew how to be wholehearted and walk and talk with god, heart to heart.

Confucius taught that true knowledge lies in the heart. If the heart is in order so too are the senses. How many people today are separated from their heart, devoid of feelings, or with a feeling of being dead inside? Another funerary text, the *Bardo Thodol*, known in the West as *The Tibetan Book of the Dead*, gives clear and precise instructions about how to experience consciousness after death, during the interval between death and the next rebirth. It is read aloud to the dead when they are in flux between death and reincarnation, in order to help them recognise the true nature of their mind and attain liberation from the cycle of rebirth. The text teaches us how we can attain Nirvana by recognising the heavenly realms instead of entering the lower realms where the cycle of rebirth continues.

Then we have great wisdom teaching from India. *The Vedas*, combined with the *Upanishads*, brought forth a most practical and holistic connection between the human individual and celestial realities. These were a collection of stories, aphorisms and dialogues between holy men and seekers of the truth. These teachings were about discovering God within one's self. In the cave of the heart dwells the Divine, waiting to merge with the mind for the embodiment of truth. The Upanishads speak of the heart as the great fulcrum of the Cosmos, the place where the enlightened self can finally meet their soul. The ancient Hindus had four goals or focuses in their life – Dharma (focused on right actions, how you live your life pertaining to one ethical and spiritual duty), Artha (how you live your life surrounded with possessions, security, and accomplishments in securing individual wealth), Kama (enjoyment of the five senses and becoming consciously aware of the pleasure that is given through the delights of taste, touch, sight, smell, listening and by exquisite objects of sensuous desires) and Moksa (focus for the liberation of the soul from the cycles of rebirth so that it can merge with the cosmic soul, the Brahman).

These four insights combine our spiritual, mental, emotional and physical wellbeing and shared a remarkable comprehension of living a life of materialism, spirituality, sensuality and awareness without any judgements of what was wrong or right. If this was applied today there would be far greater balance and harmony in the world for all of us to thrive in. The mind, the heart, the spirit and the soul would work together to restore this force of wisdom and knowledge which is thousands of years old.

Absolution of the Soul

Whilst writing this I got up to walk to another part of the house and banged my head on my prefrontal cortex. When I came back again to sit down, I again hit my head on the beam, which knocked me backwards. As I stumbled into a chair, energy was flowing down my spine and through my entire body like shock waves and all I could hear was, 'Tell the truth, tell the truth of what has happened'.

As it happens, the prefrontal cortex of the brain is all about 'truth telling' and as I felt the energy flow through my nervous system it was as if I was connected to a great universal nervous system. I sensed the ancients, the old ones, through my nervous system asking me to speak the truth of our heritage. I could feel the vibrational harmonics like great waves from a cosmic generator.

I heard them say, 'Speak your truth, share the words of your soul. Your emotions are the energies of your creation. As you create with your heart and soul you become one with your personal manifestation for the good of humanity. Know that your heart has a mind of its own and its cells are what connect you to the consciousness of the Universe. Humankind has a choice to change the outcomes and possibilities for the future by comprehending new probabilities that affect our thoughts and feelings, which manifest themselves into this reality. The truth cannot be manifested simply by writing or speaking about it, for it loses its authenticity. The truth must be felt, experienced and lived. It is time to speak from your soul's desire for love and truth. Do not be afraid to speak what has been known for thousands of years for fear of persecution from others who fear you in your power, this is no longer possible. You are living now in a time of enlightenment where for the first time in thousands of years you can speak the truth of your soul.'

I have always felt, seen, and been aware of spirits and knew they affected my nervous system when working with them. Every time they surround me I can see all future probabilities. I can also travel in the past and see what has happened before. This was like being on a super highway of neurons at very high speeds, interacting with thousands of other neurons all connected as one thought, one super-mind. As I travel on this super highway I can see billions of tiny lights representing each one of us intricately connected, but in that moment I became as one thought, one feeling, with the consciousness of the world. Even as I think about it now, the feelings keep coming back and flow through all my neurons like a fine charge. I feel connected at a much deeper level of perception and intuition. The intuitive part of my brain uses the nervous system to connect with all future probabilities created by my thought processes. It connects them to the Universal Consciousness that, in turn, communicates back to me the endless possibilities of my future.

The mind matrix is infinite, allowing us access to all that has been, is now and will ever be. No beginning, no end, the eternal now. It is available to all of us when we have an open and radiant heart centre flowing with unconditional love, joy and bliss. For how long I sat there experiencing the feelings I do not know. What I do know is the bang on my head changed my thoughts and connections. Until that point I was stopped by my thoughts and emotions relating to my past experiences and past lives.

I have had memories of persecutions ever since I was a little girl and a deep seated fear of speaking out against the false teachings that were imposed upon me. Now, today, we can again speak out to all who will listen and re-establish the true teachings of the heart and soul. When Jesus of Nazareth walked on the Earth, reincarnation was considered common knowledge. He studied in many of the ancient mystery schools in Egypt and offered teachings of wisdom and knowledge of the soul. After his death, his teachings were manipulated and edited, which meant that for the next 300 years there was a great conflict between Pagan and Christian beliefs. Many Christians and Pagans were killed for their beliefs as the struggle for power continued. Constantine the Great became Emperor in 306AD, the first Christian Emperor to rule the Roman Empire. Fifty years after his death all non-Christian faiths had been outlawed and the Christian church became a persecutor of all other faiths.

Christianity changed from a balanced system into a patriarchy and religious ideology. In 325AD the Council of Nicaea adopted the Nicene Creed, ruled by egotistical men who saw a way of controlling the masses using religion as a disguise to instigate, dominate and control people. They used their form of politics to change the course of history. The people did not stand a chance as the military swept through the whole of Europe, Asia, and Africa under a religious guise of their so-called spirituality.

The men who took control, did so with an empty heart and a devious mind. Devoid of soul, they ruthlessly wiped out all knowledge of the ancient mystery schools so no clues would be left behind. The idea of reincarnation was dismissed and replaced by a doctrine of an eternal hell or heaven depending on a person's actions in this lifetime. They did away with past lives, and taught that there was only one lifetime, that the Church was the only organisation that could offer your soul salvation. Our ancestors must have wept in their graves as they watched the desecration of all the wonderful ancient schools.

The Library of Alexandria was burnt to the ground. What was it that drove great men go to great lengths to silence this knowledge? What is it they feared by people discovering the truth – that an individual can choose free will to create their own destiny? They desecrated the vestiges of the soul and in doing so denied the presence of Spirit and Universal Consciousness from the all, to one singular individual.

Absolution comes from within – this is called personal and spiritual responsibility. I recall the violent behaviour of a childhood friend's Catholic father. During the week he would swear, threaten and verbally humiliate and abuse his wife and children, ruling over them with an iron fist, and then would promptly 'wash himself clean' every Sunday in the confessional box.

I found it most odd that only a priest or bishop can recite the formula of absolution, which forgives the sins of the penitent, in God's place. It is our spiritual responsibility to ensure that the life we live is not immoral. I have said and done things when I was not in my right mind or heart. Each time I prayed to Creator for forgiveness and each time I heard Spirit say to me, 'Self-forgiveness is the most important thing, for if you cannot forgive yourself, you will not be able to forgive others.'

This led me onto ponder what is 'good' and what is 'bad', what is 'right' and what is 'wrong'? Everyone has a different viewpoint. Good means morally positive and bad means morally negative. When we apply these principles to what I have just talked about this is what applies to the indoctrinations and philosophies of the ancestors' teachings.

I will leave the decision up to you in how you view the following: Good means a relationship with life and well-being; happiness, permanence, love, prosperity, truth, worth, virtue, beneficial, ethical, honest, honourable, wholesome, friendly, gracious, kind-hearted, integrity, morality. Bad is associated with conscious and deliberate wrongdoing; discrimination, harm to others, humiliation of people designed to diminish their psychological needs, destructiveness, acts of violence, corruption, immorality, sinfulness, wickedness, deprivation.

Which cultures promoted the teachings of the heart, the soul, the spirit, the universal oneness of all? Which cultures wanted to share all their wisdom and knowledge with the people? What teachings were given to help others become one with creation? Which cultures promoted the teachings of evil and sin? Which cultures took away all the teachings from the people and forced them to do penance? Which teachings advocated the fall of man and severed the direct link between man and God? Who created the word evil? Who created sin? These are the ones who project outwardly what they themselves have done, 'Do as I say and not as I do'.

Those who speak ill of others are in fact talking about themselves to others. If you listen to others who cast aspersions then you fall out of grace and you are no longer wholehearted, you are still the self. If you gossip, and create dramas, you are still the self. For totality to take place there needs to be a very big awakening of ethics in our everyday lives, and an awareness of self-respect and self-less-ness meaning the self-minus-ego.

Since the early 17th century there has been a great divide between the head and the heart. The Industrial Revolution of the next two centuries caused a rift between feeling and mental power, splitting our kingdoms apart, verifiable versus indescribable, seen and unseen. Our mind was apotheosised and our heart undervalued as we entered into the realms of scientific enlightenment. Gone was the wholeheartedness and in its place we became a small cog in a very large wheel. Charles Dickens wrote an amazing book, *Hard Times,* which tells the story of how Victorian children had their hearts and imaginations educated out of them by rationality.

This happened to our great grandfathers and great grandmothers who passed it on down to us without being aware of the great complications that would affect us today. This is why we are all wandering around, searching for what has been denied, and lost to our heart's legacy. In today's world of quantum physics and globalisation, we are still fragmented, depersonalised by a mindset of belief systems that do not hold true any longer to our soul's totality. In this day and age we seem to be more interested in computers and games, totally ignoring the greatest computer and game of life that we can ever play – being ourselves. How can you create a computer robot that can think like us when we haven't even mastered that thought process ourselves?

Knocking on Heaven's Door

The talk about ascension relates to how this era – 2012 and the years around it – are a time for awakening our soul's remembrance. The concept of entering Heaven alive is a belief held by many traditions and religions. They regard death as the end of the life of an individual on Earth and entering Heaven first without dying is considered a sign of God's recognition. Buddha, Jesus, Muhammad, Francis Bacon, Kwan Yin, Mary the mother of Jesus, Enoch, Elijah, Moses, Hercules, Yudhishthira, Swami Ramalingam and many other great teachers and masters have all been said to have ascended into heaven while still alive.

Each and every one of us can enter into the state of Heaven, Nirvana, if we so wish in this lifetime. We need to die well to what no longer benefits our soul's growth in human form. So how do we go about obtaining our ascension in this lifetime? How tired are you of keeping coming back over and over again? Do you want to rise above the mundane to see a clearer perspective of your true life's purpose?

It's not about dying and then working on what needs to be dealt with when you are in the Spirit World. It is about dealing with it now in this lifetime so you won't keep making the same mistakes over and over again. Are you ready to let go of what no longer serves you and join the liberation of the heart movement? All over the world, at this moment in time, people are joining together to free themselves from tyranny and oppression from dictators and rulers of soulless compassion.

This is the moment we have all been waiting for, this is our golden opportunity to listen to the call of the heart and transcend our mortal shell once and for all. If you wait for somebody else to do it for you and answer all the questions, you will be very lucky indeed. For most of us that is not going to happen. You have the answers to all the questions you have been asking about, look inside and you will find the answers for yourself. It really is that simple.

Firstly, I want you to focus on how your emotions and thoughts drive your day-to-day living. Our emotions are linked to personality, energised behaviour, and are the component to motivation in a positive or negative effect. We can behave; act out our dramas in certain ways depending on our emotional state at the time of the situation. When we no longer fuel our emotions with behavioural patterns such as crying, fighting, denial and dramas of the self, we can connect to our deep-seated emotions coming from our heart in a positive way. How you react to a given situation is vital in understanding your emotions at a very deep level.

Science has only now rediscovered what the ancients have always known for over two thousand years, that the heart thinks and the cells of the mind remember. Scientists are now coming to realise and study what the Shamans and Healers have known all along about the combined energy of the mind, heart, spirit, soul and divinity. Combining all the cells of these amazing generators of thinking, feeling, knowing and being, brings us the connection that links us to the totality of the Universe.

Emotional Rescue

My friend Rosemary, who lives in Taos, New Mexico, has worked in Kinesiology for the past fifteen years. She has talked to me about the findings and works of Dr David R Hawkins who, for the past twenty-five years, has been working on muscle testing in humans. He demonstrated that the physical and mental wellbeing of a person is directly affected by their emotional state. The negative emotions of fear, hate, anger, grief, guilt, shame, blame, envy, jealously, contempt, depression, disgust, hostility, lust, worry, remorse, can all weaken us in the body, the mind and the spirit.

This causes the body to be dis-eased and triggers mental stimulus of negative emotions, sending signals to the body that correlate and resonate with the negative emotion created. This, in turn, births many forms of illness including cancers, and liver and heart problems. The energy of the emotion becomes entrenched in entropy and is trapped, causing symptomatic complications within the body. Without any outlet, or way of knowing how to release the negatively created thought-forms, these trapped emotions cause the demise of the physical body. This is due to these negative emotions being reinforced over and over again by the belief patterns engrained within the emotional frame work.

When we focus our thoughts on positive emotions, we heal ourselves. This is personally empowering and gives back a sense of self-worth. Words have power and when you practise detachment of self-limiting beliefs you start to trust and are willing to accept and forgive others. Through this you have a reason to love and comprehend the deep joy within you, and from these feelings come a reverence and serenity for all life. All you need do is send love, peace to any part of your body that needs healing. Each organ is a living part of you and responds to you communicating with it in a positive, nurturing way.

I was just woken up this morning by the winds and heavy rains. I could hear the spirits of the elements speaking about how the emotional state of the planet is affecting the weather. There are seven billion people on this planet, a giant mind matrix. What is the balance of the world's emotions at this moment in time? We are linked to the Earth by our nervous system. Our nervous system controls the response of everything that is conceived of by the brain (thoughts) and expressed as muscular motion. Your muscles are the engine that your body uses to propel itself. They turn energy (thought) into motion (emotion).

Now if we apply this theory further; the collective consciousness of the world, which is energy is then turned into motion, which is the elements of earth, air, fire, water and ether. These are the elements of life, or elements of survival, for without them life would not exist. Now imagine seven billion people on the planet expressing feelings, thoughts and emotions, and if they were all placed together as a whole, what would be the outcome? The muscles of the world are the elements and are the driving force of destruction and creation.

The ancients knew this and honoured them through ceremonies at the volcanoes, wells and stone circles. The spirits were fed and appeased. We are made of the same elements as this planet. *'Earth my body, water my blood, air my breath and fire my spirit'* is a chant that has been sung for a very long time. Climate change, in which we play a role as we are intricately connected, has shifted the balance of the elements. Our thoughts are creating the global climate change of this world. We are responsible, and instead of exploiting them we should be honouring them and our own personal emotions. The elements sustain us; that is why, in the core principle foundations of Shamanism, the elements are the first teachers.

What will it take? Tornadoes, hurricanes, earthquakes, flooding or fires? Emotions control our actions, behaviour, and thinking. There are two basic emotions in life: love and fear. Fear-based emotions affect our immune system, the endocrine system. We need to learn how to be with our emotions, living peacefully with them, transmuting them into a higher vibration. The more we move up the scale of emotions the more we free ourselves from bodily concerns. It is important to be connected and have an understanding of how your emotions operate, and by doing so you will be living a life of high vibrational energy, enjoying a sense of completion and contentment.

When we experience unconditional love for ourselves we step into divine bliss and enlightenment, throwing off the mantle of illusion and stepping into the veil of ineffability. It's wonderful how we as human beings can experience all emotions. It is also good to feel all of them and experience all of them. The reason people are able to become aware of negative energies in the body as a healer is because they have worked and experienced all the emotions themselves.

A good detective will always find what they are looking for when they know what to look for. When you discover the negative emotions within you, you transmute them into positive ones which, in turn, empowers you. You feel whole, completely lit up with positively charged emotions, a truly enlightening experience. Emotions are the key to your well-being.

One way to liberate yourself of what no longer serves your life emotionally is the 'Papers of Regrets'. Traditionally these are burnt in the cauldron of death and rebirth on Samhain, or at New Year's Eve – 'out with the old and in with the new'. This is a about letting go. You will need a cauldron, or a suitable container to burn paper/photos in, that will hold a small fire. You also need paper and a pen to write down what you are releasing; be it a negative emotion, an illness or a relationship that no longer serves your highest good. Take your time to find a suitable place to do this ceremony in. This is all about death and rebirth, when you let go of something or someone ask for a positive replacement or understanding to appear in your life. Nature does not like a vacuum. The same goes for women – we love to fill spaces.

When you are ready and have written down your feelings you may find you have several different issues that need resolving. If this is the case please write each on separate pieces of paper. Now place a candle in the centre of the cauldron, this represents your quintessence. Now light the candle and ask the Spirit Keeper of the light to shine a bright luminosity on your situation and what you are about to release.

Take each individual piece of paper to hold and say the following… *'I release (name it) to the light, in full acknowledgment that it no longer serves a purpose in my life. I call on the highest good to surround it so that it may be released and continue on its journey for its highest good. I surround it with love, gratitude and thanks for the teachings it has taught me known or unknown, for this I am eternally grateful. I am thankful for the death of what no longer serves me and welcome in the new energies of rebirth and balance. In perfect love and in perfect trust, in the powers that watch over us, so be it.'*

Once you have done this and all the papers are burnt, take the candle and the papers outside, if you are not already there, and bury them in the earth saying the following verse. *'Earth to earth, ashes to ashes, death and rebirth awakens my passion. From this moment on I will have no fear, for my greatest teachings have now appeared. I thank the one who has shown me the way, so I may journey onwards to a new light of day. The veil has now parted, my regrets now departed, into the earth where I first started. With positive thoughts, emotions and feelings, I shape my life for all to see, enlightenment shining throughout all of me!'* (Remember this is your moment for letting go of the past and starting a new way of life, so rejoice!)

If we deny and run away from what haunts us the most we will never learn our true purpose in life. What haunts us is our ghost of Christmas past. In other words, our past lives have an energy all of their own, an energy that will push us into painful experiences in order to end our denial and find the truth. Shamanic dismemberment is a process of rediscovering our hidden truths, of dying to what no longer serves us and being reborn into a new state of awareness. Once you experience this you will come to understand that death is not to be feared, but lived. The ancients knew of this concept of regeneration just as the physicist knows that energy is neither created nor destroyed – it just changes form.

When we accept this we realise that death is a change of form rather than an end. Of course we all fear losing our loved ones, losing everything we have come to know on the Earth plane. But once you have a deep-seated comprehension of death and rebirth and have experienced it in its many forms then fear is no longer present. If we choose to walk the path of the shamanic healer we need to appreciate and to have experienced all forms of rites of passage from birth to death, for ourselves to be able to walk our talk. Only one who has experienced death and rebirth can share with others the wisdom that death brings. When we touch the realms of remembering as we die, we come to a place of clarity. This is the place of deep inner knowing that comes as the personality dissolves. We can reach the place of remembering in this lifetime and we don't have to actually physically die to discover it!

Soul Music

Our lifestyle today is causing us to question everything we have ever learnt. I am asking you to go much deeper – back to the myths and symbols – and see the correlation of how we need to reinstate the deeper relationships between our mind, heart, spirit, soul and divinity, merging them so that we can sing our soul back home. You have a unique soul sound, a heart sound that vibrates with the sounds of the Universe. All you need to do is call that sound into being and create a harmonic resonance with Source. Our minds and our hearts need to be equals, in co-operation for a greater unity, removing the competitive edge and learn to walk between the worlds in harmony, as one.

In the summer of 2011 I was having many pains in my chest. I went to the hospital and had a series of tests done. They advised me to take it easy until the problem was sorted out. I was about to go to Sun Dance in South Dakota, it was my eleventh year at Sun Dance and I was not going to miss it. On the night before I was due to go into the Sun Dance the rains started coming down. I was standing in our camp looking up at the skies and marvelling at the way the winds and clouds had formed very quickly above my head a circular moment of intense cloud formation. I had only just been saying I could do with a shower and then all of a sudden this had formed.

I spoke to Morris, who is one of the native elders at the camp and was standing beside me. 'What's that Morris?'

'That,' he said, 'is the start of a tornado. As the winds start getting stronger and stronger we best secure the camp.'

Before we had time to do so the winds had picked up greatly and the rain was driving so heavily we could do nothing.

Morris went to his car and George Fryer, who is a good friend and amazing psychic artist, got into one of the cars with me, which at that point was the safest place to be. As we sat there together being shaken around by wind and rain, the lightning started. I love lightning, having been struck by it as a teenager. I do not have a fear of it and normally I would be out and about dancing in stormy weather. This time, however, it was very different. The lightning was going across the skies vertically in all four directions. I had never seen anything like it, it was amazing to watch and observe. At this point my heart started to cause me a great pain in my chest.

George looked at me and asked, 'Are you okay?'

My answer was, 'No!' I took out my angina spray and used it.

The pain continued so after another five minutes I inhaled more spray, waited but again, nothing. By this time the fear was starting to creep in. Every time the lightning flashed my heart was racing totally out of synchronicity. The only way I could describe it was as if my heart was doing a dance all of its own. I tried slow breathing, again it just would not stop. You know the feeling when you have run fast for a while and your heart is pounding? Well this is how I was feeling. After about fifteen to twenty minutes there was still no let-up of the storm and lightning or my heart palpitating. There wasn't a hospital within reach of us.

In that moment the spirits came to me and said, 'Go to the area at Wounded Knee where the battle was fought and face the burial ground.' I looked at George in the darkness, lit up by the lightning in the sky, and he said okay when I told him what the spirits had asked me to do. We drove out of the camp, up the hill and along to Wounded Knee and parked the car opposite the cemetery. The whole sky was ablaze with the lightning forks and the pain in my chest was intense. At that point George and I experienced all the spirits of the land surrounding the car, standing together observing us. We could feel their pain and suffering.

Then I heard the words, 'Bury my heart at Wounded Knee.' I was taken back to a memory of when I was a little girl in this lifetime remembering and seeing a scene of myself as a little girl in a previous lifetime. I was running down a gully being chased by soldiers and was screaming. I remember falling in the gully and being stabbed in the back right through my heart.

As the memory faded the spirits said to me, 'This is why eleven years ago you were brought here to walk the land. This is why you came to be at Wounded Knee and to Sun Dance. This is now why you dance at Wounded Knee and not at any other Sun

Dance. The place that you now camp is where you died.'

Tears streaming down my face, the ancient memory released, I understood. As I looked around me I could see all those who were so dear to me. They were my soul family. I had come back to Wounded Knee and connected to my spirit family – meeting Gerald, Wallace, Jim, Bernard and Barbara all made perfect sense. At this point the lightning stopped and my heart pain eased. I looked at George and explained what had just happened and he said to me, 'Barbara I have seen it all, I understand. I saw the spirits of the land, I saw what happened. They are at peace now.'

'And so am I,' I responded.

The next day I danced with new awareness, I did not pierce to the tree. I had come home. No more suffering, no more pain. My heart had given me a great teaching. That final day at Sun Dance I was between the worlds, I had visions all day of an eagle dancer dancing in my heart. No longer fragmented, another part of my soul's wisdom reintegrated within me. I left the Sun Dance and went to the cemetery, to the graves, and left my crown of sage and offerings. A great peace was within my heart, I was whole-hearted once more.

After this I was called to go to Taos and travelled down to Denver with my dear friend Grandmother Jean, who is a Cherokee Elder. As we drove we talked about all that had happened at Wounded Knee. She said, 'You have sung your soul back home.' I knew then this was a very precious time together as we sang songs along the way. Once in Taos I visited the hospital where my dear sister and friend Feeny, the owner of All-One-Tribe drums, was dying. As I walked into the room my heart went out to this courageous woman who had walked her talk and helped so many people. We spent precious time together talking about all our shared memories. Then Spirit asked me to sing her a song: 'Mother I feel you', which was the first song I had sung to her all those years ago. Even though she was dying she got out of her bed held my hands and sung with me.

As I write this, tears cascade down my face, for in that moment of death there was a radiance that I will never forget – the radiance of her divine soul was streaming out of her. The light of death was beautiful, gone was all the fear and pain and in its place dignity and grace. Totality of death, heart, spirit, soul and divinity as one. She had worked through all her regrets and fears, and surrendered to the Great Spirit.

Once I arrived home in the UK I was not feeling well. I was due for a check-up in the heart department the day after I got back. As I sat in the cardiology department with my dad Dennis, I told him that I didn't feel very well. The doctor, who checked my blood pressure, admitted me straight into hospital saying I had had a heart attack. I spent ten days in there. The doctors asked me what had happened and, as I explained about the lightning, they were baffled.

'Something has happened to you,' they said. 'The tests revealed a blockage in two of your arteries, caused by an HRT build up over the past twenty years. You also had an irregular heartbeat. Now you are back and we are looking at the scans and tests that we have done here, and the irregular heart beat is now normal.'

When the surgeons went into the heart through an angiogram the blockages were only slight and nothing to how they had been before I left for Sun Dance a few weeks beforehand. I looked at my doctor and asked if the lightning might have affected my heart. He looked back at me smiled and said that he had never heard of anything like this before but it looked as though the lightning could have recalibrated my heart.

'What?' I asked.

He went on to explain that when someone has an irregular heartbeat, they stop the heart and then recalibrate it. 'Looks like the lightning did it for you, but don't tell anyone I told you this as they will think I am crazy!'

I suddenly had an image flash of Crazy Horse dancing with

lightning bolts in both his hands. I thanked the spirits for watching over me and helping me in my healing, once again lightning was in my heart. When I came home David smiled and asked me to listen to a song I had started to write and record nearly three years ago. Amongst the words I was singing were, 'Thunder in my blood, and lightning in my heart, dancing in the sun, no longer we are apart'.

Your rites of passage, both for death and for reintegrating your soul, are a personal journey only you will make. How long it will take, is up to you. How you will approach it, is up to you. It can happen in a blink of an eye, or it may take many lifetimes – the choice is yours. My life has been such a journey of initiations, experiences and I have lived them well and seen the messages that have been gifted to me. I am fifty-five years old and am looking forward to the next thirty-four years of my life here on Earth. Yes, I even know when I will leave my mortal body.

Don't let anyone ever take away what you have experienced and lived in this lifetime or any other lifetime. Hold onto those memories as if they were precious jewels and watch as they radiate out to the four corners of the Universe, connecting in a shining crown of light. Then place that crown upon your head and remember to watch over your kingdom for the shaman healer lives within. Below are reminders that there is more to this life than we have been led to believe...

- Your soul can communicate with you and desires liberation on all levels of consciousness.
- We can access Creation (God, The Great Mystery, Source) ourselves, now.
- Imposed negative habits, addictions and beliefs, keep us on the eternal wheel, repeating mistakes and perpetuating inherited, historical, mythological, spiritual and cultural untruths.

- What needs to die in this lifetime are the never ending stories of the victim, poor me, feeling sorry, the death of old habits that no longer serve.
- Remember, those who have no endeavour to improve themselves will forever sleep. It is their choice, but waiting for a prince or princess to wake you with a kiss, will be a long wait. You're the one you have been waiting for.
- Sometimes we need to walk, work, and live in the world of the dead (those still asleep). The living (those who have woken up) are taught by the dead. Knowing the difference between being alive and dead is important for our soul's growth.
- If we forgive others we receive forgiveness. When we refuse to forgive others, a part of us dies with the loss of those who we believe have harmed us.
- Only we can absolve our indiscretions, another person cannot take away what we have done.
- We can correct all our mistakes in this lifetime, and see them not as wrong or right but as a teaching through discrimination.
- Lust for sex, money, power, and the over indulgence in alcohol, drugs and tobacco binds us to a life on Earth that is not 'lived well'. By advancing spiritually we are naturally fed by an abundance of bliss which stops us 'wanting' more, allowing us to 'live well' – there is no need then to 'return'.
- Our loss of understanding death has caused a divide between the worlds. This in turn has created anxiety, resulting in a breakdown of mind and heart communication. Without the voice of the heart and soul we are lost in the wildness of psychoses.
- We can connect and view our soul's past lives in this lifetime and in the spirit world now.
- During our lives on Earth we endure hardships so we may

learn from them.
- By becoming enlightened on the Earth plane we see into the spirit world with clarity.

We have lived and died many lifetimes and will continue to do so until we are born with our souls' memories intact and do not forget them. It is when we forget our connection to our heart, soul, spirit, our divinity that we die. By using our imagination we can once again connect to our soul memories and live our lives out in full knowledge of who, what, where we have come from. We also have full capabilities to connect to and access all our souls' memories to see were we have gone wrong in our journey and to then alter the journey.

It is rather like a car journey; you get in, drive and end up at the wrong destination. You either choose to stay there or get back in the car and drive to where you were meant to go in the first place. These are our unconscious journeys along the routes of initiation. Our awareness of our past lives, dreams, soul travel are very important in accessing our soul, which transcends time and space. Being aware of our past lives helps us to fully understand our personal situations in this lifetime. Then we can stop repeating the same mistakes over and over again. Accessing our past life memories will lead us to higher states of spiritual awareness.

I have experienced many rites of passage throughout my life. The rite of passage for death while still alive helps us to face what for many of us is the great unknown. It is better to be alive and awake than to be dead and asleep when facing the greatest journey of our lives. For many people will sleep unaware of life's true gift of the oneness. To do this we must die to the ego, to the past, to become fully awake. Once we become awakened we die, for we no longer need to practise the art of forgetfulness. Once we face our fear of death then all other fears subside. When you die you are brought to the threshold of the sacred. You surrender as many do before dying and let go of the material worlds. In that moment you comprehend the absurdity of life and realise that you don't get it until you got it.

In death we surrender and release what no longer serves us. Only by giving up what to the ego is the ultimate sacrifice can we begin to realign and rebuild our framework and structure; just as in a shamanic death and rebirth we are stripped down to the bones and then rebuilt. By seeing and comprehending our own skeleton, in other words seeing our own illnesses and what caused them, we can start to rebuild. We can then take a vested interest in making sure that, having healed and understood them, we no longer carry them within our energetic energy field.

This rite of passage enables us to become The Shaman Within, teaching ourselves through our own life lessons. We have died well and rebirthed a new understanding of being sacred. I see that I am no stranger to death. Three suicide attempts, three hospital deaths, and the last one at Wounded Knee makes a total of seven little deaths.

Each time it has brought me deeper into diving into the divine. I have died to the old, leaving relationships, walking away. We die to the ego each time we make a conscious decision to change our lives for the better. By being able to walk away from a situation where your soul is dying because it is being stifled by others' fears you are able to recapitulate and choose freedom as your preferred choice. We as divine souls choose our birth and our death. I have spoken to many people who have died and each time there is an awareness of oneness, no separation.

Rite of Passage: Death

When we die we become the ancestors, souls in heaven connected once again in our remembrance of universal wisdom. Throughout human history our ancestors honoured the transitions from one phase of life to another. Today mortality is denied, respect lost for wisdom and dignity that comes with old age and dying. When we prepare for our death we get to know our fears. Death then becomes a mystery with a sense of wonderment as we strip away all fears and pains to enter into the core of the Underworld, to be in a relationship with the dead. We then awaken to the realisation that we are the ones that are dead and need to learn how to wake up.

For this rite of passage you need to find a quiet location where there is a bridge running over water. You will also need to ensure you will not be disturbed by other people. I want you to sit down if possible on the bridge facing upstream so that the water flows towards you. I want you to visualise on your left all your past lives and who you have been and what you have learnt in this lifetime and in all your other lifetimes. When you are faced with death you see all your lifetimes flash in front of you.

I experienced all my lifetimes together when I was faced with death in this lifetime. You may find it takes time to remember. Now gaze into the water flowing underneath the bridge. As you do so see the flowing water as a catalyst to release and cleanse all pain and fear from previous lifetimes until you are only holding all the good memories. Sense being merged with the water until you are one; no beginning, no end.

Next, look to your right, still facing upstream, this is the path of destiny. To walk on this path you must reclaim your personal power from others so that you can use it to create your destiny. This is the path of the awakened – a place of future possibilities. As you look to your right see, be seen and become one with all the endless possibilities of what you can create. What you create is who you will become. Take the time to see into your destiny and all the things your heart and soul desires. Again merge yourself in the water, scrying deep into its depths looking for all the future possibilities you will create. Now take both hands, with the left hand facing the left and the right to the right, hold them outwards in both directions saying these words as you focus on the water… *'Death to me has no fear, for I have now become so clear, that I can see my past and future as one and the same, my greatest teacher. Let me hold my light of truth, burning bright in all my youth. A thousand years is but a glance, of life's true purpose and our dance, to clear away all of life's illusions. And see beyond our greatest sojourns, freedom at last released from the self, coming home arms full with pilgrims' wealth. True abundance lives deep within, our finest recesses in our twin, uncovering jewels of wisdoms past, coming home to our soul at last.'*

Now bring both hands together in prayer and feel the connection between past and future married in the now. Then hold your hands over your heart stand up turn around and face the water flowing down stream saying these words… *'Water of life gift to me my visions and foresight so I may now see my past, my future, my present as one, so I can return to the land of the Sun. Heal me help me, set me free, from my mind my prison that has encapsulated me, from the truth of all ages my heart's desire, life's purpose and teaching so I may retire And reap my soul's blessings, in this lifetime's lessons, awakened, alive awareness of bliss, so I can experience death-lessness.'*

Open your hands and release. Feel your heart opening up and the river flowing through your heart centre. From this moment on you can become the observer of consciousness, centred at all times. Whenever there is emotional upheaval you can stay grounded and fearless. You will see beyond unconscious beliefs and thought patterns. You will have clarity and wisdom of foresight due to facing a great misinterpreted understanding of what death is. When you embrace love, face your fears, make friends with death and surrender to the divine, you will live forever. Look to the stars; remember where you have come from and shine brightly. When it is time to shed this mortal coil you will go home to where you have come from so that others will look to the stars and remember that you died well.

Your Last Supper

I was in Phoenix, Arizona, having just spent the week visiting with elders, friends and artisans. I had a day off to rest and relax before my flight home. I went down to the pool and made my way to the deep end. I stretched out my arms to support myself on either side of the pool with my feet touching the bottom. The water was up to my neck. I felt the Sun shining on me, the wind was gently blowing on my face, and I could feel the connection of the earth beneath my feet. Then I had a brilliant experience.

I felt the Sun flowing through my frontal lobe and I smiled remembering hitting it on the beam of the roof in my house while writing this chapter. I noticed the intensity of the Sun just on that one spot and as the Sun's energy continued to flow through my frontal lobe it ignited my kundalini. I started to experience waves of bliss flowing through my body uniting my mind, body and spirit as one. At this point my breathing deepened and slowed and I was the water, the air, the fire, the earth. I became the observer of my consciousness and the universal consciousness – no separation. I became the phoenix and flew high into the sky over the land. I could see everyone and everything.

Then I heard the calm, clear voices of the ancestors who had once walked upon the land. They told me that this city was born from the ruins of a former civilisation. They lived on the land and were nurtured by it. They came from the stars to live in peace on the land. Then the waters dried up and they moved on to another place. At this point I experienced an explosion in my entire body as if I had been torn into a thousand pieces.

I breathed deeply and then heard the ancestors say, 'You are a supernova, a child of the stars, you can never die only transform and as you travel throughout the Universe to one day connect again with other star children to birth new beginnings. This is the life of our Universe and all things here on this land. We experienced a supernova in the skies and recorded this event in the mountains for all to see. All things are recorded with those who have eyes to see. For many will see death as an ending, this is not so for when a star finally dies and explodes it travels the universe to one day come together once again for all to see.'

I then understood the feeling I had and now could believe it to be true – death is the final orgasm.

At this point I saw an old woman standing on a bridge, calling me to join her. As I approached the bridge I saw it was made of bones.

'This is the ancestors' bridge,' she said. 'Here is where you make a choice to go home or return back to the Earth. It's not dying you need to fear, it's never having lived your life on the Earth to its fullest potential and walked your soul's teachings.'

At this point she changed into a beautiful angel, smiled at me and said, 'Help people to remove their fear and pain let them know what fear does to a human spirit. Your sacred task is to align your heart and soul as one on the Earth plane. It is time to rewrite history and let people know there is nothing to fear from death.'

The next minute I was back in the pool and heard my friend's voice calling to me to tell me it was time to get ready for the flight home. So what will you be remembered for when you past to the spirit world? If you were to die right now would you have lived your life differently? Have you done what you came here to do? Can you say you have lived your life well, and consciously harmed no one? Are you at peace with all your family, friends and work colleagues? Is today a good day to die? Is there anything left to do that you have not done yet? If so, what's stopping you?

If I were to die right now I am at peace with all my family and friends and loved ones. I have lived my life well and have no regrets. I have fully experienced my rites of passage into the next journey of my life. I have asked forgiveness from those I have hurt at a soul level. As I look at my heart on the Scales of Maat (the Egyptian Goddess of Justice), that's balanced with the

Feather of Truth, I know that I have lived my life well. I am at peace. Enjoy your journey as I am enjoying mine, live life to the full, and remember to play and have fun. Celebrate each new day as a new creation, for tonight as you go to sleep you die to the old and when you awake in the morning you will start the first day of the rest of your life here on beautiful Earth.

So live your life that the fear of death can never enter your heart. Trouble no one about their religion; respect others in their view, and demand that they respect yours. Love your life, perfect your life, and beautify all things in your life. Seek to make your life long and its purpose in the service or your people. Prepare a noble death song for the day when you go over the great divide. Always give a word or a sign of salute when meeting or passing a friend, even a stranger, when in a lonely place. Show respect to all people and grovel to none. When you arise in the morning give thanks for the food and for the joy of living. If you see no reason for giving thanks, the fault lies only in yourself. Abuse no one and no thing, for abuse turns the wise ones to fools and robs the spirit of its vision. When it comes your time to die, be not like those whose hearts are filled with the fear of death, so that when their time comes they weep and pray for a little more time to live their lives over again in a different way. Sing your death song and die like a hero going home.

Chief Tecumseh (Crouching Tiger) Shawnee Nation 1768-1813
And so it begins....

Poems

The Shaman Within

He walks my path and sings my song, he dares to point where I
    belong.
He cries my tears and feels my pain, he's danced in fire and crawled in
    rain.
He sees the ancient speaks the wise, knows his heart and trusts his
    eyes.
His walk is mine as we are kin, for he is the calling, the Shaman
    Within.
Charles Antony

The Mother's Song

I am the mother of the Earth, I gave you life and your birth.
Now I watch you as you grow, through rites of passage you do show
To me the way of transformation, from birth to death to incarnation.
Gather your wisdom as you sow, life's experiences that you know.
Awaken to the beat of your drum, as you sing your song, dance and
    become
Free of what has chained you, to life's burdens and your breakthrough.
Now you see your truth at last, no more fear from your past.
Your lineage line is clear of trauma, no longer will you become the
    drama.
I am wise, strong and proud, knowing myself, standing my ground.
Walking forward with no recourse, creating my future with no
    remorse.
I am the mother, I am the Earth. I am the one who gives me birth.
Open my heart and let me see the shaman within who lives within me.
Barbara Meiklejohn-Free

Acknowledgements

Kate, my editor, manager and dear friend who has supported and shared my vision with this book. Thank you for helping me to share and speak my experiences.

My soul sister Flavia, thank you for all your hard work in editing and proof-reading my book. You are a blessing and a great gift from Spirit, thank you for being in my life.

To my spirit dad Dennis for all your support and love thank you.

My adopted family Raymond, Lillian, Karen, Douglas and Maggie, thank you for being there for me through thick and thin.

To my blood family Jim and Catherine, Michael and June and family, thank you for coming back into my life.

And thank you to all my friends, I am so blessed to have you in my life, you are my dear brothers and sisters.

About the Author

Barbara Meiklejohn-Free is renowned as the UK's best loved and hardest working 'Wisdom Keeper' – teacher, advocate and protector of the great Earth-centred traditions. Barbara has been working with Spirit since the age of twelve. Drawing on her extensive work with the Native American traditions as well as that of many other indigenous cultures including her own Pagan heritage, she is a recognised expert in assisting people to explore 'the calling', to part-take in 'vision questing' and introduce the lost arts of 'initiations' as well as hosting rites, rituals and ceremonies across the world.

She uses mediumship, psychic abilities, Shamanic healing, rebirthing, soul retrieval, past life regression and rites of passage, combining them all together in her readings and raising them to new levels of awareness in order to help people become aware of who they are and why they are here.

Barbara also leads people on guided site visits to Egypt, South America, the USA, Hawaii, and many other places to meet the native people of these lands, to gain an understanding first-hand of the way they live close to and listen to the teachings of Mother Earth. She worked at the Arthur Findlay College at Stansted as a course organiser and workshop leader and taught at the College of Psychic Studies in London. Her shop in Buxton sells all the tools of the craft, wonderful clothing from around the world and from which she also facilitates private consultations.

Barbara is a singer, drummer, flautist, dancer and storyteller – all of which she employs in weaving the ancient craft of the Shaman, Seer, Mystic, together as one. *We all carry this ability to work on all levels of awareness and intuition to heighten our gifts and talents. It is our natural birthright and it is time to reclaim it!*

www.spiritvisions.co.uk www.facebook.com/barbarameiklejohnfreeuk YouTube - Barbara Meiklejohn-Free

Moon Books invites you to begin or deepen your encounter with Paganism, in all its rich, creative, flourishing forms.

Printed and bound by CPI Group (UK) Ltd, Croydon, CR0 4YY